DEREK JARMAN
Dreams *of* England

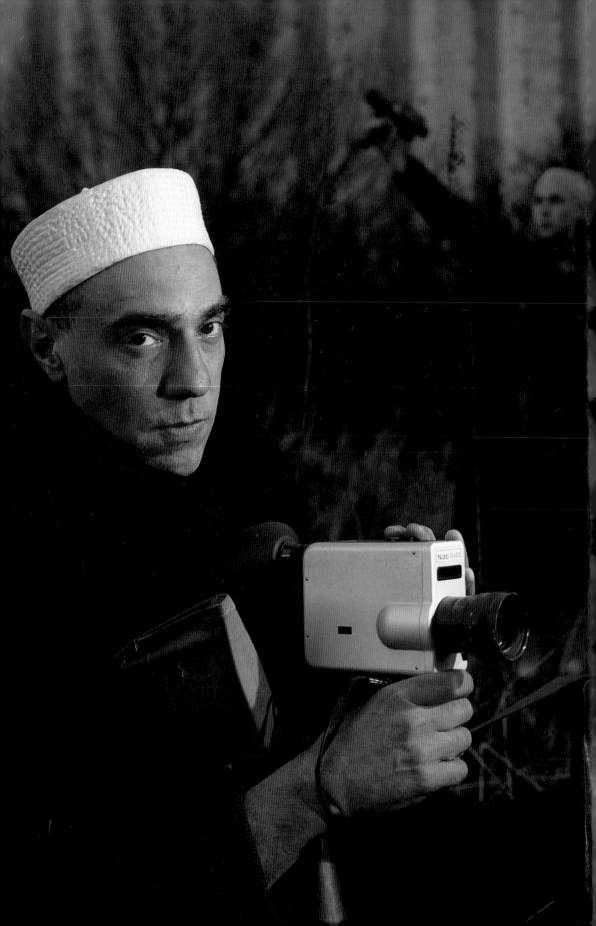

DEREK JARMAN
Dreams *of* England

Michael O'Pray

BRITISH FILM INSTITUTE

bfi

BFI PUBLISHING

In memory of Ida Mary O'Pray

First published in 1996 by the
British Film Institute
21 Stephen Street, London W1P 2LN

The British Film Institute exists to promote appreciation, enjoyment,
protection and development of moving image culture in and throughout
the whole of the United Kingdom. Its activities include the National Film and
Television Archive; the National Film Theatre; the Museum of the Moving Image;
the London Film Festival; the production and distribution of film and video;
funding and support for regional activities; Library and Information Services;
Stills, Posters and Designs; Research, Publishing and Education; and
the monthly *Sight and Sound* magazine.

Designed by Andrew Barron & Collis Clements Associates
Cover photograph by Mike Laye

Printed in Great Britain by Garden House Press,
Perivale, Middlesex

British Library Cataloguing-in-Publication Data
A catalogue record for this book is available from the British Library

ISBN 0-85170-590-1 hbk

Contents

Acknowledgments

My first thanks must go to Colin MacCabe for commissioning this book and to Derek Jarman for his unfailing support and for his friendship in the last ten years of his life.

My editor Philip Dodd was always unstinting in his role, providing patient advice and criticism. I would also like to thank Rob White of BFI Publishing for his support and comments. Vicky Wilson's initial editing was most helpful and Andrew Drummond lent valuable editorial assistance.

I would like particularly to express my gratitude to James Mackay of Basilisk Communications for his generosity in giving interviews, arranging viewings and allowing access to his archives. His co-operation and support, together with his colleague Peter Ratcliffe, have been crucial to the writing of this book. Thanks also to Tilda Swinton and Christopher Hobbs for interviews and encouragement. Tony Peake was enormously generous with his time and knowledge; he read the manuscript at a decisive stage and I am very grateful for his comments and suggestions. He and Keith Collins kindly gave permission for the use of material from the Jarman Estate.

I am also indebted to the staff of the BFI Special Collections for their help. As usual, Judith Preece and her staff at the Library of the University of East London School of Art and Design were always enthusiastic and efficient. The University of East London allowed me sabbatical leave which enabled me to pursue my research at a crucial time.

Thanks also to Richard Salmon, Paul Heber Percy, Conrad Bodmin, John Maybury, William Raban, Simon Field, David Curtis, Nicky Hamlyn, Tony Sinden, Paul Dave, Ian Shipley, Roger Wollen, Peter Wollen, and Gillian Elinor.

Finally, I must thank Sarah for her comments and criticism on previous drafts and for her love and support.

Introduction

Derek Jarman was diagnosed HIV positive in December 1986. When he died of AIDS in February 1994, England lost one of its most exceptional film-makers. It also lost a writer of distinction, an important painter, a music video-maker, an installation artist, a set designer, a champion of the gay community and an original gardener. Even when his health began to fail seriously in the last few years of his life, Jarman managed to remain prolific in almost all of these areas. In those final few years, besides writing books and making films, he also directed pop videos, gave a phenomenal number of interviews, visited film festivals, demonstrated in the streets and created one of the most famous gardens in Britain. He planned and tackled projects with an indefatigable energy that left healthy people agape with astonishment. He died a public figure.

An account of Jarman's films, which the present book aims to give, must discuss, to a fairly large degree, his life and times. The fact that Jarman was never in the cocoon that comprises the British film industry meant that his work had to be made with the resources he found in the reaches of his own life. His ideas did not have to run the sanitising gauntlet of the industry's accountants and producers. Instead, his films were formed out of his own preoccupations, and made with the support of crews, actors and backers drawn from his immediate circle of friends. However, more often than not Jarman's films also addressed the larger concerns of his social, cultural and political milieu. Given the extraordinary visibility and cultural impact of the gay world since the 60s, his activities as a gay man guaranteed this wider relevance.

Jarman was always interested in England's present and past. He had a scholarly knowledge of sixteenth-century Renaissance England and was at the same time passionately concerned with contemporary British social and political life. Even in conversation he delighted in connecting present-day

7

affairs with those of the past, an impulse that found its way into his films. His commitment to the 'home movie' denotes not only an intimate and domestic approach to his work, but also the strong presence of that other meaning of 'home' – England.

In many ways Jarman was a typical member of the British post-war generation. He was brought up in the fairly stable consensus period of the Welfare State and came to maturity in the freedom of the 60s. En route he gained what seems to be a necessary qualification for entry into British cinema – an English public school education. Both his idealism and his anarchism can be explained in part by this configuration.

Jarman had vivid memories of the late 40s and the 50s, when Britain's decline was shabbily disguised by such diversions as the Royal wedding and Coronation, the lingering obsession with victory in the war and, foremost perhaps, the grey repressive respectability which was to fall apart before his eyes as a young man in London in the 60s. From that decade to the end of his life, Jarman witnessed the process of his country's collapse – as liberalism failed as a set of values on the back of economic instability – and portrayed it in his films. In the films there is an acute, even nostalgic sense of a centre having been lost but, paradoxically, there is also an urgent desire to innovate and shock. On account of this combination Jarman is part of a long line of English radicals whose work has embraced a form of Romantic conservatism – William Blake, William Morris and, much closer to his own aspirations and times, the film-maker Michael Powell.

Jarman's first two feature films – the homoerotic *Sebastiane* and the punk-inspired *Jubilee* – made him a *cause célèbre*, a role he thoroughly enjoyed. He remained until the end of his life an ambivalent figure for what he referred to as the 'Establishment', of which he always impishly claimed membership and whose fellow-members came increasingly to his bedside in the final months to pay their respects. His death has left an emptiness at the heart of our culture. If there is an appropriate response to the blighted times we live in, Jarman seemed one of the few artists and public figures capable of supplying it. For instance, as Britain struggled to find a new sense of meaning for itself in the post-Falklands War era, Jarman created a poetic vision which expressed that crisis of identity. In the final writings, the films and eventually the paintings, he forged a language for times he saw as bleak. Yet his vision never failed to embrace some kind of humanism; it never ceased to cherish friendship, imagination and, of course, nature.

In a reversal of most directors' careers, Jarman's film style became more radical as he grew older. The inner explorations of the art movie were not to his liking, nor was straightforward nitty-gritty realism. In many ways he is more reminiscent of Brecht sieved through the *Carry On* series and music hall. The work is often gestic, polemical, loud and abrasive, yet it is also capable of sensitive poetic images of landscapes, nature and people. Jarman kept up a steady commitment, until the last few years when relatively large-budget work proliferated, to super-8 film-making – a practice usually abandoned by directors after their first commercial film. Looking back over his career, the films are fascinating in their multi-layeredness; they interweave reworkings of history, recuperations of iconic figures, avant-garde forms, personal diaries, gay polemics, political statements and social documents. The sense of engagement is strong. If there is a distance, it is usually created by a dream-like aestheticism (as in *The Angelic Conversation*) or a wilful self-indulgence.

In terms of influence, there is no doubt that Ken Russell (who introduced Jarman to commercial film) had an enormous impact. In addition, Jarman's experimental super-8s of the 70s and after are loosely connected to the avant-garde and underground cinemas of the 60s. The work of Andy Warhol, Kenneth Anger and other films seen in the late 60s had their effect, as did his friendships with the experimental film-maker John du Cane (Rishi) and others from the 70s avant-garde scene. Jarman did not see Powell and Pressburger's films until much later and in their eccentricity and radical Romanticism these were to give him a reference point, confirm his own aesthetic and at times influence his work: for instance, the club baths scene in *The Garden* owes much to *The Life and Death of Colonel Blimp* (1943). Jarman has mentioned the *Carry On* films as an influence, perhaps in recognition of an enjoyable irreverence, robust humour and campness which may have had some impact, via Ken Russell, on *Jubilee*. The Ealing comedies with which he claimed kinship seem very different from his own work, which lacks any sense of the everyday, of the frayed lower-middle classes or the innocent fun and criminality of Ealing. But Ealing comedies depict virtues and a version of nationality with which Jarman as a conservative and Englishman identified.

In fact, Jarman is not a film-maker immersed in film history at all. To

9

understand his style one is better served by looking at his education as a painter and his early forays into set design. His strong sense of artifice and emphasis on set design or *mise en scène*, together with a frontality and system of textural and colour effects which are painterly, find no real equivalent in British cinema. Equally there is a crudity, a brittle edge which some have identified as amateurishness (or incompetence) that gives his films a fresh quality. According to Jarman:

> Perfectly crafted films exclude the chance encounter that stops you in your tracks. I like rough edges, the mark of the Japanese potter who has turned a perfect tea bowl and then jabs it with his thumb.[1]

By being true to this weakness of the British film tradition, Jarman has made it a strength. His lack of film training and scant knowledge of conventional film form meant that he attempted things which those without these supposed disadvantages would never consider – putting amateurs in leading roles, mixing genres, as well as using music, dance and poetry with audacity and nerve. He has created images which have shocked film sensibilities reared on Hollywood and tasteful art movies. But these images were prescient. One could say, for instance, that Jarman's use of torture (in *The Garden*) is a precursor of films such as Quentin Tarantino's *Reservoir Dogs*.

Though probably Britain's most radical and political film-maker, Jarman was ignored, if not actively disliked, in the 70s and early 80s by the New Left of the influential film journal *Screen* and the avant-garde formalists. His radicalism was seen as heavy-handed, crass, old-fashioned, naive and suspect for its intuitiveness. The *Screen*-based theorists of that period were in thrall to the new psychoanalytical reading of Hollywood and the avant-gardism of Brecht, Novy Lef, Straub/Huillet and Godard. In other words, a strong intellectualism reigned. The call was for an analytical approach to cinema (the reading of Brecht on this count was very partial) and the theoretical attack on identificatory modes of film-making went hand in hand with avant-garde film-makers' anti-illusion manifestos. Little were the Althusserians who embraced the ideological over economic and social realities to know that by the late 80s deep economic recession and a rampant private-enterprise culture would dominate Britain and that the Left would be virtually annihilated. Jarman's emergence centre-stage from 1985 onwards coincides with this political change.

Jarman found fresh aesthetic input and support from the so-called 'New Romantics' of the early 80s. At the time, when Thatcherism decimated the Left, there was a radicalism which Jarman shared with poll tax rioters, New Age travellers and other anti-Thatcherite activists. By a knight's move, Jarman found himself at the front of the oppositional ranks, which also included old adversaries. Many who had attacked or ignored him now embraced him.

Jarman has always been at the forefront of gay cinema, making his first film, *Sebastiane*, in the mid-70s on the themes of gay love and violence long before these became bankable subjects. His depiction of gayness has always been intermingled with social critique and he has persistently located gay themes in the power nexus of politics. The merging of repressive state symbols with a certain form of gay sexuality and gay scenes involving military or police figures recur throughout his work, from *Sebastiane* with the sado-masochism of its Roman soldiers, through the violent murder of Adam Ant by the police in *Jubilee* and the torture and humiliation of the gay man by the police in *The Garden* to *Imagining October*, where young Soviet soldiers are the subject of the film's social-realist painter as well as of Jarman's camera. The identification of state repression with homosexual sadism is not uncommon in fiction – Jean Genet's *Un Chant d'amour* with its depiction of a sexual complicity between prisoners and their guards is a genuine precursor, as is Kenneth Anger's *Fireworks*, where sadistic sailors form part of the masochistic masturbatory fantasies of the young protagonist (played by Anger himself).

If authority is sexual in some sense for Jarman (and all his films seem to imply this), then it is in its refusal that an erotic violence ensues. It is this sexuality which carries the frisson in his narratives – all other forms of sexuality are casual, passive and finally indifferent. Jarman's films have often been problematic for the gay press.[2] His sado-masochistic rendering of homosexuality was seen as a narrow view of homosexual relations and he was never a gay film-maker in the sense of being a balanced spokesman for gay issues. There is a sense in which Jarman is an artist who happens to be gay, and it is his artistic concerns which fuel the films even if gayness is very much part of what is expressed. Indeed, Jarman's interest seems to lie as much

11

in social and historical comment as in a wish to depict homosexuality *per se* – he made films about history, death, politics and art, among other themes, all of which are imbued with his homosexuality. Even in the hermetic and narcissistic *The Angelic Conversation*, where Shakespeare's Sonnets counterpoint the erotic imagery, Jarman's evocation of a certain kind of love is overshadowed by the reality of gay love in contemporary Britain. In the case of the many figures who served as the subject-matter of his most explicit explorations of gay sexuality, he seemed as interested in the artistic process as in sexuality itself. In all cases, the gayness of these figures is controversial still (*Caravaggio*), ambiguous (*Sebastiane*) or rarely on the surface (*Wittgenstein*).

Jarman's attitude to his own sexuality was always a mix of pain and joy. He never quite recovered from the world he was brought up in – the dour, repressive 50s – and only in the late 60s when the assertion of gay rights began on an important scale did he find some relief from the angst so clearly expressed in his memories of his early years. He was keenly aware of being surrounded by a younger generation of artists who had 'come out' relatively painlessly.

An important figure in understanding Jarman is the radical visionary poet William Blake (1757–1827), whose pithy paradoxes were appropriated in the 60s as slogans for the new Age of Aquarius.[3] But Jarman's love of Blake runs deeper than this casual appropriation. Like Blake, Jarman was a Londoner who believed the city physically embodied the woes of its times – in sixteenth-century alchemical terms, it was a microcosm. Both created mythological systems spanning the personal and the national in which social critique was inseparable from the spiritual. (Carl Jung's description of the psyche as constructed both by self and culture is also crucial to Jarman's intellectual make-up.) Both Jarman and Blake plundered the cabala, alchemy and the occult philosophies, finding in them a symbolic vehicle for anti-rationalist and anti-materialist sympathies. On a more personal level, Jarman made ornate, hand-made diaries, notebooks and scripts in a Blakean fashion. He too was a charismatic figure, living frugally, expounding radical views, including free love. No more than in *The Last of England* do we see his Blakean spirit expressed.

The original idea of this book came out of sporadic conversations with Jarman in the mid-80s, after I had done a series of interviews with him and articles on his work. We both thought it would be a good idea and there was rather desultory talk about finding a publisher. As events turned out, Jarman was about to enter a highly productive phase with the funding of *Caravaggio*, while my own life too became busy. Colin MacCabe eventually suggested publishing the book at the British Film Institute – after the making of *The Garden*, I believe, and before *Edward II*. Jarman immediately saw me – he was in hospital, with tubes running up his nose and his breathing difficult. He promised access and interviews. Then he became busy again and his health precarious in a way it had not been before 1990.

Like others who knew him, I saw less of him in the final few years. He was extremely busy and became a public figure in a way that had been unimaginable in the 80s when I met him most frequently, working as I did in a Soho office a few streets away from his flat. I interviewed him briefly after *Edward II* and saw him in screening rooms, cafés, on the street and on the set of *Wittgenstein*. He was just as he had been on the set of *Caravaggio* seven years earlier – full of good humour with his usual boyish threats to the Establishment and praise for his crew and actors. He was physically unchanged, though I knew he was more rigorous about his routine, going to bed earlier and avoiding late nights. After *Blue* the decline in his health was steep – his physique, which had always been robust, became frailer, his eyesight much weaker and the sheer pain and frustration of the skin allergies caused by the drugs meant that at times he could barely read, write, sleep or concentrate. Meeting him accidentally on Good Friday in 1993 I was appalled at his appearance, having last seen him earlier that year at a private screening of *Blue*.

The last time I saw Jarman was in Bart's hospital one Sunday morning in September 1993. He was awaiting eye operations and was in some physical distress, but we talked about this book, Thatcherism and *Wittgenstein*. I did not stay long as I could see the effort he needed to maintain such a conversation. To the end, he made that kind of effort.

The writing of this book over three or more years has been sporadic, largely because in the two years before Jarman's death I found myself unable to write as he declined in health. At each meeting the physical signs were obvious and painful to see. Writing about him as he was dying seemed too much of a cold-blooded act and, quite frankly, I was not in a state of mind to put pen to paper about his work. Writing about someone as they are dying is not something I would want to experience again and even now his

13

memory is vivid and my thoughts are with him in ways that are not part of a book such as this.

Although never intended, this book has in the end incorporated much of Jarman's biography, culled from his own books on his life and from what I know myself. Autobiography is always a dangerous source for historians. Memory is treacherous and in any case Jarman often wrote about his life from a polemical standpoint, as in *Dancing Ledge* and *At Your Own Risk*. As a journal, *Modern Nature* reveals a different side of him; nevertheless, it was commissioned and must have been written with that in mind. *Chroma* is another kind of book – written against the background of his severe decline, it is the most abstract, discursive and in a way objective, though the descriptions of his physical states are central. Future biographers will have the task of sorting out this material as they will of the testament of his many friends and acquaintances. I have drawn back with a few exceptions from interviewing those involved in his life and films as the task would have pushed the book even further from its intention of discussing the films themselves. However, I did interview James Mackay, Tilda Swinton and Christopher Hobbs to clear up some particular areas of concern.

I have found in writing this book that it is the context of Jarman's film work that has governed my thoughts – that is to say, the British culture in

14 Annotated pages of the 'Caravaggio' script (photo: Mike Laye)

which he worked for over thirty years. There is a sense in which a survey of his films inevitably becomes a cultural history of post-war Britain, and to perform this task I have leaned heavily on historians and commentators of the period. This is the framework of the book and to that extent it is a book about a particular kind of cinema and artist, locked between notions of avant-garde, experiment and independence (all terms Jarman distrusted) and art cinema, mainstream cinema and its commercial demand.

Living on borrowed time from his diagnosis as HIV positive in December 1986, Jarman's impending death was acutely felt by his friends long before it happened. Each film was received as perhaps his last, each project seemed a race against time. No one was more aware of this, of course, than Jarman himself. In Amsterdam in June 1986 he spoke to me about the number of his friends who had already succumbed to AIDS or had contracted the HIV virus. He said that he was bound to get it or have it himself and that he had to make as many films as was humanly possible in the time he had left.

The tragedy of his death was sharpened by the fact that his discovery of his HIV status coincided with his 'rediscovery' by the British film establishment in the form of the BFI Production Board's financing of *Caravaggio*. At his death Jarman was at the peak of his powers. His films were major artistic achievements, if still controversial, and his paintings were beginning to receive recognition from an art world that had long ignored him. For the first time serious critical writings by such figures as Colin MacCabe, Peter Wollen, Robert Hewison and Timothy Murray were also appearing. It should not be forgotten, however, that until the bitter end the financing of his films was not easy and *Blue* was put together with scraps from many quarters. The begging bowl never gathered cobwebs.

---

1 Derek Jarman, *War Requiem: The Film* (London: Faber & Faber, 1989), p. 47.
2 For instance, see Stephen Bourne, *Gay Times*, January 1990, pp. 68–9: 'Another problem I have with Jarman's films is his focus on women at the expense of gay characters ... in his films gays are only partially depicted. Instead Jarman focuses on the actress Tilda Swinton as an "Earth Mother".'

3 See Kathleen Raine, Introduction to *William Blake and Prophecies* (London: Everyman, 1975).

16 Jarman's father, Michael

Jarman as a baby **17**
'Miss Gaby' (overleaf)

'The Art of Mirrors'

20 'Tarot'

'The Last of England' (photo: Mike Laye) **21**

22 'The Last of England' (above and opposite; photos: Mike Laye)
Miranda, 'The Tempest' (overleaf)

The wedding-scene, 'The Last of England' (photo: Mike Laye)

26 Promo for Marianne Faithfull's 'Broken English'

'The Last of England' (photo: Mike Laye) **27**

Jarman in front of a tableau vivant, 'Caravaggio' (photo: Mike Laye)

'Caravaggio' (above and opposite; photos: Mike Laye) **29**

'Drop Dead', 1993

30 'Maternal Nightmare', 1988
'Wittgenstein' (opposite)

EARLY YEARS

1942–1963

Derek Jarman was born in 1942, at a time when the British state was not only waging war against Nazi Germany but was also hatching one of the most profound changes to its existence. Between 1941 and 1943, Beveridge was preparing the document that was to map out the Welfare State of the post-war years. The idea of a comprehensive social welfare system with full employment as one of its axioms was to be a part of consensus politics in Britain until the arrival of Thatcherism in the late 70s. Jarman in his final years witnessed the dismantling of this system. To trace his life and art is to become enmeshed in this remarkable period in British history.

During the war years the nation in crisis consciously constructed an identity for itself. Films, paintings and books shaped images and narratives aimed at raising awareness of Englishness.[1] The dominant artistic sensibility of the period, especially in literature and painting, was neo-Romanticism. David Mellor has articulated its characteristic themes: 'the body and sexuality; nostalgia and anxiety; myth making; organic fantasies; the threat of war and extinction'.[2] Of course, these are themes projected back on to the movement from the vantage-point of the 80s, yet its commitment to the figure and engagement with the English landscape made it an exemplary vehicle for national consciousness-raising in the war years and after. It is ironic that Jarman, born in the midst of such an aesthetic, was to become at the end of his life a figure in its revival in the late 80s.

The neo-Romantic sensibility of Humphrey Jennings' wartime films (especially *A Diary for Timothy*, 1945) or Powell and Pressburger's *A Canterbury Tale* (1944) was one he shared to some extent, though as someone who experienced the decline of Britain in the post-war period he recognised the ambivalence of celebrating an Englishness corrupted by the dubious political ends it had served. Jarman's view of Englishness is similar to that expressed in George Orwell's famous wartime essay on Englishness and

32 Jarman family home movie footage included in 'The Last of England'

patriotism, which praises the English for their dislike of intellectualism, disdain for the artistic and love of flowers.[3] Indeed, part of the mythology of Jarman as a public figure in his last years was built on his compliance with the potent myth of the English gardener.

Jarman's films rarely fail to reflect on the decline of post-war England, even when their subject matter is placed far outside that time period. His own accounts of his early life, including time spent witnessing briefly but first-hand the last vestiges of a dying Empire when his father was posted to Pakistan in the early 50s, present it as a period suffused with an idealised and homosexual love and the pleasures of nature. These are passions that became the focus of his dying years, when they took on the characteristics of a final bathing in the emotional glow of childhood.

Michael Derek Elsworthy Jarman was born on 31 January 1942 in the London suburb of Northwood. His father Lancelot (Lance) Elsworthy Jarman, a squadron leader in the Royal Air Force, was a second-generation New Zealander who had lived in England for ten years when he met Jarman's mother at a dance at Northolt aerodrome in 1938. Lance's father, Hedley Jarman, had left the family farm in Devon, in the late 19th century to farm near Christchurch, New Zealand. Lance was a restless young man who dreamed of being an engineer and in 1929 sailed for England, where he believed he would find more opportunities. The day after his arrival in London he joined the RAF and soon received his commission. According to Jarman, his father's reception at the Air Ministry where he was recruited 'was as frosty as the weather'.[4] He felt that his father was a fundamentally bitter man 'obsessed by a need to belong' who as a colonial son inwardly despised the English middle classes of which he became a respectable member. He married Elizabeth Evelyn Puttock in 1940 at Holy Trinity Church, Northwood. Photographs of the handsome couple appeared in the national press. Evelyn was a beautiful woman, as her son and photographs and film testify, and she held a central place in Jarman's life. He later remarked that 'her life was as open as my father's was closed'.[5]

It would be presumptuous to believe that Derek Jarman's life was an enactment of his father's buried feelings of frustration and anger. But there is something in his awkwardness, his inability to find a niche, that echoes his father's alienation from the society in which he found himself when he arrived in England. A severe, authoritarian and apparently violent character,

34

Lance Jarman, like his father Hedley who had played first violin as a founder member of Christchurch's first symphony orchestra, had artistic interests. Lance played the piano and was a keen and accomplished amateur photographer and film-maker whose excellent documents of family and military life were to find an ironic place in his son's savage attacks on England's imperialist façade. Jarman always blamed his father's unhappy and eventually disturbed disposition on his countless wartime bombing missions.

Before her marriage, Evelyn Jarman attended Harrow Art School. Subsequently she was employed as a personal assistant to the famous English dress-designer Norman Hartnell. She was always supportive of her son's career as a painter and film-maker; a fun-loving woman who was the vibrant centre of the family, she endured cancer bravely and uncomplainingly for eighteen years before her death in August 1978. Jarman's reaction to her death was one of 'elation' at the quality of her life. He remarked that 'she had been up and about until near the end, had always been so happy with simple and homely things, never regretting anything or envying anyone'. [6]

If Jarman's relationship with his mother seemed a simple one of love and admiration, his relationship with his father was more complex and ambivalent. His father's death caused him only confusion, which he found difficult to disentangle from his own feelings at learning of his HIV positive status only months later. He characterised his father both as a 'monster' and a brave man whose personality had been poisoned by his wartime experiences. There was also the feeling that Jarman had never quite received the approval he demanded from his father, and that his homosexuality was an insurmountable problem in their relationship. By chance I bumped into Jarman on Charing Cross Road the day his father died and we had tea while he talked about him. His feelings were a mixture of relief, anger and pity. Some of these feelings surface in his book *The Last of England*, the focus of which is an anger at Thatcher's England, the sorry state of British cinema and his own HIV positive status, merged often with his conflicting feelings towards his father. During an interview for a section of that book, I suggested to him that his interest in the military was not simply a sexual one but might have something to do with his identification of his father as an authoritarian military figure in his life. Whether or not this had already occurred to him was difficult to tell, but he assented to the idea.

Following his father's death, Jarman's films incorporate, again and

35

again, images of childhood, either of his own or that of the characters he is representing. Of course, this slant may have been the result of his own heightened sense of mortality following his HIV positive diagnosis. But it is also as if he had to represent his Oedipal conflict by incorporating himself into his films by way of his presence in his father's home-movie footage (as in *The Garden, Blue,* and *The Last of England* which he started filming the month his father died). As further evidence of this return to childhood, there seems always to be a role for a child in his later films – in *Edward II, The Garden,* and *Wittgenstein.*

Love and 'The Garden'

As the son of a professional military man, the war did not end for Jarman in the way it had done for children whose fathers had been conscripted and then demobbed. His memories of life until he was in his teens, in between boarding schools, were of a series of postings in military housing quarters with their high security fences and barbed wire. In a film shot by his father of Jarman and his sister playing on the lawn, which he used in *The Last of England*, a military enclosure can be seen at the end of the garden. This experience of an idyllic period spent with his mother circumscribed by the stark brutality of a military camp finds its way into many of his films. The recurrent image of the revolving radar scanner (in *The Angelic Conversation* and *The Garden*) has its source perhaps in this military environment.

Typically the family led a nomadic life, following the father's postings. As a young boy of four years old Jarman lived in Rome and then, memorably, on the shores of Lake Maggiore. In 1953, the family followed his father to Pakistan for a brief period. Jarman's early memories of these sojourns abroad are recounted in nearly all his books. There are sharply observed, almost voluptuous descriptions of nature, flowers and gardens: 'I was always a passionate gardener – flowers sparkled in my childhood as they do in a medieval manuscript.'[7] In his final book, *derek jarman's garden*, he recalls the 'exquisite overgrown garden of Villa Zuassa, by Lake Maggiore'.[8] He was also to write of the intense pleasure he took in the flowers he saw as a schoolboy in Hampshire walking with his fellow pupils to Chapel:

> the rose pergola bisected an old walled garden – scattered with
> gnarled fruit trees. On either side, deep wine-coloured peonies

36

Derek Jarman with his mother, Evelyn, and sister, Gaye **37**

bowed, heavy with raindrops, and scattered their petals like the crinolines in *Gone with the Wind.* [9]

This love of flowers and plants found its full expression after Jarman moved to Dungeness in 1987 and began to nurture what became a very famous English garden. But garden scenes appear in his early super-8s and in *Jubilee, The Angelic Conversation, War Requiem* and, of course, *The Garden,* where they are a metaphor for pain and pleasure, for Gethsemane and Eden.

In his last years Jarman liberally sprinkled his book *Modern Nature* with extracts from the writings of the sixteenth- and early seventeenth-century English herbalists Culpepper and Gerard. [10] The connections between gardening and the early Elizabethan period are also made explicit in the setting of the John Donne poem 'The Sunne Rising' on the side of his Dungeness cottage. It is as a gardener that Jarman, once a *bête noire*, has been recuperated by English mainstream culture − his inclusion in the popular television series *Gardeners' World* [11] was astonishing in its taking for granted of his reputation and 'genius'. His absorption into English culture seemed complete.

Jarman's stay on the shores of Lake Maggiore also provided the memory of an idyllic first love which is recalled many years later in *Caravaggio*. The role played by Pasqualone in the dying Caravaggio's mind − as a sexual mentor and source of wisdom for the painter when a boy − reworks, one feels, Jarman's own encounter with Davide, the grandson of the old woman who lived in the gatehouse of the Villa Zuassa. 'This love was my great secret. If only this innocent idyll could have continued', Jarman confessed in 1992. [12] This notion of an ideal, almost Platonic love occurs again and again in his work (*Sebastiane* is an early, clumsy expression of it). It is most successfully captured in the super-8 home-movie films, exquisitely and rapturously in *The Angelic Conversation*.

With school came a quite different experience of his sexuality. At boarding school in Milford he was discovered in bed with another boy. The zealous dormitory captain reported the nine-year-olds to the headmaster's wife, who 'descended on us like a harpy ... pulled the mattress right off the bed, turning us on to the floor'. [13] Jarman was punished and threatened with disclosure to his parents but his homosexuality was a strong presence through his school years. He describes becoming reclusive as he entered puberty:

38

'The destruction first wrought at Hordle, my prep school, grew like a poison vine.'[14] School was 'bleak and soulless' and exuded 'a distressing muscular Christianity'. The two sexual experiences, one idyllic and idealised, the other sordid and punitive, were to become the polarities of sexual expression in his work.

Intimidated by communal activities at school, especially sport, Jarman took 'refuge in the art house'. He saw art as a weapon against 'the other order'. Fortunately his art master was a sympathetic figure, whose attitude to art became his own: 'Art was never mentioned in an academic context, but was a part of living in which anyone, whatever their natural ability or talent, could share.'[15] In 1960 Jarman was accepted at King's College, University of London, to study English History and Art. His father made a pact with him to support him through the Slade School of Art if he first went to King's and gained a degree. At King's his tutor, Eric Mottram, introduced him to the writings of Allen Ginsberg and William Burroughs. Jarman immersed himself in whatever literature he could find (Cocteau and Genet in particular) that would help him to come to terms with his own suppressed sexuality. He worked fairly hard, commuting for the first two years from his parents' home in the suburbs. In 1963 he moved to an unfurnished flat near Russell Square in Bloomsbury, just before gaining a 2.1 degree. A few months later he had his first full-blown sexual experience and promptly and painfully fell in love.

1 See Robert Hewison, *Culture and Consensus: England, Art and Politics since 1940* (London: Methuen, 1995), especially chapter 2.
2 See David Mellor, 'Editor's Preface' in Mellor (ed.), *A Paradise Lost: The Neo-Romantic Imagination in Britain 1935–55* (London: Lund Humphries & Barbican Art Gallery, 1987), p. 9.
3 George Orwell, 'The Lion and the Unicorn: Socialism and the English Genius', reprinted in I. Angus and S. Orwell (eds), *The Collected Essays, Journalism and Letters of George Orwell* (Harmondsworth: Penguin, 1970), vol. 2. See also Raymond Williams' brilliant book, *Orwell*, revised edition (London: Fontana, 1984).
4 Derek Jarman, *The Last of England* (London: Constable, 1987), p. 117.
5 Ibid., p. 128.
6 Derek Jarman, *Dancing Ledge* (London: Quartet, 1984), p. 185.

7 Derek Jarman, *derek jarman's garden* (London: Thames & Hudson, 1995), p. 11.
8 Ibid.
9 *Dancing Ledge*, p. 48.
10 See Nicholas Culpepper, *Complete Herbal* (London: Bloomsbury Books, 1992; first published in 1653) and Marcus Woodward (ed.), *Gerard's Herbal* (London: Senate, 1994; first published in 1597).
11 *Gardeners' World*, BBC2, 23 June 1995. The enormous commercial success of Jarman's garden book also bears testament to this cultural absorption.
12 Derek Jarman, *At Your Own Risk: A Saint's Testament* (London: Hutchinson, 1992), pp. 13–14.
13 *Dancing Ledge*, p. 49.
14 Ibid., p. 50.
15 Ibid., p. 52.

Chapter Two

PAINTING & DESIGN

1963–1970

Like others of his generation, Jarman's life was to be transformed by the 60s. Between entering the Slade in 1963 and beginning work on Ken Russell's *The Devils* in 1970 he was introduced to the art-world glitterati, he came out as gay and he experienced the phenomenon known as the 'counter-culture'. Through his friendships with the painter Patrick Procktor and fashion designer Ossie Clarke, he became part of the art scene that revolved around David Hockney. He was at one of the epicentres of the 60s era.[1] Remembering his final year at King's College, he looked back on the decade as a turning point:

> Life was much simpler, pleasures fewer and perhaps for that more intense. ... Unsophisticated as we were, we were to be part of the change that was to revolutionise life in the next few years.[2]

In 1967, as part of the liberal impulse of the times, Leo Abse's Bill to legalise homosexual practices between consenting adults in private was passed. In a climate of what seemed a national sexual awakening, art, fashion, design and photography were all filtered through sex, while aspects of pop music showed the influence of a gay sensibility.[3] The youth market was invented and 'style' became for the first time a media topic and a commodity. In the same period the British economy recovered and spending power increased – by 1971, 91 per cent of British homes had a television. Jarman remarked years later that the decade 'opened the floodgates of consumerism; and as more – much more, became available we lost a sense of the New'.[4]

At the Slade Jarman found himself spending more and more time in theatre design, where homosexuality was 'accepted quite openly' in contrast with the more constrained atmosphere of the painting studios. The painter

40 'Untitled (Archer)', 1983

Keith Vaughan, also a homosexual but of an older generation (born in 1912), was one of his tutors and was a friend of Procktor and of Hockney, whom he admired enormously. Vaughan kept a journal, published posthumously, which bears witness to the problem of internalised social disapproval many homosexuals of his generation experienced.[5] Reading Vaughan's journals in 1989, Jarman writes in his own diary:

> Sharing his troubles made me aware how lucky I am. I wish I had got to know him – but when you are young you do not realise your youth is an asset. I never thought I could do anything but bore him – I felt tongue-tied, unsophisticated.[6]

To read both journals now is to witness the differences between the gay experience of the two generations, Vaughan's moulded in the pre-war period and Jarman's in the 60s when enormous advances were made in gay liberation in terms of both decriminalisation and culture. But it is also a matter of personalities. Vaughan's introspection, self-loathing and bitter relationship with his mother compare unfavourably with Jarman's confidence. As Jarman remarks: 'Unlike Keith Vaughan, I'm not out of love with myself.'[7]

Procktor, an older man who had already done his National Service, had entered the Slade in 1958. Many years later Jarman was to play him in Stephen Frears' film *Prick Up Your Ears* (1987), based on Joe Orton's hilarious autobiographical writings. A Communist sympathiser, Procktor painted his Maoist-inspired *Long Live the Great Leap Forward* in 1966 and the following year, in a similar style, produced *Shades,* which included the figure of Jarman (twice), his friend the artist Keith Milow and Ossie Clarke.[8]

Procktor at this time was a close friend of Hockney, who had studied at the Royal College of Art between 1959 and 1962. Recalling the opening of the Lisson Gallery in May 1967, at which he and Milow exhibited, Jarman wrote: 'During the previous years both of us had "come out", and spent most of our spare time with the small band of gay artists around Patrick Procktor and David Hockney.'[9] Hockney was a leading and very public figure in the Pop Art movement and, more controversially, he was openly gay. However much Jarman was disappointed by Hockney's later career, he always acknowledged that:

42

David Hockney was the first English painter to declare his homosexuality in public. By example, he was a great liberating force, reaching far beyond the confines of the 'art world': his work paved the way for the gay liberation movement at the end of the decade.[10]

With his meteoric rise to fame, Hockney was to become a potent symbol for the success of the post-war consensus politics and Welfare State, which seemed to culminate in a so-called meritocracy as working-class figures such as David Bailey, Twiggy and Terence Stamp came to dominate the cultural 'scene'.

The northern working-class painter had attracted the attention of the art world through the 'Young Contemporaries' exhibition of February 1961 held at the RCA galleries, which signalled a new phase in British Pop Art. Many of Hockney's friends were on the executive committee, including Peter Phillips, Allen Jones, Procktor, Derek Boshier and Mike Upton. Hockney became a celebrity in the 'swinging 60s' scene of pop stars, photographers, models, dress designers and actors as well as the centre of the gay art world. By 1965 he had appeared in three popular books – David Bailey's *Box of Pin-Ups* with such figures as John Lennon, Mick Jagger, Rudolf Nureyev, Jean Shrimpton and Vidal Sassoon; Mario Amaya's *Pop as Art;* and *Private View* by Bryan Robertson, John Russell and Lord Snowdon. Hockney was featured in the quality Sunday papers' new colour supplements as much for his outrageous dress and open homosexuality as for his art. As a young gay artist following hot on Hockney's heels, Jarman respected his mentor's achievements in the 60s:

> From the beginning with his *Rake's Progress*, his 'shower paintings' including *We Two Boys Together Clinging*, and finally the exhibition of his etchings for the Cavafy poems, he produced vital new images that pulled away the veil behind which the work of older painters had had to hide. ... Those of us who came right behind had a great struggle ahead. Success was the order of the day, and it had to be instant and heady. We all believed in it.[11]

Hockney's 'shower paintings' were among the first he made after his arrival in California in December 1963. He was attracted to California

43

initially for sexual reasons. His fascination with the West Coast as a resource for his paintings – the architecture, climate, beach showers, swimming pools and billboards – came later. In *Dancing Ledge*, Jarman with the benefit of hindsight is dismissive of the lionising of American culture by British artists such as Richard Hamilton in reaction to drab, utilitarian 50s Britain. For Jarman, this simply meant that 'J. Edgar Hoover slept more soundly in his imperial bed, for the last great binge of Capital was on'.[12] Jarman's own artistic interests lay towards Europe, and in particular Italy. He was later to criticise Hockney for leading the exodus to the United States:

> The English art world quickly decided the canvas ad was bigger, brighter and therefore better in the USA. 'Go west young man!' and David Hockney did, trail-blazing for a whole generation. What price Typhoo tea or the Bradford Public Baths when you could sit in the sun by the pool in Los Angeles? What price all this? Later, we would find out that you were invited to admire, not to partake. ... The real prizes were for the home-grown product, washed around the world on an ocean of tax-deductible dollars.[13]

Revisiting Hockney's London Powis Terrace home for dinner in 1971, Jarman complained of its 'Art Deco blight' and 'antiseptic' atmosphere. He fled believing that 'the dollar dowagers' had taken Hockney over.[14] The relaxed time some years earlier when Ossie Clarke and Jarman had sat in bed with Hockney reading physique magazines after the Picasso show was gone. But if Jarman rejected, perhaps necessarily, Hockney's aesthetic project, he embraced his sexual one.

In his severity towards Hockney, Jarman perhaps failed to take into account his fellow-painter's much less privileged background. In his reaction there are also feelings of regret at the distance created by fame and loss of things past. Without doubt, Jarman's early encounters with Hockney involved a kind of hero-worship. But Jarman's own visit to America in 1964, perhaps an unconscious mimicking of his 'hero', was not an entirely happy experience.[15] The intricacies of the gay art scene defeated him and American life and culture seemed not to his taste.

By 1982, in *Dancing Ledge*, his view of the 60s is caustic; he calls the period the 'swinging decayed'. On the other hand, the gay art world of the 60s had created a context in which he could exist:

> It was easy to have a good time. You felt that to be part of this world was an immense privilege, that the lifestyle was more affirmative than any other available. As the decade wore on the 'straight' world, I realised, was a giant vegetable nightmare from which I'd miraculously escaped. Like everything mundane, it made every effort to keep young men and women in its muddy waters.[16]

Launching a Career

In 1967 Jarman exhibited theatre designs for Prokofiev's *Prodigal Son* at the 'Biennale des Jeunes' in Paris, which led to his employment as the set designer for Frederick Ashton's *Jazz Calendar* at the Royal Opera House, Covent Garden, starring Rudolf Nureyev and Antoinette Sibley.[17] This was the first step in Jarman's artistic career and perversely he began, as he always acknowledged, at the top. His designs had the architectural, minimalist precision of his paintings, a predilection that remained, belying his reputation for florid theatricality (as late as *Edward II* he used the monastic simplicity of the film studio as a backdrop). The curves and circles of colours in the *Jazz Calendar* set made the ballet, which opened in early 1969, look like 'Licorice Allsorts dancing'. The set was favourably reviewed, though Jarman's own memories are of Nureyev leading him a merry dance, sometimes cruelly, over the costumes.

In the same year Jarman was asked to design the opera *Don Giovanni* at the London Coliseum. The experience was quite different and he was later to claim that his inexperience led to his designs being sabotaged backstage by all and sundry. When the curtain fell, 'John Gielgud and I faced a barrage of hissing' and the geometric, modern sets were violently criticised. Director Gielgud accused the audience and critics of misunderstanding modern art, but Jarman believed this to be an act of kindness on Gielgud's part and that 'in his heart he dislikes my designs'. Jarman's career as a theatre designer had now 'been brought to an abrupt halt, not a moment too soon'.[18]

In one of his last autobiographical publications, Jarman recalls a verbal exchange which perhaps characterises the incestuous circles of the gay art world:

45

At Hockney's '68 Kasmin opening a friend – the painter Stephen Buckley – said 'Well, you're running out of Knights to sleep with, Derek' very loudly. I had just finished designing [Sir] Frederick Ashton's *Jazz Calendar* and was in the middle of *Don Giovanni* for [Sir John] Gielgud. Fred Ashton, who was meant to hear this (and did), laughed.[19]

Jarman's work bore no traces of Hockney's and Procktor's Pop Art style. On the contrary, his paintings have a cool, analytical and somewhat surreal feel, owing more to the canvases of de Chirico, whom he greatly admired. In 1967 Jarman exhibited in the 'Young Contemporaries' at the Tate Gallery and in 1969 showed paintings, drawings and set designs at the new Lisson Gallery in London. Norbert Lynton, reviewing the show for the *Times*, described the paintings as:

> very bare things of a few lines and occasional patches on a flat ground. The lines suggest landscape. ... He reduces his landscape data to the barest minimum. He inserts non-landscape hints. Black lines on white really have precious little of landscape feeling about them. ... When he paints gold lines on pale ochre he is tempting us to think of something else ... he is forcing us to shrug off the landscape reading and to find some other applicable reading.[20]

He ends a laudatory review by remarking that 'an easy stroll of the imagination turns out to be an adventure'.

The Counter-Culture

While Jarman's career as a painter drew on his position as part of the gay art scene, his film-making, which was some years off, was influenced as much by the 60s counter-culture or underground. He remarks in *Dancing Ledge* that he put away his earlier 'high art' tastes and replaced them with pop music, modernist-influenced literature and alternative theatre. He read Beat poets such as Corso, Ginsberg and Ferlinghetti and, of course, William Burroughs.

> Our world was one in which Britain caught up suddenly with the twentieth century. The post-war austerity was a thing of the past.

'Untitled', c. 1963 **47**

European and American influences flooded in – not Elvis, but Miller, Pound, Genet, Cocteau. ... We stumbled across this cornucopia in a jumble – editions by the Olympia Press and City Lights excitedly exchanged.[21]

In the world of film, it was an interest in American underground cinema that inspired young art radicals such as David Curtis. For Jarman, American film-makers Maya Deren and Kenneth Anger were especially influential – when he saw the latter's gay films from the 40s at Camberwell Art School, 'we expected a police raid'.[22]

This counter-culture informed the radical student movement, especially important in British art colleges, and provided some of the intellectual background for the Gay Liberation Movement, founded in 1971. For Jarman, the underground was inseparable from his sexuality:

> What did that mean to me or my friends with cock up our arses and come splattering the ceilings? We joined THE UNDERGROUND. The underground, like the bars, was illicit.[23]

Thus the 60s scene involved two intersecting worlds – one the intellectual, art-centred counter-culture and the other the glitzy world of pop stars, fashion designers and photographers in which the values of marketing and publicity were central. As Robert Hewison observes:

> While the Pop culture helped to release energies and break down former rigidities of taste and manners, the abandonment of constraints also liberated darker, irrational forces in the underground culture that developed parallel to it.[24]

In *Dancing Ledge* Jarman describes an evening in 1967 with David Medalla's Exploding Galaxy doing Artaud's *Spurt of Blood* at the Royal College:

> There were explosions in which great polystyrene rocks fell on the audience, who ducked and almost panicked. Then a whole troop of Lolitan nymphets danced, Isadora-like, in very skimpy Greek dresses

through the audience with spray cans of lavender scent, singing as they slid off the knees of the oldest men in the audience. In the row in front of me a woman in an expensive fur sat unaware of the blood dripping all over her from the cow's head and hooves suspended above the audience and hidden by the lighting grid. We were repeatedly informed, like Candide, that we lived in the best of all possible worlds. Everything went wrong. Finally the nanny lifted up her skirts and a red balloon inflated between her legs until it burst. This was the best piece of experimental theatre that I've ever seen.[25]

The shock tactics and social and cultural criticism of counter-culture artists such as the Theatre of Cruelty were to be developed in Jarman's films of the 70s. A distrust of words, a desire to penetrate the mystery of human passions and an insistence on the authenticity of personal experience as the only valid measure of moral judgment were common values.[26] This suggests that Jarman's 'excesses' owe as much to the extreme experimentation of 60s art forms as they did to the films of Ken Russell. Jarman's interest in Exploding Galaxy was the beginning of a long involvement with fringe dance groups and personalities such as Lindsay Kemp.

Another influential part of the 60s underground was the development of alternative communication systems operating outside the restrictions of the mass media. Small magazines proliferated and some, like *International Times* (*IT*), became hugely successful (*IT* achieved a print run of 50,000 in 1968).[27] Co-operative-organised magazines such as *Time Out*, which covered the alternative scene, were also important, while the Arts Lab in Drury Lane, with its mattresses for seats in its tiny cinema, typified current attitudes promoting self-help and organisation. Jarman's survival as a film-maker depended on such an ethic. His super-8 film-making of the 70s took place in his Bankside studio, in which he also held screenings on a non-commercial basis.

Despite the legal reforms of the 60s, as a gay man Jarman's lifestyle continued to revolve around an 'alternative scene' long after the counter-culture underground had effectively ceased to exist. The gay world of London had, and still has, its own clubs, pubs and public meeting-places as well as its own cultural milieu. For good reason, homosexuality was a state of being that never ceased to operate in an underground fashion and this in

49

part accounts for Jarman's lifelong suspicion of orthodox 'overground' institutions.

In *Dancing Ledge* Jarman looks back on the 60s with a mixture of cynicism and affection. He provides a collage of memories of events, people, books, films and encounters. He remembers regularly seeing the gay dramatist Joe Orton in Chapel Market, Islington; sitting in Procktor's studio or his friend Anthony Harwood's flat; demonstrating in Fleet Street against Mick Jagger's arrest for possession of drugs; seeing the dancer Wayne Sleep in the King's Road; attending *Comedy of Errors* seven times; reading Ferlinghetti, Corso, Ginsberg, Burroughs and Kerouac's *Book of Dreams*; viewing Anger's *Magick Lantern Cycle* and Warhol's *Sleep*. On a more personal note he writes in retrospect:

> I became obsessed by the beauty of young men – the obsession alternated elation with paranoia. I failed to declare my passions lest they cause embarrassment. Then rushed headlong into the back room for public sex.[28]

Much could be made of this declaration in terms of Jarman's films. Jarman always tended to idealise the love-object in his films in a non-sexual fashion, setting this Platonism against sexual violence and degradation.

Jarman was still painting throughout this period. In August 1968 he moved into a warehouse at Upper Ground at the end of Blackfriars Bridge in London, the first of a series of such homes. This coincided with a fundamental change of artistic career, brought about by a lucky accident which was to lead him to the world of film.

1 To my knowledge, the intricacies of the 60s scene of pop stars, artists, dealers and so on have never been researched. Memoirs by such as Jarman and Marianne Faithfull suggest a fine web of relationships between the different power-centres of the 60s elite.

2 Derek Jarman, *Modern Nature: The Journals of Derek Jarman* (London: Century, 1991), p.197.

3 The shifting sexual and gender perspectives of Nicolas Roeg's film *Performance*, made in 1968, are a good example of this tendency. See also Marianne Faithfull's autobiography *Faithfull* (Harmondsworth: Penguin, 1995).

4 *Modern Nature*, p. 176.

5 Keith Vaughan, *Journals 1939–1977* (London: John Murray, 1989).

6 *Modern Nature*, p. 153.

7 Ibid.

8 Patrick Proktor, *Self-Portrait* (London: Weidenfeld & Nicolson, 1991), p. 98.

9 Derek Jarman, *Dancing Ledge* (London: Quartet, 1984), p. 74.

10 Ibid., pp. 70–2.

11 Ibid., pp. 13–15.

12 Ibid., p. 62.

13 Ibid.

14 Ibid., p. 93 for a description of this event.

15 Ibid., pp. 63–6.

16 Ibid., p. 95.

17 Hockney had paved the way with his set designs for Jarry's *Ubu Roi* at the Royal Court Theatre in 1966.

18 *Dancing Ledge*, p. 88.

19 Derek Jarman, *At Your Own Risk* (London: Hutchinson, 1992), p. 52.

20 Norbert Lynton, 'Bare landscape, an invitation to play', *Guardian*, 12 March 1969, p.6.

21 *Modern Nature*, p. 194.

22 *At Your Own Risk*, p. 42.

23 Ibid.

24 Robert Hewison, *Too Much: Art and Society in the Sixties 1960–75* (London: Methuen, 1986), p. xv.

25 *Dancing Ledge*, pp. 83–4.

26 Hewison, *Too Much*, p. xv.

27 Ibid., p. 95.

28 *Dancing Ledge*, p. 95.

Chapter Three

HOME MOVIES

1970–1975

In 1969 Jarman, newly installed in his warehouse home on the Thames, had the sense of a new beginning:

> the warehouse allowed me to slip quietly away from the 'scene' which for five years had been the centre of my life – and had now exhausted itself – and establish my own idiosyncratic mode of living.[1]

At about the same time, a chance encounter on a train with a teacher from Hornsey College of Art resulted in a visit from director Ken Russell who, after perusing Jarman's set designs for *Jazz Calendar* and *Don Giovanni*, immediately offered him the job of set-designer on his new film project, *The Devils*. Following the failure of *Don Giovanni* Jarman had vowed never to do set design again, but twenty-four hours after the meeting with Russell he accepted the offer and his career in film began. It is ironic that someone who was later to be identified with 'a cinema of small gestures' was initiated into film-making through the big-budget, razzmatazz world of Russell's features.

At this time Jarman also acquired a super-8 camera and began to make short films, which he referred to as 'home movies'. These were vital years of learning his craft, experimenting with visual ideas and developing a personal style and sensibility. Interestingly, the range of approaches and scale that were to characterise his later films are already apparent in his first works.

The super-8 films of this period express Jarman's own concerns as an artist and not those of mainstream narrative cinema. His time spent in the Slade's theatre design room had not been wasted, nor had his experience in designing sets for opera and ballet. In addition he had the good fortune to work with the one director in Britain who shared his enthusiasm for *mise en scène*, wayward expressionism and strong anti-naturalism.

52 'In the Shadow of the Sun'

The Early 70s Glitterati and Other Influences

In the early 70s both the hedonism and the idealism of the 60s began to fragment and dissolve. Mary Whitehouse's right-wing Festival of Light, set up to outlaw the representation of 'permissive' ideas and pornography, was born; in 1972 members of the anarchist organisation the Angry Brigade were sentenced to long terms of imprisonment for their bombing activities. Inflation was high and unemployment reached a million for the first time since the pre-war years. In 1970 a Conservative government was voted into power.

The radicals of the 60s split into two camps: political activists who worked in the parties of the extreme left wing and 'laughing, loving, lazy, fun-powder radicals'. Jarman was part of the latter trend – fashionable, camp and artistic, and an extension of the English bohemian tradition. It was also a world in which gay fashion and ideas were in the ascendancy.

In the 70s Jarman's social life revolved around the world of artists, designers and pop stars – what he himself called the 'glitterati'. (Significantly, his exotic warehouse home was photographed for Italian *Vogue* during this period.) It was a circle which Peter York maliciously dubbed the 'Them' people and its members featured in Jarman's early super-8 films.[2] The artist John Whitney and Luciana Martinez, who according to York were at the centre of this social elite, appear together in Jarman's *The Art of Mirrors* (1973). Martinez assisted Jarman on *Sebastiane* and also appears on the arm of Borgia Ginz in *Jubilee*. This circle also included the painter Duggie Fields (the subject of a super-8 film by Jarman and a participant in *Jubilee*), Ossie Clark and David Hockney as well as musicians Bryan Ferry, Brian Eno and Amanda Lear. The artist Peter Logan occupied the studio above Jarman's at this time, before his younger brother Andrew, organiser of the Alternative Miss World events, moved in. Brian Eno, ex-member of Roxy Music, wrote soundtrack music for *Sebastiane* and *Jubilee*, as well as Malcolm Le Grice's avant-garde classic *Berlin Horse* (1970). York wickedly described *Sebastiane* as a film 'with a cost [*sic*] of hundreds of Thems'.

For York, the Thems represented a certain sensibility and style – he accuses Pop Art of teaching 'Them how to look at things in a cock-eyed way'. A major factor was camp, a defining property of pop figures such as David Bowie and Roxy Music. York, drawing on an article by John Lombardi, stresses the influence of gays on mainstream culture:

54

Lombardi showed how the assimilation of camp – once largely a homosexual sensibility – had begun to effect the marketing of all sorts of things sold to non-queer people in America. At the beginning of the seventies, homosexuals became ... the niggers of the time, the O.K. outgroup. Gay became lay. The result of this exchange was that: a) 'Straight' people learned to think and look at things in 'camp'. It was the new ghetto sensibility. b) A lot of homosexuals left the Boys'Town ghetto and became more relaxed and mainstream, and thus more influential.[3]

These were the post-Warhol years, when Warhol's protégé Paul Morrissey was directing a series of films starring Joe Dallesandro: *Flesh* (1968), *Trash* (1970) and *Heat* (1971). Shot in a quasi-realist manner, their subject matter was the world of bought or casual sex, drugs, drag queens and transvestites.[4] Andrew Logan's Alternative Miss World competitions were one of the Thems' climactic annual events – Jack Hazan's *A Bigger Splash* shows the 1972 contest and Jarman's footage of another show is included in *Glitterbug* (1994). York describes the competition of 1975, which Jarman won. It was held in Logan's apartment and its judges included David Hockney, Zandra Rhodes, Amanda Lear, Justin de Villeneuve, Janet Street-Porter and Kevin Whitney.

A further defining characteristic of the Thems, according to York, was the influence of British art schools.[5] York points out that:

Art school people and quasi art school people, post art school people, fashion business people and Applied Art media stars were ... in the forefront of this merging of sensibilities.[6]

As part of this scene, Jarman was known mainly for his design work. In 1972 he had a dismal experience staging the pop star Alice Cooper. The following year he was in Italy doing research for Russell's adaptation of Rabelais' *Gargantua* and *Pantagruel*, which never took off, and he designed a ballet, *Silver Apples of the Moon*, choreographed by Tim Spain, the Coliseum opening of which was cancelled due to a dispute about the use of flesh-coloured tights. Jarman was especially disappointed as he believed this was his best theatre design work to date – when the show was staged in Oxford, the audience, on seeing the opening scene, 'burst into spontaneous applause':

> The front cloth is painted from a black and white photograph of a
> galaxy – the set is simple, consisting of several hundred half-silvered
> bulbs in silver holders on transparent flex which hang from the bars in
> rows. Behind them is a second black and white cloth painted with arcs
> tracked by comets with small red, yellow and blue arrows. The
> costumes follow this through – the men are in black dinner-jackets
> with red, yellow and blue gloves and shoes, and silvered spectacles –
> the girls are in primary coloured tutus and the mirrored glasses.[7]

In 1976 Jarman showed ten slate drawings at the American Biennial
Exhibition in Houston, Texas, curated by Bryan Montgomery, alongside
works by Keith Milow and Mario Dubsky. In 1978 he had an exhibition of
paintings, drawings and designs at the Sarah Bradley Gallery in London. But
during the 70s Jarman, as he himself recognised, had forfeited painting for
film.

Set Designs and Collaboration with Ken Russell

Ken Russell became an *enfant terrible* of British cinema after a brilliant period
in the late 50s and 60s as a director for Huw Weldon's BBC *Monitor*
programme. His television films on composers – especially Elgar, Debussy
and Delius – showed his strong visual sense, love of music and almost
mystical view of the creative act. Russell introduced an essentially anti-
naturalist expressionism into British cinema; his view of music as a vehicle
for the composers' inner emotions, expressed through a montage of effects,
appalled the realists in the British film tradition. When he met Jarman he had
already made *French Dressing* (1963), *Billion Dollar Brain* (1967), the highly
successful *Women in Love* (1969) and the controversial *The Music Lovers*
(1970), based on the life and music of Tchaikovsky.

To see the opening sequence of *The Devils* – a high camp tableau of
the King of France cavorting in a skimpy gold lamé bikini with high-kicking
dancers and a tacky theatrical *mise en scène* watched by an aghast and
eventually bored cardinal – is to be reminded of the visual excess, camp
humour and irreverence Jarman and Russell share. Like Jarman's own
treatments of history, *The Devils* replays a historical event with a gusto and

energy that refuses to be deflated in deference to po-faced conventions about interpreting the past; it captures history as a living moment, not simply as costume drama. But the differences between the two directors run deep. In a revealing diary entry in *Dancing Ledge*, Jarman describes how a scene he had suggested to Russell for *The Devils* was transformed. Jarman had wanted Louis XIII to be shooting peacocks on the lawn as he ate, an idea which Russell changed to the King shooting men dressed as blackbirds with the quip 'Bye, bye blackbird'. As Jarman saw it:

> The idea had been transformed from the steely, vicious concentration of a scene from *The White Devil* to a farce, a flip joke in a nasty little garden at Pinewood, instead of a great abstract topiary set with strutting peacocks.[8]

A comparison of Russell's scene with the magnificent opening shot of Jarman's *Jubilee* where a dwarf lady-in-waiting walks dogs between the shadowy bushes of the Queen's palace highlights the ultimate difference in the two directors' sensibilities. While such scenes in Jarman's work have wit and humour, there is an icy tension and a metaphoric import over and above any simple visual joke.

With their futuristic, hard-edged angularity, Jarman's sets for *The Devils* are similar in feel to his paintings and theatre designs. The same style is apparent much later in the sets for *Edward II* and is expressive – as are Fritz Lang's sets for *Metropolis* (1926) – of the cold oppressiveness of institutions and the rationalist ordering of social life. The designs for *The Devils* were suggested to some extent by Aldous Huxley's book, of which the film is an adaptation.[9] Huxley's account of the true story of the 'demonic' possession of nuns in early seventeenth-century France makes reference to the 20th century, and Jarman's use of the white-bricked, futuristic St Peter's church is a deliberate anachronism: 'the architecture of the entire city is anachronistic – intentionally so, since Russell's film is about a past which warns us about the present and possible future'.[10] This placing of contemporary images or elements in supposedly historical scenarios is a device Jarman used in many of his own historical feature films. He has cited Eisenstein as a precursor in this matter,[11] but Russell's influence was surely more direct and potent.

Russell's film sets became a minefield for Jarman to work on. In

57

Dancing Ledge he makes several references to the obdurate behaviour of professional extras, an experience, budget apart, which perhaps governed his own future use of friends as extras. 'The extras can be as stubborn as mules,'[12] he remarked. He also fell foul of the hair and wardrobe people when he too enthusiastically removed tacky plastic roses from the courtiers' hair, almost bringing filming to a halt in the ensuing demarcation dispute. The year spent working on the film left Jarman with little energy for painting or social life:

> By the time I emerged from Pinewood in December, the easy life of the sixties – designing and painting – had gone for ever. It was now impossible to pick up all the threads. Painting was the major victim: I continued it over the next ten years very sporadically.[13]

Not only had Jarman had an excellent apprenticeship in feature film production, but, as he stated many years later, 'There was no better director to learn from, as he [Russell] would always take the adventurous path even at the expense of coherence'.[14] Imperceptibly transformed, Jarman was to find painting a rather unexciting experience in the following year: 'After the intense pressure under which a film is made, it seemed undemanding – and the isolation in which it was pursued, enervating.'[15]

In December 1971 Russell invited him to design *The Savage Messiah*, an account of the life of the poverty-stricken sculptor Gaudier Brzeska, who died in the trenches in the First World War. According to Jarman, he was asked because of his admiration for English painters of the period, particularly Vanessa Bell. Jarman found Gaudier 'an equivocal character' but was intrigued by the sculptor's social range – part of the Diaghilev set and at the same time a 'wild boy' keen on boxing. Jarman organised the making of period chairs, crockery and copies of Gaudier's drawings. Christopher Hobbs, whom he brought in as his assistant, carved a seventeen-foot Easter Island head out of polystyrene, and when a hired monumental mason failed to deliver anything like a convincing torso, Jarman and Hobbs feverishly and painfully carved it themselves out of a block of marble. Jarman's account of his experience of the film in *Dancing Ledge* is dominated by Russell's megalomaniac shoutings and ravings. It was a directorial style he himself avoided, partly because of his personality and partly as a result of his decision to stay away from the pressures of huge-scale productions.

58

The film adaptation of Rabelais' *Gargantua* and *Pantagruel* was offered to Russell by the producer of Pasolini's *Decameron* and *Canterbury Tales*. John Baxter, in his book on Russell published in 1973, states that the Italian director had pulled out of the film, which was scripted by the novelist Alberto Moravia. Baxter also supplies a revealing contemporary sketch of Jarman and Russell working together on the project (which never came to fruition):

> From the moment I come into the room I sense the old electricity. Prue [Russell's secretary] presses letters into Ken's hands which are signed while he goes on discussing ideas with Jarman, a calm, colourful gypsy-like young man whose ear-rings, half-boots and embroidered jacket do not detract from an air of studious absorption. ... Russell supplies the motive force, the key structure, and draws on Jarman's visual flair to fill in the spaces. Not afraid to say 'That's wrong' or 'You've done that before', Derek acts as a brake and anchor on Ken's ballooning imagination.[16]

Given Jarman's popular reputation for excess, the idea of him acting as a brake on the imagination of another director has a certain irony. Baxter's observations also show Jarman's ability to stand up to Russell's strong personality, though Jarman's own account of the experience reveals a world of 'directorial hysteria' and humiliation. Baxter goes on to suggest an interesting possibility:

> If such a relationship can hold against Ken's instinctive and abrasive methods and Derek's essentially non-filmic orientation – he worked on no other films except those of Russell and, though he was approached by Stanley Kubrick for his new film, shows little inclination to do so – it should have an important effect on the careers of both men.[17]

Of course, Baxter did not know that as he wrote Jarman was making super-8 films (*The Art of Mirrors* was completed in July 1973). However, it was true that Jarman had no serious 'inclination', at least for the time being, to make feature films.

59

The Early Super-8s

Jarman was at an impasse when in late 1970 he met Marc Balet, an American architectural student, later to become the art director of Warhol's *Interview* magazine, who stayed with him at Bankside. Jarman was neither enthusiastic about painting nor willing to follow up his experience of working on *The Devils*, though during 1971, between *The Devils* and *The Savage Messiah,* he had painted 'a series of blue capes'. Balet brought with him a super-8 camera which he gave to Jarman. This gift was to transform his life.

The super-8 had been launched by Kodak in May 1965 as a home-movie camera to document ordinary events in the way video has been marketed in recent years. This new 'amateur' gauge superseded the standard 8mm gauge and introduced a camera which was more compact, lighter and incorporated facilities such as automatic light metering to make it more foolproof. It used easy-to-load cassettes and the more expensive models had many special effects features. It was readily available from stores such as Boots. As Jo Comino noted:

> The cheapness of equipment and stock means that footage can be collected and stored for future reference, rather like keeping a film diary or notebook. ... The ease and speed with which the cameras handle make them ideal for capturing live events as they happen.[18]

The use of super-8 as a serious gauge for film-making was negligible at this time, though American avant-garde film-maker Stan Brakhage worked with it and Klaus Wyborny in Germany had been experimenting with it since the mid-60s – see the flickering, refilmed landscape scenes in Werner Herzog's *The Enigma of Kaspar Hauser* (1974). Unexcited by his painting and exhausted by the rigours of the film studios, Jarman embarked on a series of films.

Colin MacCabe has remarked that Jarman's super-8 films of the 70s 'remain irredeemably private, films which can only be truly enjoyed (as in their original screenings) by an audience entirely composed of their actors'.[19] While this is true of certain of the films, although by and large these are ones Jarman did not show publicly, it is not the case with many of the others. *In the Shadow of the Sun*, *The Art of Mirrors*, *Sulphur* and *Fire Island*, for instance, are substantial works shot in super-8 during this period all of which embrace a poetic form. (Pointedly, Jarman claimed in his final months that *The Angelic Conversation*, made in the 80s but shot primarily on super-8 and transferred to 35mm, was the film that expressed his own thoughts and feelings most successfully.) The super-8 films discussed in this chapter are often visionary and always intensely visual, with overwrought symbolic references. They have none of the social and political resonance of *Imagining October*, or of feature films like *The Garden* or *Blue*, but like any other mode of representation they are not 'irredeemably private', but form a different kind of address in the way that, say, poetry does in comparison with the novel.

Whether Jarman was aware of it or not, the 'home movie' had been a strong current in avant-garde cinema since its beginnings in the 20s. Man Ray and Luis Buñuel, and in the 30s Jean Cocteau, had all made 'home movies' in that they had used props to hand, friends as actors and their surroundings as sets – Man Ray's *L'Etoile de mer* (1928) and Buñuel's classic *Un Chien andalou* (1928) are very much home movies in this sense. Kenneth Anger and Maya Deren in the US in the mid-40s also used their own apartments and friends to make *Fireworks* (1947) and *Meshes of the Afternoon* (1943) respectively. The most systematic and committed exponent of the home movie in an avant-garde context was the New York film-maker Jonas Mekas in such films as *Lost, Lost, Lost* (1949–75). Though not a member of the London Film-Makers' Co-operative (LFMC), Jarman was certainly in touch with the burgeoning avant-garde film movement of the early 70s, in which film-makers such as Malcolm Le Grice, Peter Gidal and David Larcher were making no-budget films in a fine art context. Anger's *Fireworks* (1947) and *Scorpio Rising* (1963), which obviously influenced Jarman, were shown at the Spontaneous Festival of Underground Film organised by the underground magazine *IT* and held in London's Cochrane Theatre as well as at the newly founded LFMC in late 1966, probably their first screenings in Britain.[20] This places the screening Jarman attended between 1966 and 1970, when the films were probably in distribution. We also know that he was familiar with Warhol's films, though he was later to remark that unlike the films of Anger and Antony Balch's 'cut-up' films made with William Burroughs, these had not influenced his work.

Interestingly, Jarman's early super-8s, like the work of Anger and Warhol, do not explore the personal experience of being gay. Both Anger and Warhol were reluctant, for different reasons, to be known as gay film-makers

61

and their work asserts instead a surface style and ambivalence that can be read as a gay sensibility expressed in an oblique way. Anger's high camp theatricals are sieved through ritual and artifice while Warhol's films are often bleak depictions of the camp 'personalities' who hung out at the Factory. Jarman's own most ambitious super-8s of the 70s share these characteristics. In both Anger and Warhol, as in the underground in general, there is a strong sense of the 'home movie', the personal production of images and ideas.

During the 70s Jarman hosted screenings of a range of films in his Bankside warehouse, attended by many of his friends including Christopher Hobbs, Norman Rosenthal, Keith Milow and John du Cane from the LFMC: 'We scrambled Hollywood with the films John du Can [*sic*] brought from the Film Co-op – *The Wizard of Oz* and *A Midsummer Night's Dream* crossed with Structuralism.'[21]

Although there is an eclecticism here, Jarman's main reference point was to underground film, or what was to be called 'avant-garde' cinema. Unlike the formal film-making going on at the LFMC in the early 70s, underground cinema was not primarily concerned with formal experimentation at the price of content. Following the lead of the Beat writers, underground films were about alternative lifestyles, with drugs and 'eccentric' sexual behaviour as their main impetus, as in the work of Jack Smith, Ron Rice and to some extent Warhol and Anger. In Jack Smith's underground classic *Flaming Creatures* (1963), for instance, camp cross-dressing, richly decorated interiors and a sexual orgy overthrow mainstream values and norms. Closer to home, Le Grice's *Berlin Horse* and Larcher's *Monkey's Birthday* (1973–5) were also imagistic in style, stressing colour, texture and the almost hallucinatory quality of the film image.

This was the framework of influences in which Jarman was working when he began to make super-8s in the early 70s. Discussing gay cinema in the US in the 70s, Richard Dyer suggests that:

> Underground film was the space in which gay cinema could emerge, at that time. ... Gay film could be made in that space, partly because of the overlaps of avant-garde and gay milieux and the importance of homosexual imagery in what informed the underground (Freudianism, the novel of alienation, camp and pop art) but above all because of underground cinema's definition of cinema as 'personal'.[22]

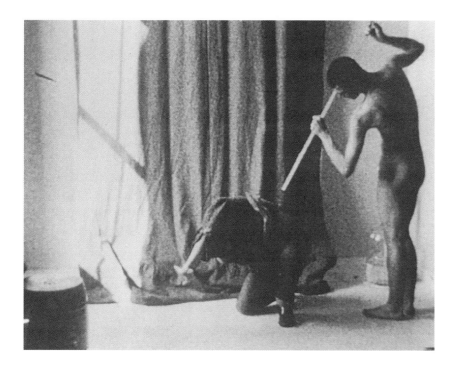

It was this idea of a personal cinema that Jarman wished to explore. His earliest super-8s can be divided into documents of his immediate environment and imaginative attempts at a form of experimental film-making. The two modes are not exclusive, though they do represent different ambitions. Jarman's autobiographical writings about the making of these films are sketchy. But it seems that in 1971 he made *A Journey to Avebury* and in 1972 *Miss Gaby, Garden of Luxor* and *Andrew Logan Kisses the Glitterati* with the more ambitious *The Art of Mirrors* being completed in 1973. The following year he made *The Devils at the Elgin, Ula's Fete, Fire Island* and *Duggie Fields*. In 1975 he made *Picnic at Rae's* and *Sebastiane Wrap* and worked on his first feature, *Sebastiane*, which was released in 1976.

Lasting about six minutes, *Studio Bankside* is Jarman's first film. It was edited in camera and is made up of a montage of static shots of his home, inside and outside. Many of the images are of photographs and are still. The camera moves only once. A motif of an electric light-bulb, its filament glowing orange, runs throughout. Friends pose for the camera, a cat walks out of the shadows. At one point we see Bob Dylan's *Blonde on Blonde* album cover and a hammock in the vast warehouse space.

'Art and the Pose' (later included in 'The Dream Machine') **63**

Twenty-five years on, the film has a charm and commitment not often found in first efforts. It reveals an artist's eye for detail – a shadow falling on the water, light reflected on a wall, a peeling surface, detritus gathered in a corner and friends posing on sofas as if in a Warhol movie. The music, provided by records and later tapes, was often changed, establishing different tones for these films – sometimes nostalgic with 30s crooners, sometimes elegiac with classical music (Jarman used Elgar to accompany *Studio Bankside* for the 1984 retrospective screening of most of his super-8s at London's Institute of Contemporary Arts[23]) and so on. Made to impress the film-maker and perhaps some close friends and very much an experiment with new technology, *Studio Bankside* has a lyrical gentleness. Following his traumatic experience on *The Devils* and lack of momentum in his painting, the film represented artistic freedom for Jarman.

A second film is always shown nowadays as part of *Studio Bankside*. It is shot in black and white and was made a few weeks before Jarman's studio was demolished (as was the area itself) in the late summer of 1972.[24] The film shows Jarman 'walking down King Street to Southwark Cathedral and back again'.

In 1972 Jarman also completed *A Journey to Avebury*, begun the previous year. In many ways less interesting than *Studio Bankside*, though obviously more controlled, it comprises a series of static shots of Avebury, its ancient stones and trees set against a panoramic horizon. An editing rhythm is attempted. Beside shots of landscape, we see a cow in a field and at one point some children sitting on a wall. The film has had various soundtracks including a medieval Provençal song which works well and a ponderous classical piece which does not help the awkward editing and conventional landscape shots. At around the same time Jarman painted the Avebury Series, a set of canvases which are geometrical and minimal in style, a good example of how his films and paintings often shared the same source of inspiration.

Garden of Luxor was made in 1972 and 'stars' Christopher Hobbs, who was also to be seen on the sofa in *Studio Bankside*. Hobbs, a close friend, designed many of Jarman's sets and built those for *Garden of Luxor*. Far more ambitious than his previous efforts, combining images and techniques that come to fruition only in *In the Shadow of the Sun*, *Garden of Luxor* testifies to Jarman's more confident handling of his medium.

The film uses a postcard photograph of the actual garden of Luxor.

A man dressed in black (Hobbs) whips something or someone off-shot, at the bottom of the frame. He has the look of a silent movie star (Valentino comes to mind) – the first filmic expression of Jarman's camp humour. At other times, in heavy romantic make-up and in close-up, Hobbs smokes a cigarette, and by means of a slow-motion reverse filming effect the smoke curls languorously back into his mouth and nose. Young men recline in exotic dress or stripped to the waist. There are close-ups of men and women's heavily made-up lips. Shadows and shapes merge. The mood is one of redolence and a heavy, erotic exoticism. With its Eastern trappings, *Garden of Luxor* is very much of its time. The imagery is reminiscent of parts of Nicolas Roeg and Donald Cammell's *Performance*, which was released in 1970 and which Jarman saw. The exotic Eastern look of *Performance* was provided by Christopher Gibbs.[25] But more interestingly, one wonders if the scene in which Anita Pallenberg films the sleeping Jagger and Michèle Breton with a super-8 camera in that film helped motivate Jarman's home movies.

Garden of Luxor is the first of Jarman's films to use superimposition. He projected two films, one on top of the other, on his living-room wall and refilmed the result. He used this primitive but perfectly adequate means of achieving such an effect without the use of an optical printer until the mid-80s. In *Garden of Luxor* images of the pyramids and the Sphinx merge with shots of the man. Towards the end we see found-footage of what looks like a desert battle-scene with men on horses, presaging Jarman's use of found-footage of Hitler, Stalin and Oswald Mosley intercut with footage from the Lewisham riots for the Marianne Faithfull *Broken English* promotion film in 1979. In *Dancing Ledge* Jarman stated that *Journey to Avebury* and *The Magician* (also known as *Tarot*) were the beginnings of a longer film which became *In the Shadow of the Sun* and into which *Garden of Luxor*'s pyramids and Sphinx were also integrated.

Miss Gaby was filmed in Andrew Logan's studio in 1972. It also has an exotic *mise en scène*, due again to the collaboration of Christopher Hobbs. A woman brushes her hair and in a repeated close-up we see her languidly blow the vivid red nail-varnish on her white hands. Her red lips are shown in close-up (reminiscent of the massive close-up of Sister Ruth's red lips in Powell and Pressburger's *Black Narcissus*, 1946). There are vivid images of flowers and pallid skin. As a portrait of a charming, eccentric French woman, *Miss Gaby* reveals Jarman's desire to deal with iconic images, with a coded

65

entry into personality through dress, artifice, *mise en scène* and colour. Like Powell's and Roeg's films, it denotes a Romanticism of visual excess and lyrical exoticism.

Another film of the same period, *Tarot*, is centred on Christopher Hobbs and shot in his Islington flat and on the river-front. Kenneth Anger's influence can be detected as Hobbs, dressed camply in an exotic fur collar, holds a candelabra. He opens a small antique drawer and fingers a piece of material. In slow motion, he claps his hands to produce a cloud of fine white dust. We then see him in theatrical formal dress with a top hat and umbrella. Photographer Gerald Incandela appears dressed as a woman in a diaphanous dress but with a black false nose similar to that worn by Max in *Sebastiane*.

The Art of Mirrors is a title Jarman used generically to describe a continually changing series of films. The film that emerged in the early 80s bearing that title was made in 1973 and shot at Butler's Wharf. It was a breakthrough film for Jarman. He received the footage through the post in July 1973 and watched it with excitement:

> This is the first film we've made on Super 8 with which there is nothing to compare. The other Super 8s of the last few months are still too close to 16mm work; whereas this is something which could only be done on a Super 8 camera, with its in-built meters and effects. At last we have something completely new.[26]

The Art of Mirrors contains themes and images that recur throughout Jarman's work: the theatrical positioning of characters in costumes, the use of a mirror to reflect light into the camera lens producing a moment of material-based abstraction and a fire, a motif derived from his fascination with Jungian symbolism. The film also includes his friends Kevin Whitney and Luciana Martinez participating in a cinema of gestures and Gerald Incandela wearing a paper-bag mask. The scene is reworked in Jordan's ballet around the burning books in *Jubilee*; in *The Art of Mirrors* the presentation is purely artistic whereas in *Jubilee* social and political implications are at the forefront.

In *The Art of Mirrors* there is for the first time the sense of a language being forged – one that rests heavily on Jarman's research into alchemy, Egyptology and Jungian symbolism. An interest in magic symbolism was not uncommon during this period – the 60s counter-culture with its antipathy towards rational systems of thought, which were seen to be part of repressive social systems, generated an enormous fascination for alternative forms of everything, including religion and belief-systems. As a result, magic and historical figures associated with it – from Paracelsus to William Blake – became part of the counter-culture of the early 70s. The Rolling Stones developed magical occult personae in their songs and stage performances,[27] while self-styled magus Kenneth Anger filmed *Lucifer Rising* (1970–80) with Marianne Faithfull as the female archetype Lilith.[28] Donald Cammell, who co-directed *Performance* and is held responsible for its 'diabolical' quality, appeared in *Lucifer Rising* as Osiris. Anger's film also used fire imagery for its symbolic-cum-magical connotations.

The Art of Mirrors was usually screened to the ethereal music of Varese, lending it a cold abstract quality of sheer artifice. The film is a difficult one and does not win audiences easily. But it was films like *The Art of Mirrors*, shot on super-8 with a strong imagistic aesthetic at a time when 16mm was *de rigueur* in the British avant-garde film movement, that were to inspire the super-8 movement of the early 80s. Young film-makers such as Cerith Wyn Evans, John Maybury and Michael Kostiff rejected the 16mm values of their avant-garde teachers and began a far-reaching change in experimental film. Jarman was an aesthetic precursor of this movement and aided it with time, money and support.

Fire Island is one of the most successful of Jarman's early super-8s. Shot in 1974 on a visit to the United States during which Jarman spent some time at the famous gay haunt, it was filmed over a single weekend and used hand-coloured theatre gels to achieve its effects. It was intended as the final section of *In the Shadow of the Sun*, though we know from Jarman's letters that until 1975 and beyond there was no clear conception of the latter film (its title, for instance, changed on numerous occasions). *Fire Island* is made up of seascapes with long-held shots of beach driftwood. There is a character with a starfish and a naked man with a fish. The dominant colour is red with a haze of purple and a blue sea with blotches of yellow. It has a similar artificial air to *The Art of Mirrors* and is the closest Jarman came to some of the minimal work being done in Britain at the time. The film is about the evocation of a mood: in its long shots it achieves a kind of reverie that resembles the mood of Jarman's early landscape paintings. With its hints of erotic passivity *Fire*

67

Island is something of a hymn to the beach pick-up.

Other films made by Jarman in the period before *Sebastiane* are often documents of events in his life. *Andrew Logan Kisses the Glitterati* has a late-Warholian feel, as Jarman's friends pose humorously on a sofa in front of the camera, though the film is decidedly light-hearted and more of a celebration of English camp. This kind of quasi-documentary filming remained a key aspect of Jarman's work – his filming of Tilda Swinton after *Caravaggio* provided footage for *The Last of England* and later footage of her at Dungeness became part of *The Garden*. The film of William Burroughs, *Pirate Tape/Film (WSB)* made in the 80s, was also a document of events as they happened dramatised only through the use of slow motion and a hypnotic Genesis P. Orridge soundtrack.

In 1974 Jarman made *Ula's Fete*, a whimsical document of a garden party organised by Luciana Martinez and Andrew Logan to raise money to pay for Ula's fine, incurred after being arrested for 'liberating a chandelier from Harrods'. Jarman called the event 'the last ghost of the sixties'.[29] The camera meanders freely among the guests being entertained in the garden. The painter Duggie Fields can be seen enjoying the proceedings. The controversial Italian film-maker Liliana Cavani came and spent her time looking for talent for her film project on Nietzsche. Little Nell (who was to play Crabs in *Jubilee*) and designer Rae Mouse were also there. Two women, one of whom's breasts keep popping out of her dress, do a high-kicking dance. Later there is a mock fashion show, Jarman's camera wittily picking out the teetering heels of the high-spirited 'models'. The music is a nostalgic-sounding 'Stalinist folksong' sung in Russian. The style of the film is casual camp. It has a remarkable air of an English summer Sunday with the innocence and confidence of a generation bathing in the last light of the 60s.

Duggie Fields, one of many films Jarman made of artists' and designers' studios, is a document of Fields' paintings and a semi-portrait of the artist. The music used for its screening at the ICA retrospective was the Rolling Stones track 'You Can't Always Get What You Want'. The film is not especially interesting except as a chronicle of Fields' paintings and the objects in his flat. *Picnic at Rae's*, made the following year, is a film of a picnic held by Rae Mouse, with Miss Gaby, Andrew Logan and Duggie Fields present. In these years Jarman seems to have acted as super-8 court portraitist for his circle, a role he never quite relinquished – his use of friends and 'scene

personalities' in his later feature films retained an aspect of portraiture. *Jordan's Dance*, shot in 1977, which not only inspired *Jubilee* but was incorporated into it in its entirety, is one of the most successful of his portraits since it merges the capturing of a personality with a symbolist setting. In 1976, after completing work on *Sebastiane*, Jarman made the pixillated *Sloane Square* (aka *Removal Party*), which used stop-frame filming techniques to show himself and his fellow occupants graffitiing a flat from which they were being evicted after a series of court cases with a belligerent landlord.

On a winter's day in 1975, Jarman shot one of the most beautiful of his super-8 films, *Gerald's Film*. At the time he was living with the photographer Gerald Incandela whom he had met in Italy while working on Ken Russell's planned adaptation of Rabelais' *Gargantua* and *Pantagruel* and who had come back to England with him after the project collapsed. Walking in an Essex wood, they stumbled across a ruined Victorian boathouse on the edge of a dried-up lake. As usual Jarman was carrying his super-8 camera, and he began filming. At first he shot from the outside and then filmed from within the skeletal frame, through which the sun streamed, casting shadows from the lattice windows and naked beams. Shooting at three to six frames per second, his camera slowly moved across the walls, skirting-board, timber beams, windowframes and floor, ending outside a window through which

Incandela could be seen sitting in a large fireplace. In a rhythmic movement, the camera zooms slowly to a close-up of the melancholic figure wearing a soft felt hat and neckerchief. Set to the intense strains of the same Mahler music used by Visconti in *Death in Venice* (1971), the film is a remarkable example of Jarman's ability to transform a simple situation into a film using the minimum of technique. It also demonstrates how adept he had become at judging how to use the hand-held camera in unpredictable situations. The high Romantic tone the film achieves is one he never wholly relinquished.

There is a temptation to treat Jarman's early home movies simply as experiments or amateurish documents of situations of little interest. But such films as *Garden of Luxor, Tarot, The Art of Mirrors, Fire Island* and *Gerald's Film* have a quality which should be tested against the burgeoning area of experimental film in Britain at the time. Jarman's use of superimposition, slow motion and symbolist scenarios owes much to the cultural overspill of a 60s drug-based aesthetic found also in film-makers such as David Larcher. He became more ambitious when he began attempting to tell stories, as when he took Christopher Hobbs and friends to Corfe Castle to shoot a medieval romance (which never actually surfaced as a film). It was perhaps a forerunner to *Bob Up a Down*, a film he never made but which existed as a script from at least the early 80s.

Jarman and the British Film Avant-Garde

The first half of the 70s saw the rise of a wave of British avant-garde film-making based around the London Film-Makers' Co-operative. The original inspiration for the LFMC members had been a mixture of anarchistic counter-culture forms and ideas derived from the Fluxus group and American conceptualism. But what began as an eclectic collection of film-makers, artists and musicians had by the early 70s become a more self-conscious attempt to construct a cinema with modernist aims coupled with a politics which regarded mainstream narrative cinema as an ideological tool for Western capitalism. This kind of film-making found its most powerful voices in Malcolm Le Grice and Peter Gidal, who forged a formalist project commonly but perhaps misleadingly known as 'Structural film'.

Around 1976 Jarman became involved, if marginally, in this scene. With its emphasis on form and 'process', it seemed far from his symbolist aesthetic. But Jarman shared with the avant-garde a desire to experiment and in particular an interest in multi-screen, expanded work, no doubt because of expanded cinema's power to overwhelm through its scale and potential for juxtaposing different films. In that year he showed at the Festival of Expanded Cinema at the ICA, organised by William Raban and Ron Hasleden to show recent multi-screen film installation work. In a letter to the organisers in 1975, Jarman states that he has been making films for five years, but 'never bothered to show them except this year to any but friends. Somehow this year everyone's interested.' He also remarks that he is about to have a screening in Brussels and another at the Museum of Modern Art in Paris.

The letter provides a fascinating insight into his attitudes towards film in general and his home movies in particular. The film he is working on is titled *In the Sun's Shadow*. He describes it as 'a sort of apocalypse' and states that it is two hours long. The film he is actually submitting, in an expanded format, is also two hours long (one might guess that it is more or less the same footage), in twenty-minute segments. It is titled *Film that Will End in Death*, and it 'can be shown independently'. As far as contemporary cinema is concerned, Jarman expresses the view that he finds 'all English film making with the exception of social documentaries and David Larcher excruciating'. At another point he describes super-8 as the opposite of 'expanded cinema', rather it is 'contraction to a point, the 20th century hieroglyphic monad' and has 'more to do with personal perception than any other gauge'. The letter betrays a guarded attitude to the festival and what it represents and a barely suppressed antagonism towards the avant-garde film scene. The film Jarman probably showed at this event was a three-screen version of the generic *The Art of Mirrors* comprising three shorts films – *Burning Pyramids*, *In the Sun's Shadow* and *Fire Film*. The festival was to be one of the last major events celebrating such a cinema in this country, though many years later I remember Jarman in conversation gleefully planning a multi-projection of one of his films with an Eisenstein classic. With *Blue* at the end of his life, there was a return to the idea of film as an event or happening, the inspiration in this case being the Dadaesque work of the French artist Yves Klein.

1976 was also the year in which the Arts Council of Great Britain's Artists' Films Committee launched its 'Film-makers on Tour' scheme, through which artists and venues were subsidised in order 'to encourage the screening of artists' films and to off-set some of the costs that are incurred in showing experimental film'. The participants were David Dye, Marilyn Halford, Ron Haselden, Tony Hill, Jarman, Jeff Keen, Malcolm Le Grice and William Raban. This list is another reminder of Jarman's involvement with the 'official' avant-garde. But while many of these film-makers are associated with so-called 'formal' film, figures like the anarcho-surrealist Keen and the performance artist Marilyn Halford cannot be so easily pigeon-holed.[30]

In an application to the Arts Council in April 1975 requesting funds to transfer super-8 footage to 16mm to facilitate distribution and exhibition of his films, Jarman clearly separates two strands in his work – an 'autobiographical' one and 'one structured around created events'. Of *Film that Will End in Death*, he says that it is 'now in its fifth section' and is 'mostly devoted to landscape'. There are eight cassettes in this section, entitled *Nostalgia, Miss Gaby Prepares a Meal, The Eye of the Storm, 1000 Molehills, The Puddle, Breakfast at the Pines, Going North* and *A Violent Moment*. These are diary films of actual events. But he also mentions a 'series of isolated sequences' entitled *The Art of Mirrors* (twenty minutes), *Burning the Pyramid* (six minutes), *A Sea of Storms* (thirty minutes) and *Archaeologies* (thirty minutes). I have attempted to sort out some of this in the section on super-8 films that forms part of the Filmography of this book, but at present many of these sections are untraceable.

Jarman also took part in the enormous 'Perspectives on British Avant-Garde Film' at the Hayward Gallery in 1977, organised by the Arts Council of Great Britain, where his work is placed under the heading of 'Expanded Cinema'. His programme notes today make fascinating reading:

> A. Reels 2 and 6, each 400 ft of Super 8 offcuts, are part of a film now eight reels long of reject footage accumulated over the last seven years. They are not chronological as the footage is pieced together from my rubbish bin which still contains footage shot several years ago.
>
> Reel 2 was made four years ago, and reel 6 last year. The editing is blind except for fragments I threw away whilst editing other films. The only unity is the fact that I shot all the footage myself: all on a N120 [*sic*] 4807 Super 8 camera in ektachrome 160.
>
> B. Diary Reel 3. Fragments 1971–74 400 ft.
>
> C. If there is time I will show THE KINGDOM OF OUTREMER

which I made in 1972–74. This film is based on my friendship with
John Dee the Elizabethan magician, and was pieced together after
reading his angelic conversations. At the time I was interested in
superimposition and refilmed Super 8 techniques which were not
available for film-makers in 16 mm. These had not been explored in
the smaller gauge and this film was one of the results. When I had
finished it I put it away. I was looking at it the other day and decided
I liked it more now than then[31]

It is not clear how the multi-projection was to work or how many
screens it involved, though the film in question again seems to be what
became *In the Shadow of the Sun*. It was probably a similar piece to the multi-
projection submission to the Festival of Expanded Cinema at the ICA.

'In the Shadow of the Sun' and Other Projects

It could be said that Jarman's intellectual framework in the mid-70s was
dominated by his study of the Elizabethan intellectual, scientist-cum-cabalist
and political adviser to the Queen, Dr John Dee. Two major film scripts –
Dr Dee: The Angelic Conversation and *The Art of Mirrors* – as well as *The Tempest*
date from this period. *In the Shadow of the Sun* is also a reworking of many of
these ideas, being in part a variant of the Dee project focusing on his research
into alchemy and the cabala. In 1975 Jarman wrote to television arts producer
Humphrey Burton and to the Arts Council enclosing his Dee script and one
of the early scripts of *The Tempest*. From the same year there also exists a
script titled *The Art of Mirrors/A Summoning of Angels* which was a rework
of the Dee scripts planned to be forty minutes in length and to use both
super-8 and 16mm when synch-sound was necessary. The sources cited by
Jarman in his introductory material accompanying the script are Jung's
Psychology and Alchemy, *Mysterium Confunctionis* and *Seven Sermons to the
Dead*; Edward Kelly's *Alchemycal Writings*; Dee's *Hieroglyphic Monas* and
Shakespeare's *The Tempest*. These same writings are cited in his notes to *The
Tempest* with the addition of Frances Yates' *Shakespeare's Last Plays*, *The Theatre
of the World* and *The Art of Memory*, plus Edward Gorey's *West Wing*.

Jarman's notebooks at this point are littered with art cinema titles.
In reference to the Dee script, he mentions Murnau's *Faust* (1926) and that
he has 'just seen Herzog's *Caspar Hauser* which uses 3 clips of super-8 to

73

wonderful effect'.[32] Antonioni's *L'avventura* (1960) is cited as an example of how grass should blow in the wind in an autumn 1974 notebook containing material on *The Tempest*. Like many of his generation of film-makers (Chris Petit, Sally Potter, Peter Greenaway), Jarman was inspired by the proliferation of art film in the New Waves of France, Germany and Italy. The films of Pasolini, Antonioni, Bergman, Godard, Truffaut, Resnais, Polanski and many others provided an education in the possibilities of cinema outside Hollywood and the mainstream.

Britain itself had witnessed a period of experimentation in films for general release in the late 60s and early 70s. Stanley Kubrick's *2001* (1968), with its obtuse storyline, lyrical slow motion, ironic use of music and optically printed 'LSD trip' sequence, offered a mainstream example of experimentation with narrative and form. Nicolas Roeg's *Performance*, made in 1968 but not released until 1970, was a film that in its complex narrative structure and themes of drugs and sexual identity stood against conventional notions of cinema. Both films dealt with mystical ideas. Lindsay Anderson's *If* (1968), with its angry blast at the British establishment and anti-naturalistic devices, heralded a more political stance, one that Jarman was to take up and develop in his own way. Like the upper-middle-class, public-school-educated Anderson, Jarman's politics smacked of a radical anarchism rather than the full-blooded Leftism of, say, Ken Loach. Richard Attenborough's *Oh! What a Lovely War* (1969), a film adaptation of a Joan Littlewood Theatre Workshop play, has an interesting sub-Brechtian music-hall style which Jarman was to exploit years later in *The Garden* (1990).

Throughout the early 70s Jarman was planning an ambitious film and many of his short super-8s were obviously conceived as sections of it. His notebooks reveal that this venture merged at times with others and had many different titles over the years. It was probably completed in 1974, although not titled until later. It eventually emerged at the end of the 70s as *In the Shadow of the Sun*, an amalgam of many of the short films which he later screened and distributed in their own right. This cumulative method of working is more akin to the artistic process of a painter or sculptor than a film-maker – a continual shaping, rejecting and reshaping of past and present work. It is a process Jarman never jettisoned, even when using scripts, and to this extent he is a film-maker who constructs much of his imagery post-filming – on the edit bench.

74

In an application to the Arts Council for a grant to make a 16mm print of the film (c.1980) he remarks that it:

> is a Fire film, an English apocalypse, starting with a journey to the stone circle at Avebury near Stonehenge. From this beginning the images develop with a dreamlike repetitive quality.[33]

In the same statement, a rare insight into his intention, he traces the film's background:

> *In the Shadow of the Sun* is a part of a series of films called *The Art of Mirrors* which were made in London from 1970–1974. The films were originally silent super 8 designed to be projected at 3–6 frames per second. At the time, the films were ancillary to my work as a painter, and were shown in my studio to friends who helped to make them, gradually becoming known outside this small circle.[34]

In the Shadow of the Sun was first shown in Berlin in 1981 and has rarely been shown in Britain. The cast includes Christopher Hobbs, Gerald

Incandela, Lucy Su, Kevin Whitney and Luciana Martinez. The film was influenced by Jung's *Alchemical Studies* and *Seven Sermons to the Dead*, which provided 'a key to the imagery'.[35] The title is an alchemical synonym for the philosophers' stone included in a book published in 1652 by Gratacolle William called *The Names of the Philosophers Stones*. The framework is based on Jung's studies of alchemy. Much of the footage had already been shot before Jarman read the Jungian texts, but he claimed that Jung 'gave me the confidence to allow my dream-images to drift and collide at random'.[36]

There are also alchemical ideas lodged in the film, especially in the use of text – which in the view of the cabala contained the hermetic secret of God in nature. The alchemical project was one of discovering in natural objects and materials the quintessence of the spirit. For the alchemists, the philosophical gold gained from alchemy was not material gold but something higher: philosophical gold was 'matter redeemed from baseness, dividedness and corruption' transformed into a matter of 'harmony and incorruptibility'.[37] Jarman remained attracted to a symbolic understanding of nature as a microcosm in which the macrocosm was present – a view shared by sixteenth-century cabala and Renaissance thinkers generally – and when he turned to his gardening in his final years he immersed himself in the assorted doctrines of herbalists of the same period.

In the Shadow of the Sun was an attempt by Jarman to resolve his ambitions for his super-8 work of the 70s. It was a film that was in the making for at least six years, taking different forms, as we have seen, during that time: Hobbs has remarked that Jarman spent a lot of time experimenting with techniques and images. He had worked out a precise structure, which he admits never found its way into the film, though many of the images detailed in his plan did. According to his outline, the first section was based on a journey to the ancient standing stones at Avebury in Wiltshire. The images include a man pointing, one tied up and another taking photographs. There are two fire mazes, one of which forms a circle in which a couple dance. Eventually the flames devour the standing stones and the whole landscape. Another figure, that of Narcissus, reflects light from a mirror into the camera lens so the image 'explodes and reinvents itself in a mysterious way'. Refilmed footage from *The Devils* of Madeleine escaping from Loudun was to be included, but what we would see is a woman in a 'blizzard of ashes'. In the second section there is an invocation consisting of black and white swathed figures walking through flames. A pharaoh figure appears in the sea and a bacchante dances. Finally a figure turns in a magic circle 'which burns the film out to white'. The third section includes typewritten messages and burning pyramids through which figures ride. Finally the image becomes abstract – a pulsating dance of atoms 'punctuated by explosions' and a rubric on a shell: SLNC IS GLDN.

If Jarman's aim was similar to Kenneth Anger's exploration of the magical world of myths, gods and occultists in such films as *Inauguration of the Pleasure Dome* and *Lucifer Rising*, then *In the Shadow of the Sun* fails. It lacks Anger's clarity of image and confident structure. However, Anger's interest seems quite different from Jarman's – for instance, in *Inauguration of the Pleasure Dome* he is concerned with the ironic depiction and expression of ritual whereas Jarman is attempting to use symbol and ritual to create emotions and moods. When Jarman discusses *In the Shadow of the Sun*, he draws attention to how the images are 'fused with scarlets, oranges and pinks'. The degradation of the film texture through refilming multiple projections (on to a white postcard stuck to the wall!) produces 'a shimmering mystery/energy like Monet's Nympheas or haystacks in the sunset',[38] a painterly quality unique to his super-8 work.

In the Shadow of the Sun uses superimposition, slow motion, choreographed staging and a modernist score by Genesis P. Orridge (performed by his band Throbbing Gristle, whom Jarman was to film in the early 80s) influenced by William Burroughs' 'cut-up' aesthetic. The effect is grating at times as the images shudder across the screen with no real purpose – a series of forms without substance. Jarman was aware of this problem and asserted in *Dancing Ledge* that the 'first viewers wracked their brains for a meaning instead of relaxing into the ambient tapestry of random images'.[39] Like his paintings, the film's landscapes contain unconnected symbolic figures and when connections are achieved, it is largely through the film's form. The image of fire is there throughout, as is that of violence (a bound man lies on the ground), while a woman dressed in sophisticated erotic clothing (pillaged from *The Art of Mirrors*) poses. Most importantly, the nude masked figures suggesting earlier classical times and the bust of Mausolos Jarman had rescued from the Slade studios symbolise an old order lost in the violent apocalyptic second Elizabethan age as well as the values of a civilisation that could embrace sexuality. The images of fire, hooded figures

77

and the photographer/film-maker were to appear often in subsequent films.

No doubt Jarman was encouraged by what he had produced in *In the Shadow of the Sun*. Against all the odds he had turned experiments with an amateur film gauge into a work of art which had some resonance for him. The film reflected a modernism he had revealed in his painting and there is no doubt that for him it was the achievement of this saturated collage effect that signalled the work's success. The film is one of Jarman's major achievements of the 70s, along with *Sebastiane*, *Jubilee* and *The Tempest*. The visual experimentation of *In the Shadow of the Sun* and the early home movies was to emerge fully-fledged in the feature films of the mid-80s and afterwards, when funding was more readily available and an audience reared on a cinema influenced by avant-garde ideas and techniques proved itself ready to take on experimental work.

From 1975 to 1980, Jarman worked mainly on three feature films. There is little doubt that this slowed down his production of home movies, though after *Sebastiane* he seems to have put his energies into showing the sections of what was to become *In the Shadow of the Sun* and finding a final shape for that film. His interest in super-8 film-making was to remain with him throughout his life and I am convinced it is this which gives his work its character and strength. I do not believe the super-8 films were made simply because he had no other more mainstream projects to occupy him; rather they signalled a need to work in an improvisational manner with friends in fluid situations, with all the control, spontaneity and sense of discovery this entails. Jarman never made a film he did not want to make. His commitment to the home movie (and eventually to video) was unique.

During the 70s Jarman still exhibited paintings and drawings quite regularly. In 1971 he showed drawings, paintings and designs for Ken Russell's *The Devils* at Bankside. The following year he was represented in an exhibition, 'Drawing', at the Museum of Modern Art in Oxford. In 1976 he had work in the American Biennial Exhibition in Houston, Texas. Two years later he had a collection of different kinds of work – paintings, film scripts, photographs, drawings – on show at Sarah Bradley's Gallery in London.

1 Derek Jarman, *Dancing Ledge* (London: Quartet, 1984), p. 96.

2 Peter York, *Style Wars* (London: Sidgwick & Jackson, 1980), pp. 112–28.

3 Ibid., pp. 115–16.

4 See Maurice Yacower, *The Films of Paul Morrissey* (Cambridge: Cambridge University Press, 1993).

5 For a full account of this phenomenon, see Simon Frith and Howard Horne, *Art into Pop* (London: Methuen, 1987); John A. Walker, *Cross-Overs: Art into Pop/Pop into Art* (London: Comedia, 1987).

6 *Style Wars*, p. 116.

7 *Dancing Ledge*, p. 132.

8 Ibid., p. 104.

9 For an excellent analysis of the film and its relationship to the book see Joseph A. Gomez, *Ken Russell: The Adaptor as Creator* (London: Frederick Muller, 1976).

10 Ibid., p. 101.

11 Alexander Walker, *National Heroes: British Cinema in the Seventies and Eighties* (London: Harrap, 1985), p. 231.

12 *Dancing Ledge*, p. 101.

13 Ibid., p. 105.

14 Ibid.

15 Ibid.

16 John Baxter, *An Appalling Talent/Ken Russell* (London: Michael Joseph, 1973), p. 229.

17 Ibid., p. 230.

18 Jo Comino in *Recent British Super 8*, Film and Video Umbrella Broadsheet, 1985.

19 Colin MacCabe, 'Edward II: Throne of Blood', *Sight and Sound*, vol. 1 no. 6, October 1991, p. 14.

20 When I invited Jarman to meet Anger at the latter's retrospective at the National Film Theatre in 1990, Jarman refused point blank, having promised a friend before he died that he would stay away from his evil influence. The story says as much about Anger's reputation gained in the 60s as it does about Jarman's superstition.

21 *Dancing Ledge*, p. 105. The boy actor Kenneth Anger has a small part in *A Midsummer Night's Dream* (Reinhardt/Dieterle, 1935).

22 Richard Dyer, *Now You See It: Studies on Lesbian and Gay Film* (London: Routledge, 1990), p. 172.

23 Jarman showed most of his completed super-8 films at the ICA Cinematheque in 1984 with his own recorded comments, from which much of the information on them has been gleaned by the author.

24 According to Jarman, the studio was on the site of the Elizabethan Globe Theatre.

25 See Peter Wollen, 'Possession', and Jon Savage's interview with Gibbs, both in *Sight and Sound*, vol. 5 no. 9, September 1995.

26 *Dancing Ledge*, p. 208.

27 See, for example, Marianne Faithfull, *Faithfull* (Penguin, 1995), pp. 211–16.

28 Ibid., pp. 297–300.

29 *Dancing Ledge*, p. 160.

30 The film under Jarman's entry in the accompanying Arts Council booklet to the Scheme is titled *In the Shadow of the Sun*. The other film titles he lists include ones that would be unfamiliar by the 80s: *Bankside* (now known as *Studio Bankside*); *New York Walk Don't Walk*; *Duggie Fields Earls Court Elegance* (now known simply as *Duggie Fields*); *Andrew Logan's Miss World* (now known as *Andrew Logan Kisses the Glitterati*); *Burning the Pyramids*; *Ula's Fete*; *Laetitia's Pot Plant*; *In the Shadow of the Sun* (forty-minute version) and *The Art of Mirrors*.

31 Notes to *Perspectives on British Avant-Garde Film* (London: Hayward Gallery, 1977).

32 These are the reverie-like scenes in Herzog's *The Enigma of Caspar Hauser* (1974) filmed by the German avant-garde film-maker Klaus Wyborny, one of the few dedicated proponents of super-8 film (always transferred to 16mm). On Wyborny, see *Afterimage*, no. 8/9, 1981.

33 One-page statement by Jarman for an Arts Council application for an English 16mm print of *In the Shadow of the Sun* at a time when he had already received German funding for a 16mm print.

34 Ibid.

35 *Dancing Ledge*, p. 128.

36 Ibid.

37 Charles Nicholl, *The Alchemical Theatre* (London: Routledge & Kegan Paul, 1980), p. 26.

38 *Dancing Ledge*, p. 129.

39 Ibid.

Chapter Four

THE FIRST WAVE
Sebastiane, Jubilee and The Tempest

1975–1979

In January 1975 Jarman had a fortuitous encounter which changed his life. At a Sunday lunch with friends he met an ex-London Film School student called James Whaley who was keen to make a first feature. Learning that Jarman made films, he asked him to collaborate with him on one. Jarman had not seriously entertained such an ambition: the projects that litter his notebooks of this period are intended as super-8s on the scale of *In the Shadow of the Sun*. When asked by Whaley for ideas, he mentioned *The Tempest*, which he had discussed with the actor John Gielgud, filling a notebook with ideas for such an adaptation. In the autumn of 1974 he had also been planning a film on St Sebastian with a friend, but the project had collapsed.[1] Whaley was keen on the idea and the deal was sealed when Whaley, to Jarman's surprise, delivered a synopsis a few days later.

'Sebastiane'

This was the starting point of five years of intense activity during which Jarman made three classic British films – *Sebastiane, Jubilee* and *The Tempest*. It was not an auspicious time to launch into feature film production. In 1975 the British film industry was collapsing fast. Cinema admissions had been falling rapidly since the 50s (in 1959 they had totalled 601 million, by 1970 they were down to 193 million and by 1975 to 116 million). The brief heyday of the 60s had gone – and the industry was largely at the mercy of the Americans. The Eady levy system – established in 1947 to assist home-produced films by allocating a proportion of global box-office receipts to British production – was in need of restructuring. Jarman's three feature films were financed from private sources[2] – often rich gay friends – and in the case of *The Tempest* by the maverick producer Don Boyd. *Sebastiane* was made in 16mm on a budget of £30,000[3] brought 'in briefcases from a shipping magnate'.[4]

80 On the set of 'Sebastiane'

Though *Sebastiane* represents a break with the poetic and experimental forms of Jarman's smaller-gauge films, it nevertheless carries forward some of their concerns, in particular an interest in the mythological aspect of the subject and a tendency to express emotions through the image rather than through the acting. But *Sebastiane* also represents a move from private to public film-making. The gentle camp eroticism and personalised mythology and symbolism of the super-8s is replaced by an aggressive directness that is both socio-political and institutional.

Probably the most innovative aspect of *Sebastiane*, besides its homoeroticism, is the Latin dialogue. Jack Welch, a Latin scholar from Oxford, translated the script, a first in cinema history. Peter Wollen has commented that the 'high camp' Latin dialogue makes the experience of the film like that of watching an opera with a libretto in a foreign language, 'thus foregrounding the role of performance and visual composition'.[5] For Wollen this feature of the film renders it modernist, although ironically so due to the films ostensible realism. The strong guttural sounds have little to do with the tones of a Latin mass; in *Sebastiane* Latin is the language of the streets, aggressive, lascivious, well suited to lust and rage.

Sebastiane was shot at Cala Domestica in Sardinia, using a ruined fisherman's house as both the set and the living quarters for the actors and crew. Jarman's toughness on the set and determination to make the film he wanted can be inferred from his descriptions of the filming in *Dancing Ledge*. When Joe Dallesandro, the star of the Warhol/Morrissey films, turned up, Jarman refused to use him despite the pleas of his co-workers, instinctively realising that such a move would 'completely unbalance the cast who are all equally unknown'. At another point there was a walk-out on the set when the crew accused him of 'fucking exploitation' and being a 'pornographer' when Adrian (Ken Hicks) could not achieve an erection for a love scene.[6] Even at this point in his career, Jarman was not afraid of being thought politically incorrect or of standing against the conventions of the gay subculture in which he operated in order to achieve the image he wanted.

Jarman was not a novice of feature film-making – after all, he had had the experience of working with a 'difficult' director on *The Devils* and *The Savage Messiah* and of major ballet and opera productions, but the weight of responsibility for his own film must have been another matter. It was obviously an intense learning experience in which he showed his ability not only to take on others' ideas but to know when to stick to his own whatever the opposition.

Richard Dyer remarks that *Sebastiane* 'astonishingly and fortuitously' received a commercial release in Britain.[7] The review of Jarman's film in *Gay News* indicates its impact on the gay community:

> Very occasionally there appears a film of such power and authority that one emerges from the cinema feeling somewhat shaken and disorientated. ... *Sebastiane* is a very special, and indeed, a quite remarkable film that represents a milestone in the history of gay cinema.[8]

Nearly twenty years later, Jarman gave his own judgment:

> *Sebastian* [*sic*] didn't present homosexuality as a problem and this was what made it different from all the British films that had preceded it. It was also homoerotic. The film was historically important; no feature film had ventured here. There had been underground films, *Un chant d'amour* and *Fireworks*, but *Sebastian* [*sic*] was in a public space.[9]

Of course there had been mainstream films in the early 70s with gay themes – for instance, Visconti's study of melancholy decadence *Death in Venice* or the more social-problem-oriented *Sunday Bloody Sunday* (1971), to name two quite different approaches to the subject. Hollywood genres like the gladiator films of the 50s aimed at heterosexual audiences also had an obvious attraction for gay viewers. (Given its Roman Empire setting, *Sebastiane* is not so far removed from some of these Hollywood epics such as *Spartacus*.) But *Sebastiane* celebrates the male body from a manifestly homoerotic perspective in a way that had never been done either in mainstream or art cinema.

The cast of characters involved in the film's making suggests that its final form was not determined by Jarman alone, but was an uneasy mix of approaches. Jarman sets out the warring viewpoints:

> James [Whaley] wants an oil and vanilla film full of ... muscle men working out in locker rooms. Paul Humfress, who is to edit, wants a

83

very serious art film, slow and ponderous. I want a poetic film full of mystery.[10]

As it turned out, the 'oil and vanilla' material is not too overbearing, the film is 'slow and ponderous' at times, and its poetry and 'mystery' are there but unresolved. For all its energy and daring, *Sebastiane* is unsuccessful largely because of its uncertainty as to what kind of film it should be. The hero is too passive and empty to engage our sympathies. Many years later, Jarman looked back on the film's central figure:

> Sebastian, the doolally Christian who refused a good fuck, gets the arrows he deserved. Can one feel sorry for this Latin closet case? Stigma Seb who sports his wounds on a thousand altars like a debutant. All fags like a good Sebastian.[11]

Jarman's lack of sympathy with and inability to do justice to the film's theme of martyrdom is perhaps its central problem. Among the sexual cavortings of the soldiers, Sebastian displays a guilt and anxiety which Jarman sees quite clearly as the result of Christian repression but nevertheless gives weight to through their presence in his 'hero'. The morality Sebastian represents is one Jarman reveals himself as ambivalent towards in his films, whatever he might say in interview or writings: this self-tortured masochist is a precursor of the self-destructive, passive, ambivalent homosexual 'heroes' of much of his later cinema (*Caravaggio*, *Wittgenstein*, *Edward II*). As with Caravaggio and Wittgenstein, there is a sublimation of sexual energies into 'higher' activities – in the case of Sebastian, religion.

In *Sebastiane* there is both a criticism of such self-defeating egotism and an understanding of its necessity in the face of the forces of oppression. Homosexual love is stifled by a system and ideology represented by the Roman platoon and besieged by a violence and aggression which is the reaction of the repressive forces of society to its potentially disordering effect (especially in its displacement into Christianity, to which Sebastian is a recent convert). It is at this point that the negative, aggressive drives of gay sexuality merge with an oppositional stance, a social radicalism. *Sebastiane* is perhaps an expression of a struggle in which aggression and death conquer the constructive and gentler qualities of love. It is remarkable that such a major theme in Jarman's films – the idealisation of homosexual love within the sadism of social and cultural historical forces – is present from the very start.

What also seems remarkable about the film today is its portrait of the collapse of an empire. Twenty years of nudity in cinema have made the display of the male body and explicit lovemaking less extraordinary, so the film's narrative and structure, which at the time seemed a peg for its homoeroticism, can be more fully appreciated. The decline of the Roman Empire, with its cruelty, introversion and paranoia, is encapsulated in the platoon of soldiers exiled to its moribund fringes. The questions of 'maleness' that obsess the soldiers, typically through Max's pining for the good old days of imperial strength, have a topicality within present-day debates on 'masculinity'.

Central to these issues is the film's depiction of soldiery, a persistent theme in Jarman's films. Part of the reason for this, as Jarman admits, is simply that the military is an area of life where men are found in large numbers. But Jarman's fondness for military characters and settings also signifies ambivalent feelings which receive their most successful articulation in *Imagining October* (1984). If the military represent the violence of the state towards its citizens, they also embody the sexual aggression and sadism Jarman seems to desire. In many cases his heroes are passive gays and their torturers soldiers or policemen – for instance, a policeman murders the Kid in *Jubilee* and another ends up in bed with Crabs before being blown up. In *The Garden* the police torture scene ascribes a repressive but erotic power to the uniformed sadists. 'If we must have troops, let's have them in bed,' Jarman wrote in *Dancing Ledge* in discussing his own sexual preferences and the problem of the homosexual image. Here he expresses sympathy for William Burroughs' idea of a militant homosexual state with its own soldiers who would deal brutally with any opposition. A 'gang of Wild Boy assassins' is 'deep down the dream of many of us', Jarman comments.[12]

The bathhouse scenes in *Sebastiane* are not only an erotic interlude but express the collapse and 'corruption' of Rome. The loss that is at the film's core is not only of a sexual object but of the Roman Empire. Max's connection of homosexuality and the loss of empire is not new: it has been argued that the maintenance of imperialism requires a bureaucratic militarism in which homosexuality, once tolerated, must be suppressed.[13] (It was the armed forces that offered the main resistance to the relaxation of

85

British anti-homosexual legislation in the 60s.) Yet paradoxically, it is Max's initiation of homosexual horseplay which binds the men together as a fighting group: for Max, the Captain's infatuation with Sebastian is not a sexual or moral transgression but a military one. The platoon falls into indiscipline and anarchy through an officer's sexual passion for a subordinate and respect, discipline and military values are restored only by Sebastian's execution.

Significantly, this execution is the only serious military action performed by the soldiers in the film. The military occupation of this lonely garrison is desultory: its defenders are passive and ultimately impotent. A strong feature of Jarman's films is here given its first elaboration – the aimless anti-narrative resulting from a lack of purpose once supplied by nationhood and imperialism. The sodomistic 'passivity' noted by Tony Rayns[14] and melancholic 'wistfulness' marked by Timothy Murray[15] in Jarman's work are at the core of this first film, but it is a passivity that is as historically and politically determined as it is sexually.

Sebastiane[16] is the simple story of the soldier-saint who as a result of his allegiance to the Christian faith falls out of favour with his protector the Emperor Diocletian. He is exiled to an isolated outpost of the Roman Empire where he is persecuted and eventually executed by his fellow-soldiers. The film begins with a text giving its historical setting. The year is AD 303 and the Emperor Diocletian (played by the painter Robert Medley[17]) has unleashed the 'last great persecution of the Christian' after his palace has been ravaged by a series of mysterious fires. On 28 December of that year Diocletian holds a huge party to celebrate the birth of the sun and to honour Sebastian, the captain of his palace guard. The scene is a glittering array of golds, blacks and reds, visually rich with an excessive theatricality absent from the rest of the film. Jarman declared he was 'always rather sad that the first scene of the film was never developed'.[18] Researched by the concrete poet and Benedictine historian Dom Sylvestre Houedard, the scene is indebted to Russell and to Jarman's own super-8 experiments in its campness – but with the addition of an aggression new to his work.

At the centre of the scene is a dance sequence featuring the painted bodies with huge carnivalesque dildos of Lindsey Kemp and his dance troupe. The dancers frantically 'masturbate' the huge phalluses, encircling Kemp who eventually collapses on to the floor covered in their ejaculations.

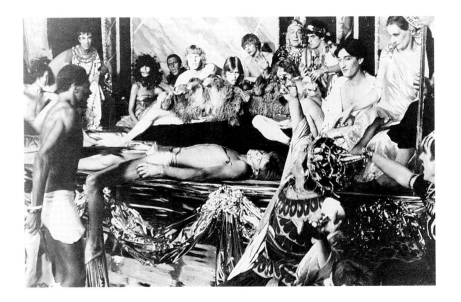

Close-ups are intercut with medium long shots. Kemp's face upside-down in the frame relishes the sperm spattered all over it. A black gladiator who kills one of Diocletian's friends he accuses of betraying him is filmed in extreme close-up, breathing harshly like a blood-crazed animal as he breaks his victim's neck. Diocletian's entrance in full regalia with huge circular earrings is also shot in extreme close-up. The camera then pans around the room to the variety of costumed party-goers among whom is the punk figure Jordan who plays the sexually voracious whore Morgana.

In a grating, sarcastic tone, Max, a hardened soldier with a black false nose, tells the story. At first in voice-over, he maliciously describes the party guests. After Sebastian has been denounced as a Christian, Max speaks direct to camera. Neil Kennedy's satyr-like Max with his soldierly brutality and sexual voraciousness is the most convincing of the film's characters. His crudity and malevolence are among the male values Jarman rejects but in some sense admires. Max tells how six soldiers including himself, plus their captain Severus and Sebastian, were sent to an isolated outpost of the Empire. The film cuts to the military post. Sebastian washes naked in the courtyard, watched by a lustful Severus. In a device repeated at similar times in the film, Severus' gaze is counter-cut with the slowed-down image in extreme close-up of Sebastian's naked body, so parts of his body move in a languorous and erotic slow motion in the 'eye' of the beholder. The scene is shot from the

The opening orgy of 'Sebastiane' **87**

Captain's point of view, so it is this the audience shares. As the Captain's sadism unfolds, we become complicit too with his sexually charged aggression towards Sebastian's uncooperative body. This opening sequence also establishes a characteristic Jarman theme of a group, isolated from the main social body, within which the tensions between an authoritarian centre and the individual are played out.

In the next scene the almost naked soldiers practise fighting with wooden swords on the hot sand, watched from a small hillock by the Captain. Sebastian refuses to fight and is later seen on horseback watching his naked comrades horseplay in the sea. The scene cuts to Sebastian kneeling beside a pool looking at his own image and reciting his poems to God. Nowhere in the film is Sebastian's narcissism more explicitly imaged. The key homosexual relationships in Jarman's subsequent films often contain a narcissistic mirroring – the twins of *Jubilee*, the two gay 'Christs' of *The Garden* and the more subtle 'twinning' of Caravaggio and Ranuccio in *Caravaggio*. The main structuring device of this 'mirroring' is the exchange of eroticised gazes through which characters become isolated from their surroundings and from one another. Invariably the 'macho' masculinity of institutions and their representatives is brought into focus by this internal space created by the homosexual gaze.

There follows a scene in which the men lounge cleaning their swords under the shade of a tree. Sebastian refuses to clean his weapon and the scene cuts to him being hung by his hands and scourged by the Captain while the men gloat over a hand-drawn pornographic image of a woman. The film's aimlessness and lack of narrative drive – often believed to be a result of its primary aim of parading homoerotic imagery – stems in fact from a realistic depiction of military life in such places.[19] The image of lassitude erupting at times into sexual frustration is one that dominates the film – at one level it is a portrait of men trained for violent action but forced into inactivity. Cut off from civilisation and its pleasures, they become the victims of their desires, fantasies and frustrations. The overwhelming sense of an empty, hostile space (the heat of the sun and barrenness of the land is almost palpable), contrasting sharply with the almost claustrophobic visual richness of the first orgy sequence, reinforces this theme.

In the dark of the sleeping quarters, Sebastian's only ally, Justin, bathes his whipped back as the martyr asserts his passivity in the name of Christian pacifism, 'he can do with me as he likes'. In the following scene the bored soldiers, with Max at the centre, bet on a spider fight. There follows a brawl with the onlooking soldiers banging stones to provide a rhythmic accompaniment. Sebastian wrestles and wins, only to be taunted by Max. Later the Captain, accompanied by Sebastian, watches the naked Anthony and Adrian kiss among the rocks, his gaze again revealing the slowed-down movement of the men's bodies in close-up. The Captain orders Sebastian to take off his boots as he watches the two soldiers making love in the sea. Again real space and time is juxtaposed with slowed-down shots of the men's bodies in the water. In reiterating the image of the Captain watching Sebastian shower, the scene consolidates the relationship between sexuality and political and military power. The political and the sexual are also merged in the identification of Sebastian as a politically disloyal Christian and as the object of the homosexual gaze.

The Captain orders Anthony and Adrian to stake out Sebastian in the hot sun. Jarman thus complicates the sexual alignments by making the two homosexual lovers complicit in the Captain's sadism. Meanwhile the soldiers play with a Frisbee on the sands. In what seems to be a trace of Jarman's super-8 work, a mysterious leopard boy holding a small bush shades Sebastian from the sun. There follows a scene in which the soldiers hunt a pig which is caught and killed by the Captain. Justin tries to reason with Sebastian, whose only response is to chant a litany to God, in which he ascribes to Him the religious erotic qualities of a beautiful man. As the soldiers eat their pork, the Captain desperately tortures Sebastian's suspended body, at times caressing it. Eventually he cuts him down. The scenes of lovemaking are stylised, idealised and ultimately unworldly and unconsummated. It is only in the Captain's frenzies of sadistic violence that the sexual act seems to find some form of representation.

In the bathhouse scene, as the men lazily wash and shave their bodies in the steam, Max mourns the decline of the Roman Empire, citing the reign of Nero with his brutal treatment of Christians as its zenith. He complains of the heterosexual orgies of his youth in Rome being replaced in recent times by homosexual ones. In the middle of the most erotic scene of the film, as the camera in close-up moves over the men's naked bodies, he comments, 'in those days men were men'. Jarman ironically chooses this homoerotic moment for Max's espousal of 'manliness', military might and homophobia.

The bathhouse scene from 'Sebastiane' (overleaf) **89**

homophobia. For Max, liberal toleration of Christianity is a symptom of military weakness and rampant homosexuality.

Homosexual horseplay or homosexual acts as a means of sexual release are differentiated by Max from the unbridled and insidious passion of the Captain, which undermines discipline and his authority over the men in his charge, and from Sebastian's 'feminine' religious pacifism. Max remarks that boys are 'OK for a quick one'. At this level, the film is a complex statement about sexual power relations in which it is difficult to locate Jarman's sympathies. Sexuality is represented as a rigid destructive force in the case of Severus and as a fluid positive one in the case of Anthony and Adrian. In the case of Sebastian it has been sublimated. It is not clear whether Anthony and Adrian's homosexual relationship is a genuine expression of their sexuality or a form of sexual pragmatism in difficult conditions. Max is rampantly heterosexual in his continuing fantasies about when they return to 'civilisation' but he also instigates much of the homosexual horseplay and innuendo. Though the male nude dominates the film visually, the narrative is structured around a complexity of notions of male sexuality and masculinity. Richard Dyer mentions that Jarman uses the film 'to lay out some of the forms that "eros" (love, desire) can take'[20] but ignores the critique of power embedded in it.

In a scene following the bath house one, Sebastian acts out a dance for Justin while Max shouts abuse: 'Christian faggot!' The Captain rebukes Max for attacking Sebastian. Max lasciviously mimics this dance in the pigpen. In stark contrast, at the water's edge, Justin and Sebastian listen to the sounds of a pearly shell. The other soldiers arrive and a fight ensues between them and Sebastian and Justin until the Captain intervenes. The antagonism between Justin and Sebastian and the other soldiers begins to become uncontrollable, as the Captain finds himself instigating a general disrespect for Sebastian yet at the same time protecting him as a love-object. As the men play dice, Max attacks homosexuals (they are 'like Greeks'), conflating sexual 'perversion' with racial 'inferiority'. The Captain gets drunk, attempts to rape Sebastian and ends up smashing up his room in drunken frustration.

There follows an image of a garlanded Sebastian crouching in a cloak beside a goatherd, watched from a distance by the leopard boy. Sebastian's spirituality and otherworldly innocence are depicted through images of pastoral idealism in this scene, the sequence when Sebastian gazes at his reflection and the one where he and Justin listen to the 'voices' in the shell.[21] This pastoral element serves to critique the corruption and cruelty within which it is set. Paradoxically Max, with his reactionary conservatism, racism, sexism and aggressive sexual urge, is the most realistic character in the film in that he recognises lust for what it is and refuses to sublimate it or idealise it. Max's political and historical sense of loss of Empire may contain elements of idealism, but even on this score he is aware, unlike the others, of the group's relationship to a broader historical picture. Sebastian and Max act as polar opposites in the film.

In the penultimate sequence, Max, hung-over, crawls out into the sun and puts a garland on the sleeping Justin. He sadistically begins to savage him with his knife and then is shown cradling his bleeding body in a mock *pietà* posture. The Captain appears and proclaims that Sebastian is to be killed, at which news Max laughs hysterically. The men tie Sebastian to a stake and each pierces him with an arrow. Even Justin, weakened by Max's attack, is forced to shoot an arrow into his friend. The films ends with a shot from Sebastian's point of view at the stake in which the wide-angle lens distorts the image into a curving horizon with figures scattered on it.

As a first film, *Sebastiane* was a resounding success. It was rejected by Cannes but taken up by the Locarno festival in June 1976 where it was loudly barracked by the audience, some of whom demanded the festival organiser's resignation. But when the film opened at the Gate Cinema in Notting Hill it played to record audiences. It was 'a stunning success'[22] in Italy and Spain, classed as a sex film in America, panned by the French and found difficult by the Germans.

The film has been unjustly criticised for its so-called controversial expression of the historical episode, especially since its imagery is very much at one with the traditional representation of the Sebastian story in paintings. Jarman mimics the *pietà*, while the execution and bathhouse scenes are handled very much in the style of classical art. By and large, though, the film lacks a rich context for its narrative. Jarman's use of the theatrical and the *tableau vivant* is limited to the first scene of the orgy, which in its campness makes a larger historical point about the Roman period of Diocletian but which carries no narrative weight. Campness and a postmodern-like bricolage were to become the methods by which Jarman made his political points. But in *Sebastiane* he is reduced to the narrow canvas and simple actions of a plot centred on the scapegoating of his self-destructive hero.

In 1976, between making *Sebastiane* and *Jubilee*, Jarman concentrated, for the last time he claimed, 'exclusively on my super-8 films. A few paintings were finished, and a set of twelve glasses engraved with alchemical texts.'[23] But the majority of his time was spent on two scripts, only one of which was to be made: *The Tempest*. The other, planned as a follow-up super-8 feature to *In the Shadow of the Sun*, seems to have been an early version of *Neutron* (what he describes as 'The John Dee' script in *Dancing Ledge*) which in part became *Jubilee*.[24] There was a third script based on Akhenaten, reflecting Jarman's interests in Ancient Egypt and sexuality. Watercolours for this were made by Christopher Hobbs and the script was reworked in the early 80s.

'Jubilee'

The opening sequence of *Sebastiane*, with Jordan dressed in punk style playing the whore Morgana, was shot last, in September 1975. At that time the punk movement was gathering force around Malcolm McLaren and Vivienne Westwood's shop in the King's Road, Chelsea. Through McLaren and Westwood's 'selling' of punk, the art school aesthetic and design ethos were once more to make a major impact on British culture. As Peter York remarks:

> the Thems pushed out the boat for the new sensibility, self-conscious, eclectic, Post-Modern. And they were much more tied into Punk's beginnings than any of the punk apologists would admit for years afterwards.[25]

Punk involved a set of elements Jarman was attracted to and which he never relinquished. It furthered the cross-dressing 'camp' aspects of glam rock (led by Bryan Ferry, Roxy Music, David Bowie and the Rolling Stones) with performance at its core. But with punk, 'performance' came closer to an anarchical theatrical 'happening'.

Westwood's remark 'I'm never more happy than when I'm parodying the English'[26] found a resonance in Jarman's work. Punk transformed a decadent apolitical music scene into one rooted in the contemporary English experience of high unemployment and inflation and the collapse of 60s liberalism and affluence. The lyrics were in the English working-class

94

vernacular, not the pseudo-Americanisms of much British pop music. There was also an eclecticism of styles which appealed to Jarman enormously, as well as the fact that costume and style were represented in a way that was neither naturalistic nor reliant on conventional associations. In both *Jubilee* and *The Tempest* Jarman used this eclecticism to great advantage. Importantly, through punk he found a device by which the present, past and future could be mingled.

Punk's demystifying of pop music professionalism and do-it-yourself aesthetic also echoed the impetus of Jarman's own home movie-making (it is no accident that *Jubilee* grew from a super-8 film of Jordan). The independent music scene that burgeoned in the aftermath of punk was to become part of the avant-garde film scene with the super-8 aesthetic and scratch video of the early 80s. Jarman was to find his natural home here among this post-punk generation.

All the energy and anti-high-art impetus that characterised Pop Art as it fed into punk is in *Jubilee*. But the film is recuperated for high art by its English Renaissance structuring device. For some of the champions of punk, such as Vivienne Westwood, the Elizabethan context of the film was unfashionably mystificatory:

> JUBILEE – I had been to see it once and thought it the most boring and therefore most disgusting film I had ever seen. ... I first tried very hard to listen to every word spoken in the flashbacks to Eliz. I. What were you saying? Eliz: 'This vision exceedeth by far all expectation. Such an abstract never before I spied' and so she went on – Fal de ray la lu lullay the day! And John Dee spoke 'poetry' according to *Time Out* ... though even now I can remember no distinguishing phrase from amongst the drone, only the words 'down, down, down' (Right On). I am supposed to see old Elizabeth's England as some state of grace? Well, I rather consider that all this grand stuff and looking at diamonds is something to do with a gay (which you are) boy's love of dressing up and playing at charades.[27]

At the time of its release, *Jubilee* was not seen as a political film. The Left was beginning its long dismantlement, with the British Communist Party in the late 70s publishing its new manifesto, 'The New Road to

95

Socialism,' which signalled its alliance with the Labour Party. Intellectual leftists were grappling with Althusserianism. In film, the theoretical journal *Screen* held sway with its Lacanian psychoanalysis, Althusserian politics and Brechtian view of independent cinema together with a persistent textual engagement with mainstream narrative Hollywood film. Jarman's film seemed to have more to do with King's Road fashion and a cultural pessimism than with the current forms of leftist politics.

But Britain had changed palpably since the 60s. Unemployment was rising steadily and the country was basically at war with the IRA in Northern Ireland, with Republican bombings in London and elsewhere on the mainland. Inflation had risen rapidly under the impact of the oil crisis of 1973. Edward Heath's Tory government had fallen apart in the face of the miners' strike and Wilsonian Labourism had long been discredited as empty and transparent. When punk arrived in 1976, it seemed perfectly fitting for the times – anti-liberal, anarchic and identified with working-class youth's despondency and frustration. Jarman's own apoliticism and anarchism found a convenient home, at least for a time, though his sympathy was tempered by scepticism:

> I thought Punk was an understandable and a very correct disgust with everything, but it wasn't focused. Youth seemed to get it right, but, in its funny way, it did end in repression with Margaret Thatcher's England.[28]

The role of women in punk was more forceful and provocative than in any previous pop music movement, and Jarman culled the cast of *Jubilee* from this scene. Little Nell had appeared in the cult classic *The Rocky Horror Show* and was later to take part in the feminist television series on women rock stars, *Rock Follies*. Toyah Wilcox, who appears in *Jubilee* with an all-female band, the Maneaters, was to appear in *Quadrophenia*. Jordan worked in McLaren and Westwood's fashion shop:

> Punk ... from the start raised questions about sexual codes. It is often argued that punk opened a space which allowed women in – with its debunking of 'male' technique and expertise, its critique of rock naturalism, its anti-glamour.[29]

96

For Jarman, *Jubilee*'s punk aesthetic and *mise en scène* opened up ways of confronting sexuality that *Sebastiane* had seemed to close down. Style, bricolage, costume, language and pose became means of exploring sexual difference. Even the drag fun of the Alternative Miss World competitions was not so far removed from punk fashion.

Jon Savage in his book *England's Dreaming: Sex Pistols and Punk Rock* remarks: 'With its persistent air of disillusion and warning, *Jubilee* captured the mood of Punk England better than anyone could have predicted.'[30] Certainly compared with Julien Temple's *The Great Rock and Roll Swindle*, which was simply about punk and the Sex Pistols, *Jubilee* is unnervingly less far-fetched in its ideas and imagery than it seemed at the time. Watching it almost twenty years later, it is striking how many of its fantasies of political life – both nationally and globally – have come true. What at the time seemed paranoid and hysterical was in fact a surer analysis of post-war Britain than many provided by the Left, then or since. The political cynicism of the electorate and influence of the media on politics and capitalist consumerism are all given voice in *Jubilee,* while the collapse of the USSR and its rampant Mafia-style capitalism are foreshadowed in the final scene as Crabs asks Ginz for a tank. Some years later, in *Dancing Ledge*, Jarman reflected:

> Afterwards the film turned prophetic. Dr Dee's vision came true – the streets burned in Brixton and Toxteth, Adam was on *Top of the Pops* and signed up with Margaret Thatcher to sing at the Falklands Ball. They all sign up in one way or another.[31]

With his interest in the music scene, Jon Savage sees the film as centred around the Kid played by Adam Ant, who like the Kid was just setting out in the pop world. When Jarman filmed Adam and the Ants at the New Victoria Theatre, they had only been going for two months. The line between fact and fiction is precarious in much of the film, but no more so than in this character, for which Adam virtually played himself, giggling at his fellow-actors' lines and awkwardly mumbling, a vacuous focal point for the rest of the characters. Jarman has asserted:

> With *Jubilee* the progressive merging of film and my reality was complete. The source of the film was often autobiographical, the

97

locations were the streets and warehouses in which I had lived during the previous ten years. The film was cast from among and made by friends.[32]

Jarman wanted a 'fantasy documentary fabricated so that documentary and fictional forms are confused and coalesce'. This is in many ways a development of the home movies where friends would 'perform' for the camera. *Sebastiane* had been an attempt to make a film proper and lacked this 'home movie' quality which Jarman was never fully to abandon again – even in the most orthodoxly funded of his films, for instance *Caravaggio* or *War Requiem*, many friends appeared in small roles.

Jubilee is about England in its decline, and as Tony Rayns remarked at the time of the film's release, it 'sees the punk renaissance in music and visuals as the first noticeable attempt in a decade or more to redefine where England is, or isn't', For Rayns, the film is located in Swiftian satire and Blakean visionary poetry and thus 'revives a strain in English thought that's been dormant for a very long time'.[33] In an interview with the critic Nicholas de Jongh,[34] Jarman revealed his ambivalence about the film's message when he conceded that 'Elizabeth I is a symbol. She is firmly embedded in the English national dream of Expansion, Capital, the new Learning, of Shakespeare and the Elizabethans.' Yet as Jongh rightly surmises, *Jubilee* is also 'a personal cry of nostalgia for a time and a security this century never knew and can only experience through reading and imagination.' This tension between an idealised past and the knowledge that that past embodied the disastrous present can only be resolved by seeing the Elizabethan period as a fantasy projection – England's dream that oiled the cogs of imperialist expansion and capitalist growth and sustains that image. *Jubilee*, however ambiguously, begins to break open that English cultural hegemony.

For *Jubilee*, Jarman cast Karl Johnson, who was to become Ariel in *The Tempest*, as the twin Sphinx, and the blind actor Jack Birkett (aka Orlando), who was later to play Caliban, as Borgia Ginz. Jordan played Amyl Nitrate and helped with the casting. His old friend Luciana Martinez – the voluptuous woman in *The Art of Mirrors* who had also assisted on *Sebastiane* – appeared in leather tied with barbed wire to a lamp-post, murdered by a gang of punks. Adam Ant was discovered by Jarman on the King's Road.

Toyah Wilcox, who played Mad, was later to be Miranda in *The Tempest*. A young John Maybury, who was to help shoot and edit many of Jarman's shorter films in the 80s, assisted Jarman and Christopher Hobbs with the sets, together with Kenny Morris of the Banshees. Richard O'Brien of *Rocky Horror Show* fame played John Dee. Ian Charleson, who was to die of AIDS in 1990, played Angel. Jenny Runacre, also a professional actress, provided a stable centre with her excellent portrayal of the two most important characters – Bod and Elizabeth I.

Jubilee is the film in which Jarman found his voice and style. With the exception of the first scene, no attempt is made to reproduce a historical or contemporary reality; instead the bricolage methods of nearly all the feature films are given full rein. The images are arresting and carefully designed while the characters are almost caricatures, almost a typology (only in *Caravaggio* and to some extent in *Edward II* did Jarman present psychologically interesting characters). Meanwhile, contemporary Britain – the Church, the royal family, the police, the pop industry – provides convenient targets for Jarman to shoot at.

In 1977, with a cheque for £50,000 from James Whaley (obtained via Tehran!), Jarman began to film *Jubilee*. Made to mark the queen's jubilee year (it was released eventually in 1978), it rode on the tide of the punk movement but was not the great success its makers hoped. Like *Sebastiane*, it deals with a post-imperialist period, this time post-war England 'seen' by the monarch of imperial reform, Elizabeth I. It again has at its centre a group of bored, decadent and largely violent victims of its times and contains idealist martyrs (the incestuous gay twins Sphinx and Angel) and a figure of authority and omnipotent power, akin to Diocletian, in the media mogul Borgia Ginz. Like *Sebastiane*, it has no true dramatic centre but rather opts for a sprawling, almost episodic structure, its protagonists lacking the motivation required to move the 'story' forward.

As in *Sebastiane*, but more centrally, *Jubilee* deals with the contrast between a society at a high point of imperialism and in its post-empire age – in the case of *Jubilee* the two periods of Elizabethan rule. As Scott Meek argued at the time of its release: '*Jubilee* is a film about England, and about the paradoxes posed by its "glorious" past in the light of its unsettled present and uncertain future.'[35] At the film's core is the merging of Jarman's 'Dr Dee' script with a typology of punk: an adaptation of Jarman's interests in

99

Elizabethan ideas and alchemy to what was going on in London at the time:

> The John Dee script was pirated and used as a framing device; Jung's *Seven Sermons to the Dead* and the *Angelic Conversations* of the good doctor Dee were scrambled with *SNIFFin Glue* and *London's OUTRAGE*.[36]

The script went through a number of drafts. In one dated April 1977, Jarman titled the film 'A New Wave Movie' and conceived of it as a portrayal of 'open war between all factions of society'. This script contains banal pornographic images from magazines showing heterosexual group sex as well as dialogue literally transposed from the 'Dr Dee' script. The film as made sprang from a super-8 Jarman was planning of punk's high priestess, Jordan. The footage of Jordan in a tutu (intimations of dancer Michael Clark) dancing around a wasteland bonfire of burning books surveyed by the mock heroes of a classical Western civilisation, naked except for ancient Greek masks of tragedy and comedy, is included in the film and also became a separate super-8 titled *Jordan's Dance*.

Jubilee is the first of Jarman's features to deal with Dee and the Elizabethan period. Jarman returned again and again to the English Renaissance – in *In the Shadow of the Sun*, *The Tempest*, *The Angelic Conversation* and *Edward II*. Caravaggio (1571–1610), who lived at the end of the Italian Renaissance, also coincides with this period. The occult beliefs which flourished in London, Prague and Hamburg in the 16th century fostered thinkers who were to be obliterated by the scientific and philosophical revolution of Newton, Descartes, Leibniz and Spinoza. Dr John Dee, Paracelsus, Fludd, Agrippa and others were to become emblems of superstition and backwardness. Yet as Frances Yates has argued, Dee was a Renaissance man mingling the sciences and mathematics with white magic.[37]

Jarman's fascination is primarily with this figure, the leading English intellectual of the Elizabethan period whose involvement with the sciences and the cabala was renowned in Europe. Dee was a close advisor to the Virgin Queen, acting on her behalf (and perhaps Walsingham's) as a secret diplomat on a long trip to Europe where with Edward Kelley he visited the Prague court of the eccentric King Rudolf II. But Jarman's main interest in Dee lies in his role as a scientist-cum-cabalist who dealt in the art of white

magic and conversed with the angels. Dee features in different ways in *Jubilee*, *The Tempest*, *In the Shadow of the Sun* and *The Angelic Conversation*.

Why this interest in such a murky figure in English history? No doubt it is partly that Dee occupies a cultural, political and intellectual space outside official tradition – a despised voice that speaks not the discourse of the Enlightenment but merges the rational with the spiritual. Dee and the alchemical tradition he embraced are part of the darker, subversive side of Elizabethan culture that is largely ignored. His ideas are also a form of psychology and mythology understood in Jungian terms (Jung is the major thinker of this century who researched alchemy and other irrational systems).

By and large, the image Jarman constructs of the period is an idealised one of England as the garden, as a repository of values he seems to suggest are long lost. There is also a conception of love in which the body and sexuality have a freedom denied by capitalist systems and the rise of bourgeois values. It is no accident that the final scene of *Jubilee* had spiritual connotations for Jarman. The Epilogue of *Dancing Ledge* is an evocation of this scene, shot at Dancing Ledge (and Winspit) in Dorset. Scenes from *The Angelic Conversation* and the last scene of *The Last of England* were also shot there. In Dee's and Elizabeth's dialogue there is a sweet, almost swooning, maternalism, laden with notions associated with Freud's idea of the 'oceanic

John Dee and Queen Elizabeth at Winspit, 'Jubilee' **101**

bliss' of the infant at the breast. But there is also an exquisite stirring from nostalgia and melancholia towards some transcendent state which, I may suggest, is never achieved:

> ELIZABETH: All my heart rejoice at the roar of the surf on the shingles, marvellous sweet music it is to my ears – what joy there is in the embrace of water and earth.

> DEE: Yea – a great elixir is the seashore. Here one can dream of lands far distant, and the earth's treasure.

> ELIZABETH: The sea remindeth me of youth. Oh John Dee, do you remember the whispered secrets at Oxford like the sweet sea breeze, the codes and counter-codes, the secret language of flowers.

> DEE: I signed myself with rosemary, true alexipharmic gainst your enemies.

> ELIZABETH: And I with yellow celandine, true gold of the new spring of learning. You were my eyes then as now, with your celestial geometry. You laid a path through treachery and opened my prison so my heart flew like a swallow.

> DEE: Sweet Majesty, to me you are the celandine now as then before, balm against all melancholy.[38]

In the past two decades or more there has been a renewed interest on the part of writers and film-makers in Elizabethan culture, the cabala and alchemy. Novelist Ian Sinclair has explored the London of this forgotten past in *Lud Heat* (1975) and *White Chappell, Scarlet Tracings* (1988), as has Peter Ackroyd in *Hawksmoor* (1985; this novel is set in a slightly later period) and *The House of Doctor Dee* (1993). Charles Nicholl has written about the alchemical theatre and the background to the murder of Christopher Marlowe,[39] while in Czechoslovakia film-maker Jan Svankmajer has looked at the cabalistic era of Rudolf II's court in Prague in the second half of the 16th century, which Dee is known to have visited.[40] At the root of the

genuine historical research into alchemy in England are the writings of the historian Frances Yates[41] while Carl Jung's books on the symbolic systems of alchemy remain important.[42] British film-makers have not returned to the period with much seriousness except to adapt Shakespeare. Michael Powell in *A Canterbury Tale* uses Chaucerian England as a narrative device while John Boorman in *Excalibur* created a flawed but fascinating image of the Dark Ages derived from Malory. Humphrey Jennings had a keen sense of England and its cultural history, using this at times as a reference point, but it is Jarman who has explored his country's history with most commitment and success.

In cinematic terms, *Jubilee* suggests much more than *Sebastiane* the influence of Ken Russell. What *Jubilee* and *The Tempest* in particular share with Russell's work is a broad-stroked anti-psychologism whereby the inner life of the characters is literally given visual shape and form. Both directors use music centrally, both have a liking for forms of popular entertainment such as music hall, fairgrounds and circus, and both use dance. Their films are reminiscent of Eisenstein's earlier work, which was heavily influenced by revolutionary Soviet theatre with its emphasis on montage methods, high spirits and strong visual images as opposed to psychological, naturalist or realist narrative.

Like *Sebastiane*, *Jubilee* is structured by a bracketing device. Queen Elizabeth I requests John Dee to allow her to see the future, the shadow of her own reign. Dee conjures up an angel, Ariel (a rework perhaps of Dee's angel Uriel), who transports her to contemporary Britain. Set in the near future, the England the film portrays is run by the pop/media industry in the person of Borgia Ginz (Jack Birkett) whose gleeful vindictiveness echoes that of many of the controlling figures in Jarman's films (Birkett's role as Pope in *Caravaggio* has the same tone). Anarchy rules, and the gang of revolutionaries, anarchists, would-be pop stars, gay twins and a lesbian artist who are Ginz's playthings philosophise, sloganise and generally create mayhem, murdering the Queen of England, a few policemen and a male pick-up. Through Queen Elizabeth I (a sympathetic character) and Dee, the beauty of poetry, mysticism and cosmological wisdom is contrasted with the violent banality and apocalyptic degeneration of England in the late 20th century.

The film opens in a beautiful, tranquil English garden. There is no soundtrack music, only the sound of birds, the wind and the rustle of leaves.

A female dwarf dressed in Elizabethan costume stands in the deep shadows of the surrounding shrubs; three large dogs accompany her as she walks to the stately home espied through the bushes. It seems to be dusk and a storm is rising. The film cuts to an interior lit by flickering candles. Queen Elizabeth I (Jenny Runacre) nervously paces the room. The female dwarf, a lady-in-waiting, sleeps on the floor against a chair. John Dee (Richard O'Brien), 'our Kingdom's eyes', sits at the end of a long wooden table. Elizabeth asks her soothsayer to call up the angels by his magic. Ariel ('the sun's true shadow'), a young man with jet black eyes bathed in a blue light, appears to show them 'the shadow of this time' – the post-70s England of Elizabeth II.

The scene cuts to the glaring daylight of London's derelict backstreets in which Mad (Toyah Wilcox) and a bunch of girls are kicking someone on the ground. Nearby a pram burns. In the background on a wall is a piece of graffiti: 'POST-MODERNISM'. We cut to a graffiti-covered classroom, patrolled by Mad, in which Amyl Nitrate (Jordan) begins a lecture on history mixed with a diatribe on anarchy. In schoolteacher fashion and with a Home Counties accent she retranslates her school motto, 'Make your desires reality', into the Situationist-like injunction 'Don't dream it, be it'. Her attack swings to art, which she asserts is necessary only if fantasies are not translated into action. She recalls that she wanted to be a dancer and the scene cuts to a slow-motion super-8 film of her in a tutu dancing in classical ballet style around a bonfire of burning books on a waste ground surrounded by motley figures, including a naked man wearing a Greek tragedian mask. A man throws books on the fire and then begins to cut his long hair.

The following scene shows the main characters in the room where they live. The twins Sphinx (Karl Johnson) and Angel (the late Ian Charleson) sit in bed (a mattress on the floor), along with the leather-clad 'au pair' Chaos (Hermine Demoriane, who is mute throughout the film), while the pyromaniac Mad creates havoc. The scene is intercut with a long shot of the present queen being chased and murdered by Bod (short for Bodecea and also played by Jenny Runacre) on some waste ground. Bod arrives back and crowns herself, much to the entertainment of the rest of her gang, for in this scene Bod is established as the figure of authority and power within the group. But if Bod leads her group, she is also answerable in some way to Borgia Ginz, who seems to control the major political powers though his

Heineken refreshes the parts ot

presence is shadowy, represented largely by the police. Within Bod's gang there exists a further subgroup, that of the twins and the artist Viv (Hilary Spurrier). Equally, Bod, Mad and Amyl are connected through their punk dress and attitude, though their relationship moves between amity and enmity. (Interestingly, it is Bod whom Jarman describes in notes to the characters as the 'epitome of all that is punk'.[43]) Sex-mad, romantic Crabs (Little Nell) is a go-between finding 'stars' for Ginz and operating largely on her own. Kid (Adam Ant) is the passive, empty-headed, narcissistic new 'find' who is the object of Crabs' lust and the twins' affection. Ultimately he is the ritualistic victim of the police state. Outside this circle is the figure of Max (Neil Kennedy), an ex-army mercenary who tends his plastic plants and earns his living as a bingo-caller. Kennedy also played the part of Max in *Sebastiane* and his role in *Jubilee* is like a retired version of that character.

This large, amorphous group does not quite make sense – it lacks cohesion and its members' views, aims and attitudes are diverse (for instance, Crabs' and Bod's connivance with Ginz is opposed to the twins' detestation of the media industry). Jarman was to repeat such groupings in later films, especially *Caravaggio* with its pimps, prostitutes, punters, models, cardinals, mutes and painters. There is a strong sense of social cohesion having broken down to the extent that it is only the existence of an external repressive force that bestows a sense of communality. This is perhaps a reflection of gay subculture, in which a shared sexuality can break down barriers, though to the Left *Jubilee*'s depiction of a fluid polymorphism of class and ideologies and its association of political activity with forms of terrorism and a lumpen-proletariat low-life seemed a right-wing response.

In contrast with *Sebastiane*, *Jubilee* abounds with women – Elizabeth I, Bod, Mad, Amyl, Viv, Crabs, Chaos. They are the supreme motivators of the action – Elizabeth demands to see the future, Bod kills the Queen and Lounge Lizard and helps to suffocate the unfortunate Happy Days, Mad and Amyl brutally avenge the twins, Crabs organises the Kid's pop career and fatally seduces the policeman – though men, in the shape of Borgia Ginz and the policemen, are the overall controlling figures. However, in a film in which the characters represent a typology of values, it is the women who are purveyors of social, sexual and political views. Crabs is the only one who articulates a position as a woman *per se* and it is a standard one – always falling in love with the wrong person and desiring a romantic family life, for which she is reviled by Bod and Mad in the scene in which Happy Days' body is dumped in the mud of the Thames. The cut from this image and its sentiment to Viv's bare hermetic room where she and the twins swear their love for each other is poignant in its juxtaposition of viewpoints.

In the scene leading to the death of Happy Days, Crabs is having sex with the young boy, while Mad taunts her for her anachronistic need for sex. Bod watches in disgust, half-naked eating yoghurt, and also chastises Crabs for her sexual 'needs'. As the boy climaxes, Crabs dons a leather mask and the others smother him in the crinkly red plastic bed sheets. Crabs is presented as typifying 'normal' female heterosexual desire with its accompanying fantasies of romantic love and eternal domesticity. Bod's sexuality is purely masochistic with a lesbian tinge (at one point she strokes Mad's short cropped hair then bares her back so that Mad can carve the word 'love' on it with a knife, finishing it off with a generous sprinkling of salt[44]). Mad's sexuality is sublimated in her pyromania and sadism, while Amyl's is in the grip of her narcissism as she continually preens herself in a mock-middle-class fashion. For both Bod and Mad extreme emotion is present only at the moment of killing, as we witness when Bod visits Lounge Lizard's home and murders him with her bare hands in a state of sexual arousal, watched with studied indifference by Mad and Amyl. Mad's disembowelling of the policeman is committed in a similar frenzy, leaving her crying uncontrollably as if in despair at her own viciousness.

Interestingly it is Bod who represents the historical notion of Elizabeth I, the Virgin Queen – ice-cold, cruel, manipulative, almost asexual (both roles are played by Jenny Runacre). She is dressed as a man throughout the film and her cohorts treat 'feminine' virtues as weak and contemptible. Bod rules by her silence, quick rebukes and calls to action. There is a restless and aloof quality to her character that sets her apart, yet, when she does speak, she is as banal as the others. Her masochistic demands are articulated in a flat, matter-of-fact tone, in contrast with Mad's gleeful sadism. In true masochistic fashion, Bod is controlling and powerful in her very submission to Mad's knife. Her personal masochism is also the other face of her public (social and political) sadism.

The twins have the only clear-cut homosexual relationship in *Jubilee* and theirs is an incestuous love articulated dramatically through a third party, the woman artist Viv. In an arrested moment in the film, Angel sings a

109

traditional Scottish love song in Viv's darkened room, cut off from the mayhem outside. A similar triangle is set up in *The Garden* between the two men representing Christ and the Madonna figure played by Tilda Swinton and in *Caravaggio* between the painter, Rannucio and Lena. In these films there are also such 'moments', desexualised ones in which love affirms itself against the incessant pain and cruelty of sado-masochistic relationships. This love finds its closure with the casual shooting of the twins in the arcade, witnessed by Viv. Thus the only relationship founded in emotion as well as sexual desire is negated. In *Caravaggio*, by contrast, Jarman seems consciously to eschew sado-masochism as the central motif and to place the love triangle at the film's centre.

The character of Elizabeth I is depicted as sensitive and vulnerable, unlike the popular image of the aggressive and frosty Virgin Queen of Hollywood biopics. Her emotional reactions to what she finds in twentieth-century England are the shaping ones of the film. In much of Jarman's work women express the emotions elided in the male heroes. If his female characters are often reduced to being bystanders, they are nevertheless representatives of the good and the ideal or of its opposite, malevolence and aggression.

Jubilee reached America in September 1979, nearly two years after the Sex Pistols' tour there and the film's opening in London. Sixteen minutes were cut from it, including the Elizabeth I and Dee framing device, making it a very different film.

'The Tempest'

With its eclectic costumes, mixing of voices and menacing atmosphere, Jarman's film interpretation of Shakespeare's *The Tempest* shares something of the punk-like sensibility of *Jubilee*. Jarman stated that he had had the idea of working with *The Tempest*, a play he had loved since his university days, as early as 1975 when he had worked on some designs for a production at the London avant-garde venue the Roundhouse, interpreting the play as one in which 'a mad Prospero, rightly imprisoned by his brother, played all the parts'.[45] Peter Greenaway's later film version, *Prospero's Books*, has a similar idea at its centre, with John Gielgud, with whom Jarman had discussed his own ideas in the mid-70s, as Prospero.

The film cost £150,000, most of it raised by the producer Don Boyd

On the set of 'The Tempest' **111**

who was later to produce *War Requiem* and the portmanteau film *Aria*. Alexander Walker cites Boyd as remarking that he provided the money in 'a mad moment of commitment'.[46] According to Lorna Sullivan in an article on the funding of the British film industry for the *Sunday Telegraph* in February 1980, *The Tempest*, along with films such as Alan Clarke's *Scum* (1979) and Claude Whatham's *Sweet William* (1979), were made possible by a complex financial manoeuvring involving the setting up of limited partnerships which could be legitimately offset against tax. As Sullivan remarks, it 'transforms tax avoidance into tax deferral'.[47] These tactics, along with the use of holding companies in countries more 'hospitable' to film investment, allowed independent companies such as Boyd's to survive.

Some scholars have argued that Shakespeare's Prospero is in fact a portrait of John Dee.[48] Certainly, Dee seems central to Jarman's conception of Prospero. In a draft version[49] of the film written in June 1976 Jarman has Prospero in a 'costume like Robespierre', which suggests that his view of Dee was associated with terror, authority and revolution, an interpretation that supports Colin MacCabe's view of the film as a comment on the Elizabethan 'police state'.[50] Jarman's Prospero has all the attributes of a wily, Machiavellian politico – again not incompatible with Dee, who was one of Elizabeth I's diplomats. Years later Jarman was to analyse his obsession with Dee:

> Part of my interest in the magician John Dee was his preoccupation with secrets and cyphers. … Why this obsession with the language of closed structures, the ritual of the closet and the sanctuary? the prison cells of Genet's *Un Chant d'amour*, the desert encampment of *Sebastiane*; Anger, insulating himself with magick, screening himself off; Cocteau's *Orphée*, an attempt to steal through the screen into the labyrinth and usurp the privileges only the cabal of the dead may confer; the wall of unreality that girds the house in *Salo* and its victims, who are told: What is about to take place here will have never happened, you are already dead to the world outside.[51]

In citing the work of other gay directors, Jarman suggests that his – and their – interest in closed worlds and secret codes is perhaps a reflection of the gay culture in which they operated and its relation to wider society.

112

Jarman's interest in the English Renaissance is at times couched as a form of conservatism:

> Our culture is backward-looking and always has been. Shakespeare is backward-looking. What interested me is that Elizabethan England is our cultural Arcadia, as Shakespeare is the essential pivot of our culture. It seemed really important to deal with it. ...The whole myth of Camelot, Blake, Tennyson – you can go through all the English artists – there's that dream of Arcadia. We seem to be the only European culture which really has that dream background.[52]

Despite the 60s, when mysticism was largely Eastern served up via California, Jarman's interests lay in a distinctly English strand of visionary thought which, in the case of William Blake, incorporated political and social critique.

Made in the year of the death of Jarman's much-loved and perhaps idealised mother, *The Tempest* is a play of mortality, reconciliation, magic and love of different sorts: paternal, maternal, sexual, humanist. For Jarman, the subject matter brought him to thoughts of film itself:

> Film is the wedding of light and matter – an alchemical conjunction. My readings in the Renaissance magi – Dee, Bruno, Paracelsus, Fludd and Cornelius Agrippa – helped to conjure the film of *The Tempest*[53]

Like the play, Jarman's film is confined to an island in which the story is resolved without the interference of the real world in which its complications arose. Only in Ferdinand's love for Miranda does the outside world cut into Prospero's omnipotent manipulations. If *The Tempest* is about reparation and forgiveness, as has been generally accepted, it is at the cost of displacing reality. The play's implicit pessimism lies in the fact that only magic can bring about such things, not real political or personal understanding. Reparation is achieved in a fantasy world, a view that Jarman subscribed to throughout his films.

Jarman's view of Prospero from the earliest draft scripts is of a tyrant who 'is unable to see his exploitation of Caliban and Ariel'. His character throughout is sinister, intense, secretive and cruel, signalled by the first

113

appearance of Caliban before him, when he stands on the latter's fingers in an act of calculated sadism. Jarman remarks that however Prospero 'resolves his own tragedy the maxim that all power corrupts remains essentially true'.[54] But his Prospero is also the first of his characters to display the tense energy of a seer, and in this respect is a model, much more than the anaemic Sebastian, for the film-maker's future 'seers' – Caravaggio, Wilfrid Owen, Wittgenstein and finally, in the last films, Jarman himself. Prospero is treated as an artist – as someone with the insight and imagination to see what others cannot and to transform that seeing into something good and spiritually satisfying. Acted by the 60s poet Heathcote Williams, Jarman's Prospero is a dark, cabalistic figure working in the moving shadows of candles, spiders scuttling across his books – images at times reminiscent of Jarman's first film, *Studio Bankside*. The brooding figure of Prospero alone in the darkness of his study at the end of the film echoes a recurrent image in Jarman's work that refers without doubt to Jarman himself, locked away from competing systems but always caught between them. *The Garden*, for instance, opens with a similar scene of Jarman himself writing in his room.

Unlike *Jubilee*, where Jarman had attempted a reconstruction of costume and sets from the early Elizabethan period, *The Tempest* is the first of his anachronistic portrayals of historical pieces. With the exception of the masque scene, the action takes place in deep shadows, the flickering light coming from a fire, candles or the moon. Jarman and Peter Middleton, who lit the film, decided early on 'to let shadows invade' so that 'boundaries disappear'.[55] The setting of the huge rambling mansion with its many dark passages and back stairs locates the play in some ruined English aristocracy, held together by dreams, spells and displaced characters.

The film begins with a sequence which intercuts the shipwreck (found-footage of sailors in a storm) with the disturbed sleep of Prospero, his breathing magnified to become a rhythmic part of the soundtrack. A patterned veil covers his face. The room is momentarily lit by the lightning of the storm. Miranda (played as a coquettish tomboy by punk singer Toyah Wilcox) wakes up frightened by the storm. The soundtrack mingles the mariners' calls with Prospero's dream-voice pleas for his wife and child. In a particularly violent moment of the storm Prospero awakes as if from a nightmare. Jarman suggests that the subsequent events are perhaps a dream or that Prospero's omniscient powers have invaded his sleep. But with the

waking of father and daughter there is a sense of an awakening to all things – love and knowledge for Miranda and revenge, forgiveness and the return to his past life for Prospero. The storm, as Prospero knows, introduces a reckoning. Jarman ends the film with Prospero asleep in his chair as Ariel sneaks out to his freedom, a bracket of sleeping or unconsciousness he was often to use in his films.

Jarman's idea for Caliban in the 1976 script was that he should be 'black and beautiful' and dressed in livery. One of Shakespeare's most controversial characters, Caliban's association with the New World has been widely discussed and there seems little doubt that he alludes as much to contemporary conceptions of the 'primitives' discovered in these new lands as he does to European satyr-like beasts.[56] Jarman shuns these models and in the film as made uses Jack Birkett (Borgia Ginz in *Jubilee*) with his strong north-country accent, bald head and butler-like garb to suggest something rather different. As Miranda creeps through the dark kitchen where Caliban surprises her, the 'monster's' maniacal laughter at her fright is accompanied by sexual gestures. At a later point, as Miranda bathes semi-naked by the fire, she is again disturbed by Caliban, whose ribald laugh she returns after she

The masque ending 'The Tempest' **115**

pushes him out of the door. At this level, Jarman reduces Caliban's lust and sexual threat to a ribald laugh and lewd gestures – at no time is he Shakespeare's sexual ogre.

Ariel, played by Karl Johnson (one of the twins in *Jubilee*), is a slight, fey creature dressed in a white shirt and leggings, a 'look' influenced by Cocteau's messengers of death.[57] His feelings of injustice at Prospero's drawn-out endgame are tempered by nervousness as we see him practise his demand for freedom in front of the mirror. When Ferdinand clambers naked through the waves from the shipwreck in the cold blue moonlight he is watched by Ariel sitting on the nearby dunes. The cut between Ariel's gaze and the naked man suggests a homosexual desire. In a more revealing moment, as Ariel and Prospero mimic the sounds of animals and the hunt to frighten Caliban and the drunken Stephano and Trinculo, we see Ariel's face in extreme close-up, waggling his tongue lasciviously (a popular gesture in Jarman's films). There is some room for the view that Ariel's freedom is a sexual one – after all, the camp masque is Ariel's concoction – though there is no evidence for a homosexual relationship between Prospero and his sprite in Jarman's rendering of the play. In the flashback sequence Jarman uses to accompany Prospero's story of how Ariel was a tormented prisoner of Caliban's mother, the witch Sycorax, we see the naked adult Caliban sucking on his naked mother's breast, while Ariel is dragged into the scene naked on the end of a chain. The tremulous Ariel is no doubt an image of a feminised gay male as Caliban is the 'old queen' figure who masquerades as the heterosexual lustful for Miranda. A further representation of maleness, Ferdinand, by contrast, is portrayed as a suitably handsome, rather wooden matinée idol.

If *Jubilee* was an enactment of the collapse of the class system and its replacement by power, then in *The Tempest*, with its country mansion setting, we are witnessing the ghosts of the English aristocracy. The original play has been identified with Shakespeare's attempt to regain the Elizabethan dream of 'sacred imperialism' during a short-lived Elizabethan revival in the Jacobean age.[58] (As Jarman knew, the play was presented at court to mark the marriage of the young princess Elizabeth, daughter of James I, to the Bohemian prince, an attempt to cement the Protestant alliance and part of a revival of Elizabethan ideology that occurred in the first decade of the 17th century.[59]) Jarman does not set his interpretation of the play in contemporary Britain, but its dream of a lost community nevertheless has a much broader

116

historical frame for him. It is the loss that seems to be incurred after the Elizabethan period with which he so strongly identified in its merging of knowledge and magic, of science and morality and of nature and culture.

The Tempest is one of Jarman's most accomplished and satisfying films. Elizabeth Welch's rendering of 'Stormy Weather' is one of the great scenes in British cinema, its majestic quality throwing into relief the other levels of representation within the film from nineteenth-century Romanticism to

Hollywood pastiche to high camp. The darkness that characterises some of Jarman's other works is mitigated here – as in Shakespeare's original – by reparation, young love and forgiveness. Miranda is the childlike innocent at the film's centre. As all around her manipulate and are in turn manipulated by her father, she alone has a pure emotion that motivates and thrills her – her love for Ferdinand and her wonderment at that love. Central to Shakespeare's rendering of Miranda is her joy at meeting mankind – 'O brave new world'. And her conjoining in marriage with Ferdinand symbolises not only the reconciliation between the two brothers and the end of Prospero's magic but also the playwright's transference of optimism to others. But if Jarman uses *The Tempest* for optimistic ends, its optimism is limited. The cabalistic microcosm of the shadowy house on the island where sexual knowingness and lust in the shape of Caliban meet the sweet innocence of Miranda suggests that if all can be put right in the world, it is only through magic, not through human relationships.

The Tempest did well in Europe, but it suffered irredeemably in the US at the hands of the critic Vincent Canby, who famously described it as 'very nearly unbearable ... a fingernail scratched along a blackboard, sand in spinach'.[60] Years later Tilda Swinton recalled that what hurt Jarman about Canby's criticism was its insult to his knowledge and research of the play, and indeed the film has been praised by Shakespearean scholars who have seen it as one of the most successful screen adaptations of Shakespeare.[61] Russell Jackson, for instance, is of the opinion that purist adaptations of Shakespeare for film and television have resulted neither in very good films nor in capturing the original text. Discussing adaptations of Shakespeare's comedies, Jackson remarks:

> I favour Derek Jarman's *Tempest* more than, say, Christine Edzard's *As You Like It* or Peter Hall's *Dream* because his film seems to manage 'mainstream' appeal ('gothic' horror, camp humour, a sense of festivity) on a 'fringe' budget.[62]

For Jackson, Jarman's ruthless cutting back of the original dialogue allows cinema's image-making ability to speak. He compares the energy of Jarman's film with Peter Greenaway's *Prospero's Books*, which though more reverential towards the play's text does not succeed as well in capturing its mood. Nevertheless, Canby's criticism took its toll – Alexander Walker, writing in the mid-80s, recounts how the 'poor American box-office cost Jarman finance for his next project, which was to have been a study of Caravaggio'.[63] Jarman's future in the British film industry was to prove bleak for over five years.

According to Walker, 'the absolute beginners [among British film-makers] were the truly poor of the Seventies'.[64] Without a Channel Four and with the National Film Finance Corporation systematically starved of funds, even those young film-makers who managed to make a feature film during this period found it difficult to finance follow-ups. Of the film-makers who made their reputations in the 60s, only Ken Russell and Nicolas Roeg 'produced work fairly consistently and consolidated their reputations'[65] within British cinema in the 70s. Others, such as Stephen Frears and Ken Loach, worked largely in television while John Schlesinger and Tony Richardson moved to Hollywood.

Walker singles Jarman out as the 'most prodigiously gifted' of the young independent film-makers of the 70s. He justly compares his achievements to those of Herzog and Fassbinder in Germany. Jarman was to complain many years later that in any other European country, following such a start, he would have found funding on a fairly regular basis, as did his German and French counterparts. This was not the case in Britain, however, where he had to wait until 1985 before receiving any substantial money to make his long-nursed project, *Caravaggio*.

1 For more details of this earlier attempt, see Derek Jarman, *Dancing Ledge* (London: Quartet, 1984), p. 142.

2 According to gossip columnist William Hickey in the *Daily Express*, 3 February 1975, the Marquis of Dufferin and Ava, David Hockney and Lord Kenilworth backed *Sebastiane* to the tune of £35,000.

3 Jarman cites this figure in *Dancing Ledge*, p. 161, but Alexander Walker cites £15,000 in *National Heroes: British Cinema in the Seventies and Eighties* (London: Harrap, 1985), p. 232, – a figure he seems to have got from an interview with Jarman on 16 July 1982.

4 Derek Jarman, *At Your Own Risk: A Saint's Testament* (Hutchison: London, 1992).

5 Peter Wollen, 'The Last New Wave: Modernism in the British Films of the Thatcher Era', in Lester Friedman (ed.), *British Cinema and Thatcherism* (London: UCL Press, 1993), p. 44.

6 There are two accounts, one in *Dancing Ledge*, p. 150, and a rather more explicit one in *At Your Own Risk*, pp. 72–4.

7 There had been an underground cinema tradition in America which had celebrated gay sexuality, e.g. Markopoulos, Anger, Warhol. See Richard Dyer, *Now You See It: Studies on Lesbian and Gay Film* (London: Routledge, 1990), for an account of this tradition from a gay perspective.

8 Quoted in *At Your Own Risk*, p. 73.

9 Ibid.

10 *Dancing Ledge*, p. 142.

11 *At Your Own Risk*, p. 73.

12 *Dancing Ledge*, p. 236.

13 See Christie Davies, 'Buggery and the Decline of the British Empire', in *Permissive Britain: Social Change in the Sixties and Seventies* (London: Pitman Publishing, 1975).

14 Tony Rayns, 'Submitting to Sodomy: Propositions and Rhetorical Questions about an English Film-maker', *Afterimage* no. 12, 1985.

15 Timothy Murray, *Like a Film: Ideological Fantasy on Screen, Camera and Canvas* (London: Routledge, 1993), especially chapter 5.

16 As Alexander Walker points out, 'Sebastiane' is the Latin vocative, translating as 'O Sebastian' and not, as some have thought, simply a pretentious spelling. See Walker, *National Heroes*, p. 232.

17 Jarman planned a documentary on Medley in 1983.

18 *Dancing Ledge*, p. 155.

19 See Richard Holmes, *Firing Line* (London: Pimlico, 1985), on the problems of boredom and inactivity in military life. Jarman's own father commended his son's film for the accuracy of its portrayal of garrison life.

20 Dyer, *Now You See It*, p. 169.

21 Early Greek pastoral verse included homosexual work by Theocritus. See Anthony Holden (ed.), *Greek Pastoral Poetry* (Harmondsworth: Penguin, 1974).

22 *Dancing Ledge*, p. 165.

23 Ibid., p. 162.

24 According to Christopher Hobbs in interview with the author, August 1994.

25 Peter York, *Style Wars* (London: Sidgwick & Jackson, 1980), p. 128.

26 Vivienne Westwood interviewed on 'Punks and Pistols', *Arena*, BBC2, 20 August 1995.

27 Quoted in *At Your Own Risk*, p. 76.

28 Jarman quoted in Jon Savage, *England's Dreaming: Sex Pistols and Punk Rock* (London: Faber & Faber, 1991), p. 377.

29 Simon Frith and Howard Horne, *Art into Pop* (London: Methuen, 1987), p. 155.

30 Savage, *England's Dreaming* p. 377.

31 *Dancing Ledge*, p. 172.

32 Ibid., p. 176.

33 Tony Rayns, 'Queendom Come', *Time Out*, 24 February – 2 March 1978, p. 11.

34 Nicholas de Jongh, 'History is punk', *Guardian*, 2 February 1978.

35 Scott Meek, 'Jubilee', *Monthly Film Bulletin*, vol. 45 no. 531, April 1978.

36 *Dancing Ledge*, p. 172.

37 See Frances Yates, *The Occult Philosophy in the Elizabethan Age* (London: Ark, 1983).

38 Lines reproduced in *Dancing Ledge*, pp. 252–3.

39 Charles Nicholl, *The Reckoning: The Murder of Christopher Marlowe* (London: Picador, 1993).

40 See my article on Svankmajer, 'Between Slapstick and Horror', *Sight and Sound,* vol. 4 no. 9, September 1994.

41 See especially Frances Yates, *The Rosicrucian Enlightenment* (London: Ark, 1986), and *The Occult Philosophy*.

42 See especially Carl Jung, *Aion: Researches into the Phenomenology of the Self* (London: Routledge, 1991), and *Alchemical Studies* (London: Routledge & Kegan Paul, 1983).

43 Script dated April 1977 in Derek Jarman Special Collection, BFI, London.

44 Jarman describes how at his first meeting with Adam Ant the latter had the word 'fuck' carved by Jordan on his chest, see *Dancing Ledge*, p. 168.

45 Ibid., p. 183.

46 Walker, *National Heroes*, p. 237.

47 Ibid., p. 156.

48 For the association of Prospero with the figure of Dee, see Yates, *The Occult Philosophy*, pp. 159–63. For the influence of Agrippa on Shakespeare's conception of Prospero, see Yates, *Shakespeare's Last Plays: A New Approach* (London: Routledge & Kegan Paul, 1975), a view pioneered by Frank Kermode in his classic introduction to his edition of *The Tempest* (London: Arden, 1983), first published in 1954. Jarman was familiar with these texts.

49 In Derek Jarman Special Collection, BFI, London. There is also a notebook with sketches of the project dated autumn 1974.

50 Colin MacCabe, 'Edward II: Throne of Blood', *Sight and Sound*, vol. 1 no. 6, October 1991. Extended version, 'A Post-National European Cinema: A Consideration of Derek Jarman's The Tempest and Edward II', in Duncan Petrie (ed.), *Screening Europe* (London: British Film Institute Working Papers, 1992).

51 Derek Jarman, *The Last of England* (London: Constable, 1987), p. 66.

52 *Afterimage*, no. 12, 1985, p. 49.

53 *Dancing Ledge*, p. 188.

54 Draft script dated June 1976, Derek Jarman Special Collection, BFI, London.

55 *Dancing Ledge*, p. 194.

56 For a review of these debates, see Kermode's introduction to his edition of *The Tempest*.

57 Draft script dated June 1976, Derek Jarman Special Collection, BFI, London.

58 See Yates, *Shakespeare's Last Plays*, pp. 17–37.

59 Jarman sets out this historical background to the play in his draft script dated June 1976.

60 Quoted in Walker, *National Heroes*, p. 238.

61 See Russell Jackson, 'Shakespeare's Comedies on Film', in Anthony Davies and Stanley Wells (eds), *Shakespeare and the Moving Image: The Plays on Film and Television* (Cambridge: Cambridge University Press, 1994), pp. 107–9.

62 Ibid., p. 99.

63 Walker, *National Heroes*, p. 238.

64 Ibid., p. 216.

65 Andrew Higson, 'A Diversity of Film Practices: Renewing British Cinema in the 70s', in Bart Moore-Gilbert (ed.), *The Arts in the 1970s: Cultural Closure?* (London: Routledge, 1994), p. 217.

A CINEMA
OF SMALL GESTURES

Chapter Five

1979–1985

Following *The Tempest*, Jarman was to spend six years in which his energies were thrown into super-8 home movies, painting, music videos, writing and occasional set designs for Ken Russell. These were the years of the early 80s when Britain under Thatcher suffered one of the most reactionary governments of the century. By 1984 cinema admissions had fallen to an all-time low of 55 million and only 700 cinemas with 1,200 screens remained.[1] One of the few positive achievements of these years was the setting up of Channel Four in 1981 (it began broadcasting the following year). Meanwhile, the British film renaissance which the Oscar-winning success of *Chariots of Fire* (1981) seemed to promise proved to be illusory. As Alexander Walker points out, in 1985:

> At the very moment the Government was dismantling the British film industry, and putting only short-term, prefabricated structures in place of it, the industry itself announced that it was going to celebrate 'British Film Year'. It all looked like the last reel of an Ealing comedy.[2]

Shortly after Jarman had completed *The Tempest*, he met James Mackay, who was to produce many of his subsequent films, in particular the shorts, music videos and more experimental projects like *The Last of England*. Born in Scotland, Mackay had been an art student in the late 70s, specialising in film at North East London Polytechnic,[3] a stronghold of avant-garde cinema. His taste was broad, including Fellini, Godard, Welles, Warhol and Anger. In the late 70s he programmed the cinema at the London Film-Makers' Co-operative and invited Jarman to show his super-8s. Mackay remarks:

> It was through discussing the problems of working with Super-8 with

him that I got involved with production and why a lot of the work I have subsequently done has been produced on Super-8.[4]

The partnership was a fertile one. Mackay raised money and organised production, distribution and exhibition so Jarman could get on with writing scripts and making films. On his return to feature film-making with *Caravaggio* in 1985 Jarman benefited from a new audience and a developed aesthetic which he had honed over the years in experimental super-8s such as *TG Psychic Rally in Heaven*, *Pirate Tape/Film (WSB)*, *The Angelic Conversation* and *Imagining October*.

Also associated with Mackay was a group of young film-makers – John Maybury (who had assisted on the set design of *Jubilee*), Cerith Wyn Evans, Michael Kostiff, Steve Chivers and Holly Warburton – who helped to displace the formalist avant-garde of the 70s as the cutting edge of experimental cinema. Their cultural framework was not the fine art sensibility of predecessors such as Le Grice and Peter Gidal but one which embraced the American underground films of Jack Smith, Ron Rice, Warhol and Anger with their emphasis on sexuality, artifice and the pleasure of the text. They were also sympathetic to the European art cinema of such directors as Godard, Werner Schroeter and Andrei Tarkovsky and to popular culture itself. The impact of feminism on the avant-garde meant that the human figure, especially the female one, had become problematic for many film-makers – Gidal, for instance, had rejected the possibility of representing any figure, male or female, on screen. Wyn Evans' material, by contrast, was sexually explicit – naked young men kissing and masturbating in scenes that had the sensuous and sumptuous imagery of Rice or Smith – while one of Maybury's first works, *Tortures that Laugh* (1983), was a homage to Warhol's minimalist classic *Thirteen Most Beautiful Women* (1964). Maybury and Wyn Evans, both gay film-makers, were also inspired by Jarman, at the time an awkward figure who did not belong either in the avant-garde or in mainstream British cinema. Jarman's representation of the punk sensibility in *Jubilee* also endeared him to post-punk film-makers like Maybury.

Maybury and others were part of the burgeoning London club scene which merged fashion, music and dance with an eclecticism that had not been seen since the 60s. In 1981 Maybury and Wyn Evans showed their super-8 work at the ICA in London under the title 'A Certain Sensibility'.

In the accompanying notes, Wyn Evans speaks of 'the catwalk as a metaphor for existence' and the 'coffee table as the ultimate mode of exhibition'. Like Jarman, Maybury and Wyn Evans enjoyed the possibilities offered by super-8 and were happy to show to small groups made up mainly of friends. Maybury's own notes to the programme sum up their conscious break with the past:

> Our criteria for visual response have been permanently altered – sophisticated advertising and slick promotional videos have picked up the line from where the Surrealists and German Expressionists left it. Experimentation was sidetracked up the blind alley of structuralism which effectively murdered underground film.[5]

The relationship between Jarman and these film-makers seems to have been a mutual learning process – for instance, he was to use slow motion much more widely in response to the younger film-makers' work.

Jarman was also to be connected, though more obliquely, with another growing area of film-making in the early 80s – black independent cinema, centred initially on Sankofa and the Black Audio Film Collective. These two groups attended the 1986 Edinburgh Film Festival and saw *Imagining October* in which they recognised an aesthetic in which the political, personal and filmic were fully integrated. No other independent film-making offered them such a well worked-out resolution of the kind of problems they too were encountering. Both Isaac Julien's *Territories* (1985) and Sankofa's *Passion of Remembrance* (1986) use found-footage, fragmented structures, music and notions of memory and cultural resonance that owe to Jarman as well as to Godard. *Territories* shares with *Imagining October* a reliance on poetic imagism to convey complex ideas of politics and gay sexuality.

During the early 80s Jarman had one of his few forays into party political activity when the actress Vanessa Redgrave coaxed him into working for the Trotskyist Workers' Revolutionary Party (WRP).[6] In November 1980 he attended a WRP rally in Liverpool, one of 'several marches this year'. But in January 1981 he left a meeting of the WRP held at Kensington Town Hall to celebrate the party newspaper's eleven years of publication unimpressed by the fact that 'not one printing worker takes the rostrum, nobody involved in the actual production of the newspaper'.[7] At that point his interest ended.

125

Super-8s, Videos and Pop Promos

In 1979 Jarman made a film to promote Marianne Faithfull's punk-influenced album *Broken English*,[8] which was described by her unofficial biographer Mark Hodkinson as an exposition of 'Jarman's individualistic bleak style'.[9] The film covered three of the album's tracks – 'Broken English', 'Witches' Song' and 'The Ballad of Lucy Jordan' – and used fragments from *In the Shadow of the Sun* together with found-footage, most memorably of fascist soldiers on the march.[10] 'Witches' Song' begins with original black-and-white footage of an elfin Faithfull in a leather jacket and miniskirt walking at night through London's West End. The rest of the film is made up of imagery from *Jubilee* – the super-8 book-burning scene with Jordan dancing – plus men in paper-bag masks reflecting light into the camera as in *The Art of Mirrors*. This section, titled 'Devil's Brew', threatened to become a separate film with the gay club personality Marilyn (Boy George's boyfriend) playing the role of the bride and a tattooed Dave Baby as the groom.[11] 'The Ballad of Lucy Jordan' has the black-and-white West End footage of Faithfull superimposed over images of a woman looking into a mirror and ironing. The final track 'Broken English' has Faithfull in an amusement arcade intercut with images of atomic explosions, found-footage of Mussolini and Hitler plus shots of the late-70s National Front demonstrations. There is also footage of the London blitz, of Oswald Mosley and of East End anti-fascist demonstrations of the 30s.

The first two films are very much like Jarman's home movies with the accompaniment of pop songs rather than 30s jazz, arias or medieval songs. For Jarman, 'Broken English', a response to the rise of fascism in Britain in the late 70s, was the most successful:

> We used old footage of Stalin and Hitler, cut together so that they smile and wave to each other in a ballet of destruction. There's footage of Mosley, and video material that the Oval Co-op have given me of the police at Lewisham. The film starts with the Bikini H-Bomb explosion monitored on a space-invaders machine; and ends with the destruction in slow motion of the huge concrete swastika that crowned the Nuremberg stadium.[12]

It seems that for films aimed at the pop music market, Jarman was content to raid his own image-bank, though masked or tattooed figures, bonfires and reflecting light off shiny surfaces into the camera lens are undeniably strong motifs whatever the context. Faithfull was pleased with the results and became friends with Jarman. He used her version of 'The Skye Boat Song' in *The Last of England*.

Jarman found himself drawn into the world of pop promos in the early 80s, mainly for financial reasons but also to gain experience with video (the Marianne Faithfull promos were shot on film). Interviewed in 1984 by the author, he claimed that he was 'not very good' at making them:

> I know how it should be done but my mind doesn't work that way – eighty cuts per minute. I always ask for previous videos of the groups, and I've noticed that the people who make them don't relate to the singer at all; they relate to some technical thing in video. I don't have that technique; I don't understand it, and in a rather deliberate way I've stopped myself understanding it, because it leaves me more involved with the people in front of the camera.[13]

In the previous year he had made promos for the Lords of the New Church ('Dance with Me'), Carmel ('Willow Weep for Me'), Wang Chung ('Dance Hall Daze') and Steve Hale ('Stop the Radio'), with the Aldabra production company. They are unremarkable pieces, shot in a simple style with the accent on the band or individual's performance. At the time they looked rather naive in comparison with larger-scale, more sophisticated work of the same period.

Jarman's first production with James Mackay was *TG Psychic Rally in Heaven* – an eight-minute film of Genesis P. Orridge's band Throbbing Gristle's 'Psychic Rally' in Heaven, one of the most popular London gay clubs of the early 80s. Shot in December 1980, it cost around £350 to make. The film has the shifting slow-motion aesthetic Jarman was to use throughout the early 80s and a pulsating, almost abstract feel. According to Mackay, 'it was shot, processed, blown up to 16mm and shown at the Berlin Film Festival within two weeks of its inception'.[14] For Jarman, it was a film that 'takes experiments with superimposition and refilming, begun in 1972 with *In the Shadow of the Sun*, as far as I can go'.[15] Afterwards he was to simplify his style, relying more on slow-motion effects achieved by

127

projecting at three frames per second. The film was not received very well, largely because the sound is extremely loud and aggressive. The imagery achieved with the Nizo camera veers towards a strong abstraction, with Genesis' figure seen only in fuzzy outline. Jarman describes how he used wax earplugs while shooting as he had to manoeuvre near the speakers to get the right angle. The film was shouted down at the Melbourne Film Festival in 1981 according to Tony Rayns, who reported this to Jarman.

In 1983 Jarman made *Waiting for Waiting for Godot,* a film of a RADA production of Beckett's play designed by John Maybury. It was more abstract in conception than any of his previous super-8s, involving filming in super-8 the image from a video monitor, which was then transferred back to video. The Beckett film did not attempt seriously to document the performance or set. Rather it achieves an abstract, internally degenerated image thanks to the transfer from one medium to another. The colour is dispersed into washed-out oranges, pinks and pale yellows. Figures and their shadows can be detected moving about a room but the image slips continually between representation and abstraction – for instance a close-up of a leg transforms into a dark-coloured mass which subtly changes shape. The surface texture owes more to the reshooting than to the slowed-down camera effect. It is a confident and striking film which is rarely shown, though it was released on video by James Mackay's production company Dark Pictures.

Pirate Film/Tape (WSB), also released on video by Dark Pictures, was made by Jarman from super 8 footage he had shot of William Burroughs when he arrived in England for the notorious Final Academy Event at B2 Gallery in September 1982. Jarman accompanied Genesis P. Orridge, one of the event's organisers, to Heathrow Airport to meet Burroughs and on the way back to Chelsea in a taxi began to film him with the Nizo. The film is shot in the slowed-down (three to six frames per second) style he used much in these years and shows Burroughs entering a bookshop with his 'bodyguard'. On the soundtrack Genesis P. Orridge's electronic music is collaged with Burroughs' voice saying repeatedly 'Boys, school showers and swimming pools full of them'. The soundtrack and slowed-down visuals achieve a sinister quality while the shifting moments of frozen gestures and looks have an erotic quality.

In the wake of this event, Jarman, Maybury, Kostiff and Wyn Evans collaborated on a portmanteau film, *The Dream Machine,* produced by

Mackay. Jarman's contribution was a piece he had filmed in New York a few years earlier in black-and-white super-8 of two young men (the photographers Gerald Incandela and Jean Marc Prouveur), one naked and the other not, in a room – one at first coyly behind a curtain – where they embrace in a slow erotic dance similar in style and mood to sequences in *The Angelic Conversation*. The slow-motion image begins in long-shot, moving to medium close-up, and is an exquisite rendering of innocent gay love. Wyn Evans' film is an abrasive montage of images, locating gayness in urban London. It uses video effects to achieve one memorable scene, a superimposition of a skinhead sitting giant-like in London's West End making obscene gestures at his Lilliputian world.

'Neutron'

During 1980 Jarman wrestled with a script which was never to be made but which is worth discussion because of its intimations of the apocalyptic vision he would foster in *The Last of England* and *The Garden*. *Neutron* came out of an ongoing political quarrel with a young politico, Lee Drysdale, who had been hired to guard the set of *Jubilee*. Scripts were produced (including one dated November/December 1979) and actors cast – pop star David Bowie and actor-playwright Steven Berkoff. Christopher Hobbs designed some sets. Don Boyd was interested, as was Bowie, though he would only come into the project if money could be raised without using his name. The time Bowie could afford was short and the money could not be found quickly enough, so the film was shelved. Jarman described it as 'the Book of Revelations ... worked as science fiction'[16] and to judge by its sketched-out visuals, it would have been a precursor of mainstream films such as *Escape from New York* (1981), *Blade Runner* (1982), *Brazil* (1985) and others of the post-punk apocalyptic genre that surfaced in the 80s. Jarman writes:

> We set it in the huge junked-out power station at Nine Elms and in the wasteland around the Berlin Wall. Christopher Hobbs produced xeroxes of the pink marble halls of the bunker with their Speer lighting – that echo to 'the muzak of the spheres' which played even in the cannibal abattoirs, where the vampire orderlies sipped dark blood from crystal goblets.[17]

129

Once again there is a trace of John Dee in the parody of the magician's music of the spheres and the symbolism of 'anti-heroes Aeon and Topaz':

> *Neutron* is the Sleeping Film – the shadow of the activity surrounding the *Caravaggio* project – a trailer for the End of the World based on the self-fulfilling prophecy of the Apocalypse. A dream treatment of mass-destruction, of the world's desire to be put out of its misery, the now-established place the unthinkable has in the popular imagination. *Neutron* sleeps between its covers like a Cruise or a Pershing in its silo, and is overhauled every eighteen months.[18]

The ideas here are not dissimilar to those Jarman was to express in *The Last of England* except that by then he had no need of a sci-fi framework. Two years later he was still working on the script, now with the pop music critic and historian Jon Savage. In 1987, just after completing *The Last of England*, Jarman discussed *Neutron* again, remarking that it was based on Jung's *Aion*:

> The script was a conflict between the active and the contemplative life. Topaz, a revolutionary, and Aeon, an artist, meet in a desolate shadowy world, a purgatory where neither of them has an audience any longer. They criss-cross each other's lives in a perpetual conflict; at the end we discover they are the same person. It was a very strange script. Based on the Revelation of St John.[19]

Jarman was to say later that he did not think *Neutron* could have been financed as the budget needed would have been enormous. He also felt that it bore too strong a resemblance to Terry Gilliam's *Brazil* which had come out in the meantime and which he admired. The other script Jarman was nursing during this period was *Bob Up a Down*, described as a medieval allegory, which had been in existence even longer than the *Caravaggio* project. In 1981 he visited Granada Television in Manchester to discuss the script, but it came to nothing.

In 1982 Jarman designed Ken Russell's production of Stravinsky's *The Rake's Progress* at the Pergola theatre in Florence:

I'm embarking on this project for three reasons: first, after a year of waiting for *Caravaggio* I'm broke; secondly, I've always enjoyed working with Ken; and thirdly, it's a kind of revenge.[20]

The production was a characteristic Russell/Jarman collaboration:

We have the brothel-keeper, Michael Aspinal, in Queen Mother drag, leading the chorus who are dressed in Falklands fatigues. The Rake wears a T-shirt depicting Mrs Thatcher as a vampire holding a skull – 'Alas, poor England I knew her well.' He croons with a set of scarlet Mohican dancers from Milan.[21]

While in Italy Jarman shot a short super-8 film which became *Pontormo and Punks at Santa Croce* showing tourists and a group of punks messing around in the square outside Santa Croce in Florence. During these years of fairly free experiment Jarman developed a visual language that was to be the mainstay of his future work: 'Looking back, those years were not wasted, they were years of distillation; I was in the retort, screwed down, I drew in my horns.'[22]

'The Angelic Conversation'

In 1985 Jarman completed his only major film of this period – *The Angelic Conversation*, shot largely on super-8 in the previous summer. The leading players were Paul Reynolds and Philip Williamson, the music was by the group Coil and Benjamin Britten. Shakespeare's Sonnets were read by Judi Dench. Jarman made his own connections: '*The Angelic Conversation* moves through the same landscape as *Jubilee*. Elizabeth and John Dee are wandering along the same cliff, at Winspit, as Philip.'[23] *The Angelic Conversation* was blown up to 35mm for distribution by the BFI, which expected a theatrical release film. As it was, it would have survived better with a 16mm print (which does not exist), making it available for audiences in small venues, art clubs and colleges. The film was a failure at the box office, though it was well received by critics.

The scenes were shot with friends on location over the summer of 1984:

It was really a silent film. All the things that happened in that film were things that happen in 'home movies', like down on the beach

131

swimming, walking through the landscape, going to the stately home. Most of the things in the film were what anyone might do, except rather carefully chosen locations. It comes from a visual response to the place and so forth and it is non-dramatic in that sense. The drama is restored by the sonnets.[24]

The Angelic Conversation is one of the most moving and beautiful of Jarman's works; through the combination of its images and the use of Shakespeare's Sonnets it creates a testimony to love. Jarman thought of the different films that make up *The Angelic Conversation* as poems, while *Caravaggio*, for instance, is a novel. He was aware that he was:

> exploring a landscape I had never seen on film: an area of psyche that hadn't been projected before. I have seen very few on male love which are gentle, they usually have a violent subtext. ... *The Angelic Conversation* is gentle.[25]

The films were not conceived originally as visual accompaniments to the Sonnets but rather as a Jungian reading of the Anglo-Saxon poem 'The Wanderer', reaching back to Jarman's Jungian ventures of the 70s, especially *The Art of Mirrors* and *In the Shadow of the Sun*:

> I came to the ideas after I made the film, as we cut it together. ... The beginning had symbols of industrialism – the burning car. The cross related to industrialism – a sort of Buñuel moment. The weight of received thought. The fog and night journey is the idea of a journey which is so important in Jung ... the caves were places where analysis began ... the place where the world might be put right. A sort of ritual. The descent into darkness – that is like Rimbaud – the descent into the other side is necessary. Then I saw the swimming sections as ablution, the ritual washing of the world ... and the sunlight comes out and one is out in the fresh air. I saw the section with the emperor as service for others. It's based on the first poetic elements of our culture – the wanderer, the giver of dreams. ... The psychotic wrestling match is with oneself ... an incredible struggle goes on ... and there is a sort of restitution, a sort of homoerotic scene. ... The signal – the

The gentle eroticism of 'The Angelic Conversation' **133**

radar thing – which at first is so menacing ... is eradicated by the flowers. This is almost back to the beginning and this time the sunlight is there.[26]

The film is a supreme example of the use of English landscape in Jarman's work. It merges the cultivated gardens of the Tudor house Montacute with the wild seashore of Dorset, abstracted through super-8 slow motion and dense swirling mists (using sea rescue flares). The film has a Blakean quality, as if Jarman rejected 'the sordid drudgery of facsimile reproductions' which Blake described and eschewed in his painting. (In the 60s, while at King's College, Jarman had been a student of Nikolaus Pevsner, who described Blake's antipathy to anything like realism in *The Englishness of English Art*, which it is highly likely Jarman read.) The images of place are stylised but highly evocative. For example, the slow, shifting rhythms of the shots which open the film – of fretwork windows looking out onto the lawn of Montacute – enhance the depiction of the young man's melancholy gaze.

The painterly colour and texture are achieved by refilming at a very slow speed (usually three frames per second), the last time Jarman extensively used this effect, developed over many years of super-8 experimentation. The aesthetic is reminiscent of that of the early impressionist avant-garde of post-First World War France, which included film-makers Abel Gance and Jean Epstein and the critic Delluc. With its use of technique in order to privilege style over narrative, it moved towards an idea of pure cinema. In *French Film Theory and Criticism 1907–1939*, Richard Abel lists the techniques employed by these French film-makers as:

> variable speed recording (especially slow motion), various optical devices (superimposition, vignette masks, distorting filters and lenses), 'punctuation' devices (the fade, iris, and dissolve), and accelerating montage.[27]

The Angelic Conversation also involved an innovative production method:

> The film was generated on Super-8 and a VHS video camera linked to a U-matic deck. The Super-8 footage was transferred through that

video camera by a projection on a wall at about 3 frames per second. The resulting U-matic was time-coded by Research Recordings onto VHS video cassettes. We did a preliminary edit, here in my flat, on VHS with a simple camera, home movie editor with two decks and a television set. We chopped it together. Then using the time-coded VHS we edited the U-matics and put them onto 1 inch tape. That tape became the master tape. This is all silent at this stage. And then the whole thing was transferred to 35mm film.[28]

Jarman manipulated the white balance to obtain unusual colours and used red paper in front of it to get a greenish tint and green paper to get a reddish tint.

Like *The Art of Mirrors* and *In the Shadow of the Sun*, the narrative of *The Angelic Conversation* is made up of a series of ritualistic actions. The film uses Jarman's favoured bracketing device, in this case of a reverie, the film opening with a man gazing through a Tudor-like window and Dench's voice-over reading a sonnet and ending in the grounds of a Tudor house as the young man walks through the blossoming shrubs and trees fanning his face, a figure and action from the Elizabethan period. In a high Romantic mood, the final shot is a freeze frame as the young man collects blossoms to his face.

The central narrative is the journey of two male lovers. We watch them walking through the mist and the gloom of caves, swimming in dappled pools and eventually wrestling before making love. The background to the early scenes is modern-day – a burning wrecked car, a high fence beside which a man walks, revolving radar antennae. Like *Jubilee* the film implies a comparison between the brutal realities of the present and some ideal past in which love, tenderness and well-being were possible. But the distinctions between the present and the past are not so clear-cut – for instance, the scene with the car and fence, suggesting contemporary reality, is shot in the dream-like slowed rhythms of super-8.

The film is Jarman's testament to his love of filming his friends, especially young men whom he found attractive. It is also the film in which he most substantially celebrates the body. The male nude forms the centre of his films of this period – *Imagining October* and *Caravaggio* – and in *The Angelic Conversation* one has some inkling of what *Sebastiane* might have been like

135

had Jarman had more control over its aesthetic.

Tony Rayns criticised *The Angelic Conversation* as the film 'in which Jarman comes closest to a homosexual version of heterosexual kitsch'. For Rayns, Shakespeare's Sonnets are simply trappings 'intended to dignify what would otherwise be straightforward carnal representations'.[29] This criticism would have some force only if one neglected the long passages in the film in which such carnal representations do not occur, for instance the journey through the cave and waste ground in which the young men carry a barrel and a crucifix-like piece of wood, and the washing ritual. On the other hand, kitsch was never far away in Jarman's work; with the retreat of modernism, kitsch became less despised. The Elizabethan material in Jarman's films provided a framework within which his idealism could flourish, in particular in relation to love, which is often contrasted with a down-to-earth, sado-masochistic and 'realist' portrayal of sex as in the brutal drunken rape of the soldier in *The Last of England* or the death of Happy Days in *Jubilee*.

The Angelic Conversation also falls within the English pastoral tradition, found in some of the work of Michael Powell and Humphrey Jennings. Jarman shares their idealisation of an English rural past, contrasted in *The Angelic Conversation* with an other-world of urban blight and institutional repression associated with the social decline of England and its attendant brutality. The anonymous rotating radar antennae are part of the 'real' social world against which the pastoral of the men swimming and making love takes place. There is a strong sense of exile. The world of love, articulated in the Sonnets, is shown through the film's imagery as impossible to obtain in the real world, which is depicted as distant, broken-down and intolerant.

Edmund Spenser's epic poem *The Faerie Queen* (1596) embodies the Elizabethan pastoral ethos. Traditionally, pastoral has been used for satirical or critical ends. The pastoral scenes of *The Faerie Queen* are fleeting, unattainable moments set against forces of corruption and evil. Similarly in Jarman's *The Garden*, the scenes set at the house on the beach (Jarman's own cottage at Dungeness), where the tattooed young man and the young boy live, represent an idyll in which life is simple, counterposed against the 'sophisticated' world of the metropolis with its cruel queens, repressive police and harassing press. This idyll is shattered in two key scenes – when the photographers attack and 'rape' the Madonna figure and taunt and humiliate the transvestite. *The Angelic Conversation*, with its world of ritual, sun-dappled

136

bathing and magical saunterings through picturesque gardens, is more thoroughly pastoral, its idyll disrupted only implicitly by the turning radar antennae and burning car which represent the institutional forces ranged against it. Unlike Jarman's other Elizabethan films, *The Angelic Conversation* lacks a historical setting: the world it constructs is a dream one and the Shakespearean material acts simply as an inspiration for and counterpoint to the abstraction of the images.

Jarman did not set out to explore the world of Elizabethan England in any systematic fashion. For instance, there are contradictory impulses at work between his renderings of *The Tempest* in the late 70s and *Edward II* in the early 90s. Although both are tales of exclusions and power, the differences between Shakespeare's idealised vision and Marlowe's much darker one are exaggerated in Jarman's adaptations.

The Angelic Conversation was financed by about £3,500 of development money for *Caravaggio* granted to Jarman by the Production Board at the British Film Institute, headed by Peter Sainsbury. Jarman promptly set off for the Dorset coast and filmed large chunks of material intended for *Caravaggio* but which ended up as *The Angelic Conversation*. (At that point *Caravaggio* was to be a super-8 film.) Jarman held a private screening at the ICA of some new super-8 material which he said was for *Caravaggio* but which became *The Angelic Conversation*. The ICA allowed Jarman to use the Cinematheque to shoot material, often involving superimposition. At one point the young projectionist was stripped to his waist and placed in front of the screen while a film (*The Pantheon*, 1978) was projected on to him. This was to become one of the most successful scenes in *The Angelic Conversation*. Only when the *Caravaggio* film deal was firm did Jarman complete *The Angelic Conversation* with more money from the BFI to transfer it to 35mm.

'Imagining October'

In September 1984 Peter Sainsbury invited Jarman and other independent film-makers – Sally Potter, Peter Wollen, Ed Bennett and head of BFI distribution Ian Christie – to show their films, including Jarman's *The Tempest*, in the Soviet Union.[30] Jarman took his super-8 camera and ten cassettes of film, hoping to capture enough footage for a short film promised to Derek Malcolm, who was director of the London Film Festival at the

137

time. Jarman shot the Stalinist monumental architecture of Moscow, the street life in Baku and Peter Wollen reading John Reed's *Ten Days that Shook the World* in Eisenstein's study. (Controversially Wollen showed Jarman's camera the censored passages where Trotsky's name was blocked out in black ink.) When they returned to England, Jarman had forty minutes of film but no structure. He then employed the artist John Watkiss to paint an epic social-realist style tableau of some of his young friends dressed as soldiers which was interspersed with his home movie footage.

Imagining October, which cost £4,700, was for many a turning point in Jarman's career. A critical success, it transcended its home-movie roots to become a brilliant merging of sexuality, politics and history in a form that was to be influential. Jarman inserted polemical intertitles attacking both East and West, but in particular President Reagan and Mrs Thatcher, throughout the film. The first intertitle boldly stated:

> Scenario of Repressions riot police in the streets?
> Films censored by the IBA?
> Books seized by customs?
> Bookshops closed down?
> Politics of Regression through economic idolatry[31]

The film ends with the statement:

> Private solution
> Sitting in Eisenstein's study
> With a home movie camera
> Imagining October
> A cinema of small gestures

The last line was timely. As so many younger film-makers struggled to finance their films, Jarman seemed to be pointing to a cinema that was cheap and effective, capable of subverting the Hollywood machine and able to run against the reign of the city financiers that marked the ascendancy of Thatcherite England.

Imagining October was the first film in which Jarman placed himself – in this case through the figure of the painter John Watkiss, an artist who

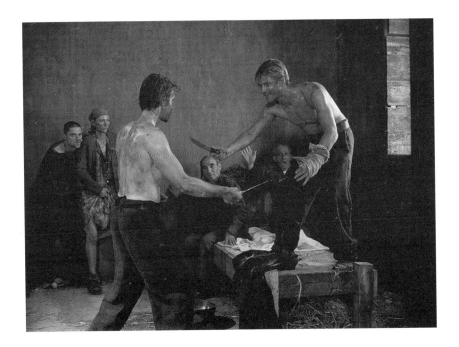

attempts to capture a reality that is a fusion of state ideology and homoeroticism. The artist's dilemma does not entirely dominate the film; rather there is a tension between the subjective act of painting and the objective world of politics and history that is to be painted. The sexual aspects of history and politics are crystallised in the image of the male models/soldiers who are transformed into brutal, sullen authoritarian symbols of a regime which is at one and the same time repressive and erotic. The ambiguity of such figures is expressed here without recourse to sado-masochistic imagery. The film is gentle, melancholic and carefully constructed, utterly economic.

The silence of the studio, broken only by the paint being brushed on to canvas, and the centrality of the gaze of the painter are motifs common to both *Imagining October* and the later *Caravaggio*. The gaze of the camera as well as that of the painter is felt, especially in the scene where the gold-toothed young man in the streets of Baku smiles into Jarman's lens. The ease of this smile is contrasted with the artifice of the young men in the studio who do not catch the film-maker's eye. These studio scenes are tense and artificial, constructed ideals unlike the more playful reality of the home-movie shots. Jarman weaves the home movie with the narrative in such a way

'Caravaggio' (photo: Mike Laye) **139**

that the former remains outside the narrative space; nevertheless coherence is achieved through Jarman's poetic vision.

The home-movie footage is a personal expression of sexual desire for a particular young man. It is as if we were seeing Jarman's holiday snapshots. In the studio scenes with the posed, semi-naked Soviet soldiers, on the other hand, we have a depiction of military and artistic repression. Yet sexuality is present alongside state authority in the hint that the young men who act as soldiers are objects of erotic desire outside their film roles. Such scenes are not simply expressions of a social reality. They are also projections of Jarman's own desires. Very few film-makers have so explicitly combined the personal and the social in terms of sexuality.

At the end there is once again the image of Peter Wollen in the dark shadows of Eisenstein's study reading history and its construction, in this case its repressive construction. The strobe-like, shifting movement of the image, a consequence of the slowed-down speed, gives it a painterly quality and an almost sinister, dream-like feel. The contrast between the super-8 material shot in the Soviet Union and the static normal-speed studio footage creates a distance between two worlds, two points of view, two politics, two kinds of film-making, two kinds of representation and two kinds of sexuality.

Painting

Over a period of time Jarman's films forged a radical visual language which used poetry and imagination to portray a particular time and place – Britain in the late 20th century. His paintings were also part of this struggle for expression, especially from the early 80s to the end of his life.

Jarman started painting again in December 1981 in response to an invitation from David Dawson to show with John Maybury, Duggie Fields and Andrew Logan at his short-lived B2 Gallery in London's pre-developer Docklands. This was to mark a change of style:

> I collected together the few landscapes that I painted with varnish glazes, pencil and metal dust last year. Apocalyptic visions of fire, with skulls and minute people lost in eternity under strange moons. Then I took up my brushes again and painted dark canvases of a different kind – Night Light, Canvases of Fire, Fire of the Soul. Icons to spark off reveries.[32]

140

This show was a low-key affair at a time when Jarman was in the wilderness. But it was a crucial one in the development of his paintings, leading to an upsurge of new work in the mid- and late 80s. The first group of paintings drew on 'the fragments of Heraclitus, the technical drawings of Robert Fludd, Athanasius Kircher and seventeenth century hermeticism'.[33] They are largely in black and scarlet and are 'austere', to use Jarman's description. They are also quite small due to the confines of his flat. With gold leaf obtained in Florence to gild the sets of Russell's *The Rake's Progress*, he made grounds for a second series based on 'nineteenth century photographs of the male nude mixed with sexual and religious iconography' deeply affected by Caravaggio.[34] The eroticism of these paintings is not highly achieved and in their brooding artifice and archaic form they recall the work of William Blake and perhaps Samuel Palmer. The mood is reminiscent of *The Angelic Conversation*, which Jarman began working on shortly afterwards.

A reference point for this work is perhaps the British neo-Romantic movement of the Second World War and after – painters like John Minton, Leslie Hurry and David Jones. Along with an intimacy and organicism there also seems to be a shared interest in mythology and in the case of Minton an idealised and romantic homoeroticism. The organisers of the recent British neo-Romantic exhibition define the movement as follows:

> Emblematic of the artists' vision and the Neo-Romantic sensibility is 'the quest' ... a search whose object is the shrine, an Eden or Arcadia; a quest made by artists sensitive to the spiritual loss of their day, a society which was to be broken by a tidal wave of war carnage and subsequent consumerism.[35]

In 1982 Jarman had a show of twenty-two paintings at the Edward Totah Gallery and in 1984 a show of paintings, installation work and films at the ICA. Here the cool abstraction of the late 60s was replaced by dark canvases in black and gold in which nude male figures were depicted in interiors reminiscent of *The Tempest*. Jarman remarked: 'I have broken the stranglehold of my landscapes. They had become tedious, a fine balancing act that I had mastered. They were no longer an adventure.'[36]

The cape installations at this show took England and nuclear threat as

141

their subject matter. The capes were huge and made of transparent material enclosing small objects like keys. Some of the paintings at the time used the image of Britain's outline painted in reds and yellows. Other paintings used darker colours in an impasto of swirling circular shapes in which were embedded small glistening coloured crystals. John Roberts was perceptive in his praise of this show:

> These paintings are about the derangements of British nationalism and patriotism, about how Britain is the most class-divided, xenophobic country in the West. ... In a sense the reality of nuclear annihilation has unfurled the sacred, placed it on the contemporary horizon of meaning, as it was at the height of the Industrial Revolution in the 18th and 19th century. Jarman's passionate indignation is not so different in spirit to Blake's images of Urizen or John Martin's visions of hell bursting the banks of the living.[37]

The same aesthetic seems to be working in *The Angelic Conversation*, which also has a religious intensity and like the black and gold paintings uses deep shadows and light from flares as its only colours. For the first time there seems to be a common sensibility between the films and the paintings.

142

1 As Alexander Walker points out in *National Heroes: British Cinema in the Seventies and Eighties* (London: Harrap, 1985), only 5 per cent of the population went to the cinema once a month.

2 Ibid., p. 270.

3 Dave Parsons ran the department at the time and experimental film-makers like Guy Sherwin, John Smith, Lis Rhodes, Cordelia Swann and John Maybury had been taught there.

4 James Mackay, 'Low budget British Production: A Producer's Account', in Duncan Petrie (ed.), *New Questions of British Cinema* (London: British Film Institute Working Papers, 1992), p. 54.

5 Quoted in David Curtis (ed.), *The Elusive Sign: British Avant-Garde Film 1977-1987*, catalogue (London: Arts Council of Great Britain/British Council, 1987), p. 8.

6 With the exception of Gay Liberation Front whose founding meetings he attended at least once, and gay marches in the late 80s and early 90s, Jarman seems to have distanced himself from political activity. His relationship to the gay liberation movement is not mentioned in *Dancing Ledge*, leading one to believe that it was fairly tenuous. His remarks on political organisations in general, gay or otherwise, are often sceptical if not downright cynical. Christopher Hobbs confirmed in interview with the author (August 1994) that Jarman was only politically active in the final years around Clause 28 and the debates about the age of consent for gays.

7 Derek Jarman, *Dancing Ledge* (London: Quartet, 1984), p. 215.

8 The poet Heathcote Williams, who played Prospero in Jarman's *The Tempest*, sent Faithfull the most controversial song on the album, 'Why D'Ya Do It?', which he had originally performed in Amsterdam in 1968. See Mark Hodkinson, *As Tears Go By: Marianne Faithfull* (London: Omnibus Press, 1991), p. 172.

9 Ibid., p. 179.

10 A description of the making of the film is in *Dancing Ledge*, pp. 208–11.

11 Dave Baby, according to Boy George, is 'a psycho tattooed builder from Stoke Newington'. See Boy George (with Spencer Bright), *Take It Like a Man: The Autobiography of Boy George* (London: Sidgwick & Jackson, 1995), p. 130.

12 *Dancing Ledge*, p. 214.

13 Michael O'Pray interview with Derek Jarman, 'News from Home', *Monthly Film Bulletin*, vol. 51 no. 605, June 1984.

14 Mackay, 'Low-budget British Production', p. 54.

15 *Dancing Ledge*, p. 214.

16 Ibid., p. 209.

17 Ibid.

18 Ibid.

19 Derek Jarman, *The Last of England* (London: Constable, 1987), p. 182.

20 *Dancing Ledge*, p. 223.

21 Ibid., p. 224.

22 *The Last of England*, p. 68.

23 Ibid., p. 145.

24 See Simon Field and Michael O'Pray, 'On Imaging October, Dr Dee and Other Matters: Derek Jarman in Interview', *Afterimage*, no. 12, 1985, p. 55.

25 *The Last of England*, p. 134.

26 Field and O'Pray, 'On Imaging October', p. 52.

27 Richard Abel, *French Film Theory and Criticism 1907–1939 Vol. 1 1907–1929* (Princeton University Press, 1988), p. 109.

28 Field and O'Pray, 'On Imaging October', p. 52.

29 Ibid., p. 64.

30 On the background to this trip, see *The Last of England*, pp. 92–101.

31 The intertitles are printed in *The Last of England*, pp. 101–3.

32 *Dancing Ledge*, p. 222.

33 Ibid., p. 229.

34 Ibid.

35 David Mellor (ed.), *A Paradise Lost: the New Romatnic Imagination in Britain 1935–55* (London: Lund Humphries & Barbican Gallery, 1987), p. 7.

36 *Dancing Ledge*, p. 223.

37 John Roberts, 'Painting the Apocalypse' *Afterimage* no. 12, 1985, pp. 37–8.

Chapter Six

THE SECOND WAVE
Caravaggio, The Last of England, War Requiem

1985–1988

In December 1986, during the production of *The Last of England*, Jarman discovered he was HIV positive; earlier in the same year in Amsterdam he had told me that he knew he was going to get AIDS and had only a few years to live and must therefore work flat out. The following years were to be his most prolific, resulting in a series of astonishing films that gained him his second popular reputation.

'Caravaggio'

Caravaggio signalled a move back to the more mainstream style of Jarman's feature films of the late 70s and away from the innovative, poetic work of the previous six years. He was rarely to go back to the short home movies again. The early 80s had witnessed the beginning of a transformation in the British film industry. Channel Four began broadcasting in 1982 with a brief which included support for innovative film-making. In the general excitement about the new channel *Screen* devoted a whole issue to a debate on what it might offer independent cinema.[1] Documentarists and political film-makers were expected to gain most and there were plans to establish film workshops throughout the country to train film-makers and foster a progressive social cinema. Avant-garde film-makers wary of the threat to an individualist film-making approach were on the whole more sceptical.

The ambitions of feature film-makers were also to find support in the channel's drama department. As Duncan Petrie remarks:

> It was the production finance made available by commissioning editors such as David Rose and Alan Fountain which lay behind the resurgence in British film-making in the early part of the decade, and which has effectively propped the industry up since then.[2]

144 The death-scene, 'Caravaggio' (photo: Mike Laye)

In the early 80s the British film industry seemed to enjoy a renaissance. *Chariots of Fire* scooped up Oscars in 1981 to the sound of Colin Welland's war-cry at the ceremony of 'The British are coming!' The following year Richard Attenborough's *Gandhi* repeated the act. In retrospect, however, it is films such as *The Draughtsman's Contract* (1982), *My Beautiful Laundrette* (1985), *Letter to Brezhnev* (1985), *A Room with a View* (1985), *Caravaggio* (1986) and *Distant Voices, Still Lives* (1988) – all with financial backing from Channel Four – which are most representative of British cinema in this period.

Jarman's own view of the opportunities Channel Four offered was more cynical:

> Channel Four, in spite of a much-vaunted alternative image, was to turn out all beaujolais nouveau and scrubbed Scandinavian, pot plants in place. It wasn't our alternative: independent cinema was to remain independent, disenfranchised by a channel for the slightly adventurous commuter.[3]

The 'our' in this passage is ambiguous. Jarman during the period between feature films did not fall comfortably into any film-making camp: the mainstream had failed to finance his work yet he did not fit with the Independent Film-Makers Association (IFA) notion of independent cinema with its workshops, leftist political agenda and strong documentarist aesthetic that had grown from the theories and debates of the 70s (in fact, Jarman was despised by many of these 'theorists'). Somewhat ironically, Jarman became identified with the super-8 experimental film-makers during this period – the new avant-garde. In the first flush of buying, Channel Four did, however, acquire *Sebastiane*, *Jubilee* and *The Tempest*, though these were not shown for several years, a state of affairs which rankled. What amounted to an embargo was only broken when the film critic David Robinson chose the three films for a critic's choice series in 1985.

With the funding of *Caravaggio*, Jarman's long-nursed project came to fruition.[4] *Caravaggio* was his first film shot in 35mm and was made for £450,000 by the British Film Institute's Production Board, headed by an academic, Colin MacCabe, who had replaced Peter Sainsbury. Sainsbury had had a major success with Peter Greenaway's *The Draughtsman's Contract* in

1982 after the board had decided three years earlier (in a change of policy) to fund feature films, beginning with Chris Petit's *Radio On* (1979). Sainsbury left the BFI at the time the Eady levy was abolished, a cirumstance which threatened the existence of the Production Board as an active unit. MacCabe made an agreement with Channel Four to grant the board £500,000 annually if the government matched that sum. The channel would have television rights on material produced. *Caravaggio* was one of the first films MacCabe financed, though his predecessor had already committed the board to funding it.

Sebastiane, *Jubilee* and *The Tempest* were screened on Channel Four in autumn 1985, just before *Caravaggio*'s release. According to Channel Four controller Jeremy Isaacs, 'the time had come to show some of our most difficult pictures'.[5] Knowing that these films would cause a furore, he brought in *Times* critic David Robinson, whose views he believed 'would command respect', to front a critic's choice series. The channel's purchase of Jarman's films had made the headlines in the tabloids in the early 80s, at which point Channel Four issued a statement denying any intention of showing the films in the forseeable future. In addition to the Jarman films, Robinson's series (billed as *Robinson's Choice*) included Ron Peck's gay film *Nighthawks* (1978) and such classics as Bresson's *L'Argent* (1983), Ozu's *Tokyo Story* (1953) and Visconti's *Ludwig* (1972). The Independent Broadcasting Authority agreed to the season on condition that an erect penis was electronically disguised in the first sequence of *Sebastiane*. *Jubilee*, with its violence against the police (which Isaacs quite rightly judged in retrospect as 'prophetic enough in all conscience'), provoked most viewer complaints.

The casting of *Caravaggio* proved momentous for Jarman. To play the prostitute Lena, he chose a young actress who was to be a major influence on his films thereafter – Tilda Swinton. Swinton came from the world of theatre where she had established a reputation with roles in *Measure for Measure*, *Mother Courage* and *The Devils* for the Royal Shakespeare Company (RSC) and in Peter Arnott's *White Rose* for the Traverse Theatre. She had just resigned from the RSC when Jarman hired her and had had no film experience beyond a part in a student film.

Jarman and Swinton became inseparable for some time after making the film. It was with his lover Keith Collins and Swinton that Jarman chose his cottage in Dungeness, purchased with money inherited from his father.

147

Shopping locally for plants, Swinton and Jarman were mistaken, much to their amusement, for a married couple. The mingling of Jarman's life and work is nowhere more clear than in his relationship with Swinton; her influence on *The Last of England* and *The Garden* is difficult to separate from Jarman's own input. Her vibrant on-screen presence is crucial to the success of many of his later films – for instance, her role as the nurse in *War Requiem* gives the film a poignant emotional centre that rescues it from a Russellian brashness. Similarly, her 'performance' in the final sequence of *The Last of England* creates a profound climax to the film's emotional thrust. Swinton's sympathy with Jarman's critical stance, his anti-naturalism and poetic experimentation led to a formidable artistic relationship. It was important to Jarman that he created space for his performers, allowing them to establish their own responses, gestures and moods. This, together with Swinton's intuitive understanding of how she figured in his work, contributed to a collaboration based on mutual trust and a genuine sharing of the project in hand.

Nigel Terry, who was cast as Caravaggio, was also to take part in subsequent works – *War Requiem, Edward II* and the major voice-over in *Blue*. Sean Bean, who plays Ranuccio, appeared in *War Requiem* before his acting career blossomed in television drama. Swinton, Terry and Bean form a potent trio in *Caravaggio*, negotiating the emotional ambiguity between their characters which the script demands. Jarman had never had such a strong cast under his direction and their excellent acting, combined with a sturdy script, helped much towards the film's success. He remarks that the 'film is the first in which I have developed acting parts and bowed to narrative'.[6]

By comparison with the super-8 experimentalism of *Imagining October* and *The Angelic Conversation*, *Caravaggio* seems conservative in its narrative style, use of actors and script. A professional crew and small studio distanced it even further from the home-movie aesthetic. After the film's completion, Jarman complained of the rigidity of the format in terms of the lighting and focus required by a 35mm camera; having to set up scenes in a more formal manner than usual left him feeling frustrated and believing that the film was more controlled than he would have liked.[7]

Characteristically *Caravaggio* uses a framing device – the dying artist attended only by his mute assistant Jerusaleme – with the film structured as a series of flashbacks over the protagonist's life. The narrative revolves around

Caravaggio's relationships with his patrons in the Catholic Church and his models, the prostitute Lena and her lover Ranuccio. 'As in Jarman's three previous features, the story unfolds from the point of view of a central character standing outside events (in *Sebastiane* Max recounts the story of Sebastian, in *Jubilee* Elizabeth I 'sees' a future England through the magic of John Dee and in *The Tempest* Prospero controls and comments on the events on his island). Although in *Caravaggio* the painter's involvement in the action described is more intense, his position in the film is still that of an omniscient, detached narrator.

Caravaggio is a film about painting as a mode of representation that is both personal and historically placed. It is uninterested in the painter's biography – what we learn about his early life, for instance, serves only to establish his sexuality and its relationship to his art and to power. Indeed, it is the interconnections between art, power and sexuality that the film explores, in particular the mutual attractions between Caravaggio, Lena and Ranuccio sieved through money and sex and the structure of power and corruption within which they are located. Jarman's film connects the personal with the political, using the making of art as a focal point.

As a film about painting, *Caravaggio* is remarkable. It makes no claims for artistic inspiration, the uniqueness of artistic sensibility or the idea of artistic genius but rather portrays the reality of the working context of the artist – the atmosphere of the studio and the system of patronage in operation at the time. There are two key studio scenes. In the first, Caravaggio's patron, Cardinal del Monte, watches him struggle with the *St Matthew* canvas. The studio is hot, 'flies buzz, the clock ticks away' and Del Monte stifles a yawn. In the screenplay there is a voice-over by Del Monte which expresses his concern about the painting's realism and Caravaggio's standing in the Academy.[8] But in the film as made, the only break in the stifling, concentrated silence is when Del Monte giggles, causing the models to snigger. Caravaggio rebukes them: 'You are paid to be still.' Thus the relationship between the patron, the artist and the model is effortlessly established in a scene with the bare minimum of dialogue. Del Monte, as a gay man, shares Caravaggio's sexual desire for the models. But as Caravaggio's rebuke reminds us, the scenario is underpinned by economics: Del Monte pays Caravaggio who pays the models. Jarman has thus transformed what could have been a sentimental scene about artistic genius into one suffused

149

with sex and money. Caravaggio is neither a defender of artistic integrity against state patronage nor a protector of the exploited lower classes (his models). The painter is thoroughly compromised.

In the other key studio scene Caravaggio is painting Ranuccio as the executioner in *The Martyrdom*. Lena, Ranuccio's lover, falls asleep in her chair and Jerusaleme throws light on to the model from a golden reflector. Throughout the long session, Caravaggio throws pieces of gold to Ranuccio who stuffs them greedily into his mouth. The length of the pose is determined by the supply of money. The only sound is the metallic tinkling of the coins. Finally Caravaggio places the last coin between his own teeth and in a profane kiss Ranuccio takes it with his lips. Lena and Jerusaleme look on with a mix of fascination and shock. It is as if the expression of Caravaggio's love for Ranuccio is possible only through an economic exchange, though despite the financial and essentially exploitative context, it is love nonetheless. Jarman also insists here on the justifiable sexual involvement of the artist with the model, too often romanticised or in recent times deplored. One cannot help surmising that the scene both reflects and is perhaps a justification for Jarman's own practice of using friends and lovers as the subject-matter of his films. Jarman later remarked ambiguously about the home movies:

> In all home movies is a longing for paradise. How have the victims prepared themselves for their brief immortality? Who smiles when they are told? Where is the serpent lurking?[9]

The eroticism of money is expressed in another scene in which Ranuccio and Lena swing in a hammock and use their newly acquired coins in the foreplay to a lovemaking provoked by the excitement of wealth. Caravaggio's payment fuels their desire. Financial exploitation and its connection with sex is shown in a literal fashion.

In another studio scene Caravaggio indolently watches the androgynous Pipo perform a series of slow acrobatic moves to a melancholic Spanish dance song. No word is spoken and a palpable intimacy arises, almost as if Pipo's performance – which is spontaneous and lies outside the cash nexus – were a projection of the painter's inner life. The scene also highlights Caravaggio's essential passivity.[10] In many ways the artist is the passive viaduct through which all flows – through his painting and Prospero-like exploitation of his models the power and corruption of the Church and state invade the passions and aspirations of the prostitute and pugilist thief.

Very few of Caravaggio's actions outside painting have any narrative impact. Lena loves him in her fashion, finds a rich lover and is then murdered by Ranuccio. Ranuccio loves him in his fashion, is accused of Lena's murder and is finally killed by Caravaggio in one of his few acts of any impact, though it is one that leads only to death. Around him swirls the history of the final years of the Italian Renaissance and he stands at its still centre, in the eye of the storm which is the darkness of his studio. Like Elizabeth I in *Jubilee* and Prospero in *The Tempest*, Caravaggio is a prisoner of his memories and of an early ideal love – in his case for Pasqualone. The device of voice-over also removes him from the narrative and is another element in his passivity.

Caravaggio develops ideas about the painter-model relationship expressed schematically in *Imagining October*, which may have been an attempt to deal with some of the themes of the elusive feature film project. The tense presence of the tableau of male figures, the erotically charged silence of the studio broken only by the sound of brush on canvas, the centrality of the painter's gaze and the blank look of the models are all elements shared by the two films. Timothy Murray discusses *Caravaggio* as a text organised around the gaze, primarily of the painter himself.[11] Intrinsic to this analysis is the notion of a melancholic yearning for a lost love-object. In the super-8 films this was expressed through slow-motion, by which Jarman portrayed 'the eroticisation of the senses'.[12] According to Murray, Jarman's films often begin with a loss already established. The bracketing device creates a framework in which a death, or social collapse, or a series of events is presented, and the film proper is the story of the failure to recover that loss. In *Caravaggio* such a loss is embedded in the figure of Pasqualone, the painter's mentor and the 'innocent' sexual partner of his childhood – surely, at one level, a filmic representation of Jarman's childhood passion for the Italian Davide. At the end of his life it was Davide whom Jarman called his truly great love.

Tony Rayns has suggested that the intrinsic passivity of Jarman's films is a filmic form of 'submitting to sodomy'.[13] His male characters are often passive and masochistic; where objectification of the homosexual state

151

occurs, guilt, violence and anxiety are paramount. Unlike the idyllic eroticism of *The Angelic Conversation* and some of the super-8 home movies, in the larger, more ambitious projects the central character passively accepts the aggression aimed at him.

This is the case in some respects with Caravaggio, yet among his models and hangers-on he also stands in for the authority of the Church and the Pope, who financially sustain him through commissions. His paintings are an ideological instrument through which the Pope obtains the loyalty of his flock as well as representations of sexuality destined for the erotic consumption of the ruling elite. But ultimately Caravaggio is a victim who succumbs to the violence of the state. The film is the memory of a dying man with the coins of the realm on his dead eyes; his sexuality is figured by the knife clutched between his fingers – an image of the division between the intimate truths of sexuality and authority's purveying of sexuality.

Like Miranda in *The Tempest* and Elizabeth I in *Jubilee*, Lena, the young prostitute in love with Ranuccio (and perhaps Caravaggio too), represents an innocence not found in any other character. Swinton's Lena is very much a character part – a naive and impish young woman who is sucked into the world of power, made pregnant by Cardinal Borghese and killed by her lover Ranuccio. As both a prostitute and the model for the Virgin in Caravaggio's painting, she is literally madonna and whore. Lena is very much the victim in *Caravaggio* – a woman used by all: Ranuccio, Caravaggio and eventually the establishment itself in the figure of Borghese. Her love is compromised by her poverty. Interestingly, the love between Caravaggio and Ranuccio is mediated through Lena.

Lena first appears in the film as a hand entering right frame to cut the cloth binding her lover Ranuccio to his wrestling opponent. From then on she is portrayed by and large as someone who waits and looks, often at the edge of the action. In her only opportunity to shape her own life, albeit under the control of Borghese, comes death. Her transformation from dirty-faced but loving prostitute to a hardened mistress of the cardinal is a variation and inversion of the Elizabeth I/Bod transformation in *Jubilee* or the transformation in *Edward II* of Isabella from loving wife to the violent and ruthless queen determined to bring about her husband's downfall.

When Caravaggio gives Lena the dress that is to transform her into a beautiful aristocratic-looking woman for the fateful party, he draws her to

152

centre stage and kisses her. The party she attends is a corrupted version of the masque staged for Miranda at the order of her father Prospero in *The Tempest*. Like Prospero, Caravaggio celebrates his charge's entrance into a new world by providing in a paternal fashion the artifice necessary – in this case the dress – for her to leave the old one. Lena's seduction at the party takes place in a scenario of excessive theatricality – a degraded mirror image of the painter's studio where poses are struck and nothing is as it seems.

Lena's passive role as onlooker is paralleled by Caravaggio's role as the wistful surveyor both of the characters he assembles around him and of his own paintings. Many scenes show the painter staring at his canvases and at the models and a circuit of looks is set up between Ranuccio as model, Lena watching the model and painter and Jerusaleme with his reflecting metal watching them all. The series of looks is brought to an end by the gold coins placed on Caravaggio's dead eyes as the film is brought to an end.

Various motives have been put forward to explain Caravaggio's murder of Ranuccio. It has been argued that Caravaggio will not allow Lena's death to be the price of achieving his own aim of having a homosexual relationship with Ranuccio (Ranuccio says he has killed Lena for them). Or is he simply avenging the murder of a woman he also loved, even if this requires the death of his own lover?

The confines of the film studio lend *Caravaggio* an enclosed quality. There are no exterior locations and the outside world is perceived only through street sounds and sunlight. With its dominant chiaroscuro lighting, the film is stylistically close to *The Tempest*'s claustrophobic atmosphere. Both films have a central character played with brooding intensity, a master – servant relationship (Caravaggio – Ranuccio and Prospero – Ariel) and an 'innocent' female at their narrative core. And in each case love pierces the main character's art, but with quite different consequences. Jarman tightens the similarities by making Miranda a more sexually knowing character, though Lena's 'brave new world', unlike Miranda's, is not one at all.

Caravaggio was a critical and commercial success and heralded Jarman's second and final wave of feature film-making.

'The Last of England'

Between *Caravaggio* and *The Last of England* Jarman made a series of promo music videos for the Smiths, the style and stance of which fed into the latter

153

film. Morrissey, the band's lead singer and lyricist, has been described as 'ambisexual' and was strongly associated with the gay scene of the 80s when sexual ambiguity or gender-bending was part of many pop performers' personas. The band was of the same generation as film-makers John Maybury and Cerith Wyn Evans and like them had assimilated punk into a form of Romanticism. In their music the Smiths portrayed Thatcher's England with wit, insight and sarcasm.[14] The film-maker and band seemed a perfect match with their shared interest in the current state of Britain which was explored through a Romanticism tinged with hard-hitting realism.

The films of 'The Queen Is Dead' and 'Panic' were shot on super-8 and are notable for their use of the jerky, fractured pixillation technique Jarman was to develop more fully in *The Last of England*. Gone is the slow-motion, erotic pulsation of *Imagining October* and *The Angelic Conversation*. At about this time Jarman met the young super-8 film-maker Richard Heslop who had graduated from Malcolm Le Grice's film department at St Martin's School of Art in 1985. Heslop's 'scratch' films used aggressive, relentless split-second editing of brutal imagery culled from war newsreels, medical documentaries and so on. He was to shoot much of 'The Queen Is Dead' in a similar style. Parts of the promo were edited by Maybury, who was embarking on a successful music video career with Sinead O'Connor and others while Wyn Evans and Christopher Hughes (another former St Martin's student) also shot material. The joint venture aspect of the commission resulted in a film that is markedly different from any of Jarman's previous work.

If *Imagining October*'s politics were schematic (East versus West) and embedded in historical and iconic forms, the music videos Jarman made for the Smiths depicted contemporary Britain's run-down streets, derelict waste grounds, graffiti-streaked walls and the new-style opposition – for instance, a young girl with a short-back-and-sides haircut wearing a loose white dress spray-paints a tenement wall. Jordan's dance from *Jubilee*, made nearly ten years earlier, is reworked with a new aggression, ending with the unveiling of her naked body in a jubilant gesture of revolt. An old-fashioned rock guitar revolves in the space created by video effects, as does a flower. The videos mark a more socially aware Jarman whose feelings of opposition had merged with those of a younger generation who wanted to express the reality they experienced as unemployment soared, yuppie values reigned and

154

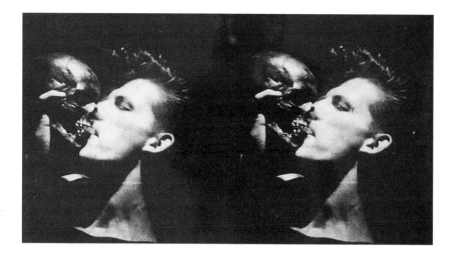

the left was demolished by the crushing of the NUM in the miners' strike of 1984-5. But the social realism so endemic to British film culture held no attraction for this generation: if their films contained a realism then it was expressionist, with the camera hand-held and pixillation and artifice merging with one another.

The Last of England was the first of three films made in the last seven years of Jarman's life which contain his own private and public self (the others are *The Garden* and finally *Blue*). Filming began in summer 1985 with super-8 footage of Tilda Swinton shot on a casual basis, though with a larger project in mind. Jarman and Swinton discussed a version of *St Joan* during these months, much of which they spent in each other's company. Some of this footage ended up in *Aria* and, of course, *Glitterbug*. Filming for *The Last of England* as such began in earnest in August 1986. It was shot on super-8 by Jarman, Wyn Evans Hughes and Heslop. The budget was small (it eventually cost £240,000) and the majority of the cast were friends (I ended up in the film as a refugee). When asked why he made *The Last of England*, Jarman replied, 'For the camaraderie'.

In contrast with the studio filming of *Caravaggio* using an unwieldy 35mm camera, Jarman shot *The Last of England* outdoors, on the Royal Victoria Docks, Millennium Wharf and in Liverpool. Some footage was shot in America. The cameramen often worked in threesomes, moving constantly about the action and deftly remaining out of each other's shots. Jarman remarked that he used super-8 because 'the Super 8 camera is free. 35mm is chained by money to the institutions'.[15] The jumpy, edgy, speeded-up pixillation technique bristled with anger and tension and was unlike anything he had done before. (*Jubilee*, for all its hard-hitting venom, was conventionally shot and edited.)

The Last of England, *The Garden* and *Blue* enjoy a marriage of talents. Simon Turner's symphonic orchestration of the aural elements (there is no synch sound, only voice-over, music and found sounds) is extremely important for the final result, as is the lighting and camerawork of Christopher Hughes. Hughes, Heslop and Wyn Evans brought to the films the aesthetic of the late 80s – visual, raw and energetic. The colours – night blues, mauves and a burning orange reminiscent of London as painted by Turner – have a visionary beauty Jarman had never achieved before. The cast included Nigel Terry as voice-over, Jordan as a member of the royal family, Spencer Leigh and a large number of friends. Christopher Hobbs looked after the production design and James Mackay raised the money and saw everything brought to a fitting end.

The film's title refers to a work of the same name by the pre-Raphaelite painter Ford Madox Brown. It was painted in the mid-19th century when emigration to the British colonies was at its height. A heterosexual couple look dolefully at the receding shores of England, symbolised by the white cliffs of Dover in the top right-hand corner of the painting. The couple in Jarman's film are perhaps his own version of this despondent pair and the film itself is what we might imagine a modern-day couple 'seeing' as they leave the country – a series of images as visionary, nightmarish and fragmented as we might expect from anyone with memories of the 20th century.

The Last of England is arguably Jarman's most brilliant film, a major artistic achievement, although a commercial disaster. One of the key British films of the 80s, if not of the post-war period, its stylistic influence on other film-makers and on advertisers in the 90s has been widespread. It also carries Jarman's critique of British post-imperialism to its furthest point: it is his account of 'Little England'. It is studded with his father's home movies which include footage of the Raj, of Second World War Wellington bombers taking off and of the cosy upper-middle-class world of the post-war years as Jarman and his sister play ball with their mother on the lawn. The cruel, even bitter, juxtaposition of these images with the monochrome shots of contemporary

Jarman with fellow film-makers **157**
(from left) Richard Heslop, Christopher Hughes, Cerith Wyn Evans (photo: Mike Laye)

urban dereliction, with Spring crouched in a doorway injecting heroin into his arm, exposes both a national and a family romance: one cannot help but draw the conclusion that Jarman felt that both were shams and that his feelings towards his country are as ambivalent as those for his family. There is no separation, as the film as a whole testifies.

The warmth and communality of Jarman's family circle contrasts tellingly with the plight of the anonymous and pained individuals who pick their way through the rubble of the decaying city. The only image in these sequences that implies any human warmth is that of the refugees who huddle together in front of a fierce fire on the dockside before their expulsion or death. Jarman's allegiances in the film are with outsiders – the cast-offs, junkies, refugees and homeless who populate England's margins. But equally, opposition must reside here: mainstream politics can no longer sustain a coherent body of humanist values. As with the eclectic, marauding gang of *Jubilee*, the protagonists are scattered on the edges where if they are fortunate they can find comfort in their shared misery; the centre is defined negatively as where they are not. The film is bleak and filled with despair, but the energy and vivacity of its image-making is so extraordinary that it now seems a visionary work that touches an open nerve in our culture.

Annette Kuhn has compared *The Last of England* with Humphrey Jennings' wartime classic *Listen to Britain* (1942), made at a time when neo-Romanticism was mobilised to promote a sense of national identity.[16] Kuhn highlights the contrasting effect of the use of montage in passages in the two films, which juxtapose images of British landscape and ordinary events with the pomp and circumstance of military parades:

> If *Listen to Britain*'s montage unites a discrete series of icons – the military, heavy industry, rural life and landscape – under the aegis of an anthem of national victory, producing an imagination of nationhood as harmonious in its internal differences, *The Last of England* offers a larger, less tidy, perspective.[17]

For Kuhn, Jarman's film 'asserts while it condemns the significance of the memory of an imperial history'.[18] Paradoxically, it seems that at this point in his career Jarman was dealing with the very public matter of the state of England in the last years of the present century in a personal and

158

experimental work, while the more 'private' drama of an individual's sexuality was played out in the more mainstream *Caravaggio*. There is no emphasis on homosexuality in *The Last of England*: the 'heroes', who serve as symbols for contemporary Britain, are heterosexual. Perhaps, as Kuhn suggests, *The Last of England* is 'a less personal film ... than it might seem'.[19]

An 'improvised' film,[20] its quasi-narrative organised around a young woman and her male lover, *The Last of England* depicts a future in which the military, often masked in balaclavas like terrorists, rule England with repressive violence. It is constructed through sequences which are often linked only thematically, giving it a collage-like structure which owes more to the super-8 home movies than to Jarman's other state-of-the-nation feature film, *Jubilee*. There is a strong sense of Jarman struggling to find images to express his feelings – a naked man tearing a cauliflower apart, a tattooed young boy jacking up in a doorway, a group of prisoners huddled on a dockside guarded by terrorist-like soldiers, a young woman in a field of flowers, the same woman as a bride tearing her dress from her with scissors, a stooped man pushing a pram through a night slum while holding on high a burning torch. The carnivalesque air of *Jubilee*, with its black humour and theatrical excess, is replaced by the unrelieved anger of a poetic documentarist who uses the wasteland of London's docklands to create an atmosphere of hysteria, paranoia and pessimism. The urban landscape – London housing estates bathed in red, metallic blue-green interiors and orange-red sunsets above the desolate East End docks – has a frightening, futuristic beauty that prefigures that of Jarman's later paintings. Asked what the film is about, Jarman replied with a quote from Oliver Cromwell's angry address to Parliament on its dissolution in 1654:

> For the day of vengeance is in my heart and the year of my redeemer is come. ... And I will tread down the people in mine anger, and make them drunk in my fury.[21]

The editing of *The Last of England* is determined by poetic and imagistic demands rather than the telling of a story. The opening sequence, for instance, juxtaposes monochrome images of Jarman at his table writing, Spring dancing on Caravaggio's painting *Profane Love*, a pen racing across the page, and a searing white welding light in the darkness. The film begins with

159

a young man (Spring), stripped to the waist and with the cropped hair and tattoos of a lumpen proletarian, moving through a landscape of urban dereliction. He savagely and mindlessly kicks Caravaggio's painting *Profane Love*, in which Cupid tramples over symbols of culture and architecture – almost as if Jarman were rejecting his own *Caravaggio*. Later, a thin, almost wasted naked young man (cameraman Christopher Hughes) tears at a cauliflower with his teeth among the debris and wrecks. Refugees huddle in the cold escorted by sullen soldiers in balaclavas who could be a new form of military or terrorists – it is hard to tell which, and that is perhaps Jarman's point. Others are rounded up and shot, one a young man who it seems is the lover of the woman (Tilda Swinton) who appears in a simple dress in a field of wild flowers. Two soldiers fuck aggressively on the Union Jack. In the final electrifying sequence the young woman marries a yuppie buffoon in a bizarre mock royal wedding with male bridesmaids in drag and a crying baby in a pram wrapped in the front pages of a tabloid newspaper with screaming headlines on the Falklands War. The rising music (Simon Turner's montage of sounds including the wailing voice of Diamante Galas) evokes an atmosphere of hysteria as Swinton establishes without words the panic rising in the bride of a twisted nation state out of control. Outside on the dockside in a twilight that pervades the entire film, she takes scissors and swaying in a mad dance of horror and despair cuts savagely at her wedding dress. The final shot is a haunting one of figures, torches held high, rowing out into the night sea.

Film-maker Gus Van Sant acknowledged Jarman's film as an influence on his own work, especially its technical production method of shooting on super-8, editing on video and transferring back to 35mm: 'I liked the way Derek cut *The Last of England* together, similarly the way he cut his videos for the Pet Shops Boys and the Smiths.'[22] For Van Sant, Jarman represents aspects of the 'underground film-makers of the sixties' in his use of slow-frame filming and projection and, one imagines, in his fragmented narrative structure. Van Sant used similar techniques in his own music videos for the Red Hot Chilli Peppers.

For the novelist Will Self, *The Last of England* has already, it seems, achieved classic status:

> The truth of the matter is that Jarman was a great Englsh film-maker. And in *The Last of England* he offered us a set of discursive and yet

plangent images of our own divided nature: its beauty and brutality, its sensuality and its darkness. Each frame that Jarman contrived in this film appeared to me to be at the one and the same time wholly arbitrary and yet exactly right.[23]

Self's understanding of the film as a lament on our 'divided nature' probably reflects the Jungian conceptions that informed *The Angelic Conversation* a few years earlier.

Robert Hewison has placed *The Last of England* firmly at the centre of an argument for a 'new art of the nineties'. He sees in the film an example of an art that refuses to take the given external world as its foundation, rather 'the materials of the external world have to be used in a different way'.[24] It is a film of 'sounds and images that are constantly running into one another, across each other, against each other'.[25] Hewison argues that in the work of certain primarily British artists there is a mapping of a way forward for art which through its notion of social responsibility goes beyond post-modernism, embracing a pluralism in art and all other aspects of society that will suggest future possibilities. Alongside Jarman he places artists Gilbert and George, Tony Cragg and Helen Chadwick; novelists Iain Sinclair, Salman Rushdie, Ian McKewan and Martin Amis; and dancer Gaby Agis. In Jarman there is a provocative lack of distinction between fact and fiction, between a film that documents aspects of England today and an apocalyptic vision of the future. Jarman himself tried to define the film along such lines:

> The film is a documentary. I've come back with a document from somewhere far away. Everything I pointed the camera at ... had meaning, it didn't matter what we filmed. The film is our fiction, we are in the story. After all, all film is fiction, including the news, or, if you want to reverse it, all film is fact. My film is as factual as the news.[26]

This echoes his own comments on *Jubilee*: 'JUBILEE is a fantasy documentary fabricated so that documentary and fictional forms are confused and coalesce.'[27]

Through his super-8 home movies of the early 80s Jarman crafted a film form which was innovatory in its merging of documentary and fiction. The combination of the two modes in *The Last of England* makes it a home

161

movie with irony dripping from the word 'home'. Here Jarman creates his own home against the 'home' laid down by the politicians, land developers and broadcasting institutions that have taken control over 'reality'. The nostalgia of *Jubilee*, provided mainly through the John Dee sequences, has been shed, leaving fragmentation, brutality, loss of identity and a maelstrom of words and images that never quite connect.

An important element in the film's sound is the reflexive voice of Tilda Swinton watching the film's images. Jarman appears in the opening black-and-white shot sitting in his room writing – a modern-day 'necromancer', as Hewison calls him. This is a variation on the opening of *Jubilee*, except that here Jarman does not need a John Dee to conjure the near future but instead uses himself as the seer. The home-movie technique implies a documentary sensibility – the capturing of the moment, of 'reality', in front of the camera. Eschewing any characterisation or narrative figuration, we witness the responses of *people*, not characters, to a situation which is by definition that of the moment. Spring stamping and masturbating on Caravaggio's painting exemplifies the uneasy mix of a set-up situation, yet one to which the performer responds through his or her own feelings and perceptions.

Jarman had been developing a cinema that would be capable of this kind of representation throughout the 80s. Swinton's contribution was to recognise this aesthetic in Jarman and, as she readily admits, to use it as a space for her own 'agenda' as an actress. Brechtian acting theory – the notion that a distinction between the actor and his or her role must be enforced – has been particularly influential on Swinton's approach. While Brecht did not rule out emotions in actor or audience, he thought that empathetic acting, whereby the performer and spectator identify with the character's feelings, led the spectator to abandon his or her critical position. Swinton discusses this distinction in the context of Brecht's leading actress (and wife) Helene Weigel:

> Helene Weigel cried on the opening night of one of Brecht's plays and a critic commented that she was identifying with the character, she has lost herself in the character. Brecht replied ... that Helene Weigel was crying for the character. There is always a commentary there. The performer is always there.[28]

Swinton's final dress-tearing sequence in *The Last of England* can therefore be read as the behaviour of Swinton the actress towards the role of the bride.

Brecht doubted that the alienation effect, created by the distance between actor and role, was possible to achieve in cinema since the performance is fixed on celluloid; the alienation effect would seem to depend on the idea of a role being created anew with each performance. However, the relationship between actor and 'real person' in Jarman's home movies militates against actor-role identification. That we watch Jarman playing himself in the opening shot of *The Last of England* signals the tenor of the other 'roles'. To this extent, Swinton's claims for a Brechtian method in the films seems valid.

Jarman's unconventional mode of editing also helps reconcile his film work with the tradition of Brechtian theatre. Jarman's camera is continually moving in the super-8 films (partly because of its lightness compared with cumbersome 35mm cameras). The rhythms set up do not comply with the narrative demands, making the vocabulary of shot-reverse-shot, 180 degree rule, eyeline matches and so on redundant. The rhythms are determined by the emotional shaping of the film, by associations set up between visual images. In other words, the structure is more poetic than novelistic – the aesthetic of the *gest* Brecht wrote of in relation to his own poems in 'On Rhymeless Verse with Irregular Rhythms' (1939),[29] where he eschewed language with the 'oily smoothness of the usual five-foot iambic metre' in favour of 'everyday expressions' with the 'tone of direct and spontaneous speech'. The 'shifting, syncopated, gestic' rhythm Brecht recommended is that of Jarman's *The Last of England* and *The Garden*.

In 1987 Jarman contributed a short section to producer Don Boyd's portmanteau film *Aria*. The other directors involved included Robert Altman, Bill Bryden, Nicolas Roeg, Jean-Luc Godard and Jarman's former mentor Ken Russell. Each was asked to make a short piece based on an aria of their choice, and Jarman picked Gustave Charpentier's 'Depuis le jour' from *Louise*. The segment was shot in super-8 then blown up to 35mm; it was produced by James Mackay with Tilda Swinton, Spencer Leigh and Amy Johnson as the actors. *Aria* is a broken-backed venture with little but the music to recommend it, though Godard's sequence of two naked women in the midst of a bunch of male body-builders unaware of their presence is an

'Aria' (overleaf) **163**

interesting oddity among the otherwise awful sex scenes. Jarman's sequence, which involves the two doomed lovers from *The Last of England* beside the sea, playfully chasing each other through a garden, sits awkwardly with the high production values of the rest of the sections. Jarman rarely mentioned the film except at one point to acknowledge it as 'a ship of fools'.

'War Requiem'

Jarman received two commissions in the last few years of his life, each revolving around very different figures from the present century: the philosopher Ludwig Wittgenstein and the gay composer Benjamin Britten, whose *War Requiem* was a musical setting for the poems of Wilfrid Owen. Both Wittgenstein and Owen fought in the trenches in the First World War, while Britten was a pacifist and conscientious objector in the Second World War. *War Requiem* was not a narrative project but a more poetic one along the lines of *The Angelic Conversation*, *The Garden* and *The Last of England*.

Don Boyd informed Jarman that the film on Britten's *War Requiem* was a 'possibility' in December 1987, the same year that *The Last of England* was released.[30] Jarman had used Britten's music in *The Angelic Conversation* and *Imagining October* and claimed that 'the music of Benjamin Britten has always made the perfect foil to my more intuitive film-making'.[31] He had been familiar with *War Requiem* for some time (and had listened to it throughout the editing of *The Last of England*) but was unable to use it in the film as the royalties would have proved too expensive. Boyd arranged the finances for the later film by offsetting the demands of the trustees of the Britten-Pears Foundation with funding from the BBC. Jarman remarked: 'I've had to move carefully, given my reputation as an enemy of narrative film, since the recording company obviously want a conventional narrative.'[32]

Like Jarman's previous historical feature films, *War Requiem* is a history play in that its main character acts and is acted upon within a specific historical context. However, the notion of a central character is less important here than in *Caravaggio* or *Sebastiane* since the subject matter of *War Requiem* is to a large extent Britten's music.

Unlike Britten, Jarman was never a pacifist in either his films or his writings. But in notes published with the script of *War Requiem*, he examines his own 'revulsion for war', coming up with recollections of the effect his father's wartime career had on him and a strong boyhood memory of being

166

in a military hospital with wounded soldiers. The war Jarman refers to in his notes on his present-day feelings is the controversial Falklands War waged by Britain on Argentina in the early 80s and his anti-militarism is presented as much as a dislike for that particular war as it is a strong anti-war sentiment. *War Requiem* is also a film that fits neatly into Jarman's ongoing exploration of post-imperialist England.

The constraints on the film were largely the result of the anxiety of the Britten estate at allowing such a film-maker to interpret the composer's work. In the end, the narrative is slight; Jarman described the film as 'a collage. A cut-up.'[33] The fragmentation occurs along four main fault lines. First there is the narrative in which Owen joins the army and unintentionally causes the death of the Unknown Soldier, a member of his company. Second there is the poetic symbolism of certain events such as the moss growing on Keats' poems which Owen reads and the apocalyptic scene of his death watched by ghoulish banker-like figures. Third there are flashbacks shot on super-8 and involving the Nurse and Mother figures – one the mother of Owen and the other of the Enemy Soldier, although this connection is not obvious in the film itself. Fourth there is the often horrific found-footage of war – both the grainy stock of early black-and-white documentary and the harsh washed-out colours of television coverage of contemporary conflicts. The technique goes back to *Imagining October* with its drift in and out of narrative and intercutting of this with home-movie material and agit-prop intertitles. There is a rich patterning of visual surfaces and textures but a strong sense of a compromised sensibility in Jarman's failure to marry thematically these different kinds of images.

At first Jarman did not find a role for a woman in the film to reflect the soprano voice, but eventually he and Tilda Swinton constructed her part as the Nurse. It is a testament to Swinton's understanding of the film and of Jarman's aesthetic that her role embodies some of *War Requiem*'s most intense emotional and visual moments.

In the first scene, set in contemporary England, the Nurse pushes the Old Soldier, a war veteran (Laurence Olivier), in his wheelchair. He shows her an old snapshot of a nurse who resembles her. The Old Soldier remembers. Owen lies in state on a stone altar attended by the grieving Nurse. Owen and his mother hang out washing while the Nurse tends the garden. Owen is recruited and at the parade he helps his comrade doomed

167

to become the Unknown Soldier to remove a thorn from his foot. Owen prays in a church and then breaks bread with the Nurse. The chorus sings in front of a screen filled with images of exploding shells. Owen writes in the trenches watching his fellow-soldiers sleep, intercut with a scene of him playing soldiers as a child. The Nurse does her night round on the ward and helps a sick young soldier. She then sees the young Owen at the window. Owen is recruited by men in drag dancing the cancan in front of a huge Union Jack watched by four enormous businessmen clutching scythes. This is intercut with a scene of the nurses playing blind man's buff in the darkened hospital ward. The Nurse reads a letter and with the Mother places flowers on an altar. Owen and the soldiers prepare for battle. In the battle, the Unknown Soldier and an Enemy Soldier throw snowballs. Owen misreads their behaviour and shoots the Enemy Soldier who in the confusion kills the Unknown Soldier with his knife. The German as a boy blows bubbles with his mother. Owen collapses in front of the dead British soldier and they are all taken away by stretcher-bearers. The soldier is buried. The biblical figure Abraham ritually kills Owen before a bloodthirsty audience of bankers, generals and clergymen. Owen lies on the altar as in the first scene and the Nurse grieves. The Unknown Soldier is revealed to be Christ who is holding *pietà*-like the corpse of Owen. There are war scenes of horrific carnage. Owen appears in a cave filled with dust-covered dead soldiers and the Enemy Soldier rises from them to bless Owen and then blows a trumpet which awakens the soldiers who wash in a crater filled with water. In the final scene, the Enemy Soldier appears holding a wreath of poppies watched by the Nurse and the Mother. The Unknown Soldier stands on the tomb and four soldiers sleep at its base. The Nurse places the white poppies on the tomb and follows the Mother out.

As this attempt at a synopsis shows, the film depends largely on associations between images and a logic that is not determined by narrative. Scenes are transformed from realistic depictions to biblical ones. There also seems to be a shifting of identity between Owen, the Unknown Soldier and the Enemy Soldier. Similarly, the Mother and Nurse figures appear in slightly different scenarios that render their separate identities uncertain (at one point the Nurse seems to be Owen's sister as they are both shown at home with the Mother). The naturalist or realist scenes (Owen tending his fellow-soldiers; the Nurse tending her patients) are penetrated by fantasy – for

instance, as Owen's book becomes covered in moss or the Nurse sees the child Owen's face at the hospital window. There are also two scenes of theatrical melodrama – the recruitment scene and Owen's death, which are both played out in a Russellian style reminiscent in its caricature and hyperbole of Eisenstein, whom both Russell and Jarman admired. The fast-editing montage technique of the film is very different from most of Jarman's previous work.

For Jarman, film biography was never an invitation to inspect an inner life but rather an exploration of the relationship between the subject and their means of expression. In the case of Britten and Owen, Jarman has provided an interpretation of the music and poetry in which the film obeys similar rules to those art forms – metaphor, rhythmic and rhyming groupings, the impacting and condensation of images and of time and space.

The difference between the exaggeration of the set pieces and the delicate sensitivity of the memory scenes is abrupt and total. In other words, there is a continual shifting of levels of 'reality' and meaning within the film – from hectoring agit-prop caricature with its blatant political attack (the Establishment's murder of Owen) to scenes based in love and human relationships. Jarman seems caught between these two modes, as if he had little faith any more in the power of realist emotional expression to do the work of political passion. After the vibrant poeticism and formal and conceptual clarity of *The Last of England*, *War Requiem* is disappointing. Perhaps Jarman was too anxious about the Britten estate, or the subject matter was too distant from his own concerns.

The film is haunted by the sombre mood of the super-8 footage used for memories or to depict the pasts of certain characters, though it is not always clear whose memories we are witnessing – at times the Enemy Soldier's family merges with Owen's. These super-8 scenes are some of the best in the film and point perhaps to a more subtle rendering of the film's topics of the horror and shame of war. One of the most brilliant scenes in Jarman's entire output, in which the understanding between him and Swinton is epitomised, is a long static take (of about seven minutes) in which Swinton, sitting at the base of an altar dressed in a loose, almost classical dress, her hair a mass of plaits, performs a mime of body and gesture to the moving soprano voice of the Sanctus. It is not a bodily accompaniment to the music but a response to it, a personal 'choreography' of astonishing intensity, beauty and awareness. Swinton describes her approach and motivation:

> It is my method ... to creep up on the image and deconstruct it from within. The music was playing and I'm showing an awareness of that and also showing that there is both a pernicious and a celebratory aspect to war. ... While this is a performance there is also the inevitability for me of the work being to some extent autobiographical.[34]

As an image redolent of the high-art-cum-kitsch expression of emotion in nineteenth-century neo-classical painting and sculpture (Pre-Raphaelite painting is awash with such images), this sequence is also a response to that essentially imperialist tradition, its vacuous posturing

170

Tilda Swinton in 'War Requiem' **171**

'deconstruct[ed] from within' in Brechtian fashion by Swinton's consummate acting skills.

Unlike Russell, who uses hyperbole to depict the unconscious of his subject, Jarman is an Eisensteinian political film-maker without the Leninist framework. For him, the Establishment is the root of all power and repression, whether social, artistic or sexual. The subtle analysis of how power operates within the Establishment that we find in a director like Alan Pakula is not the point for Jarman, whose subject matter is the struggle between the individual and Establishment power. Whether located in Roman times, sixteenth-century Italy or England, turn-of-the-century Europe or contemporary Britain, the same issue remains central to Jarman's films. The numbing effect of Establishment repression is personified in the passive 'heroes' of these films: suffering, martyred, meek and almost silent. Owen is a Jarman hero in the same mould.

In its religious themes and images *War Requiem* is a precursor of *The Garden*. The *pietà* of the Enemy Soldier and Owen, the altar on which the dead soldiers lie and the characterisation of the women – the suffering mother of Jesus and the Mary Magdalene sister character – contribute to this religious atmosphere. A fascinating comparison is with Pasolini's *The Gospel According to Matthew* with its passive apostles and active, aggressive Jesus. One of the film's strongest features is that because it is set to music it looks like an early silent film. The acting style is often Eisensteinian, with a strong use of grotesque, expressionistic facial contortions. Against this is set the naturalism of the scenes in the trenches and hospital.

In just over two years (1986–7) Jarman made three feature-length films. During this time he was also adjusting to knowing he was HIV positive. The relative tranquillity of *Caravaggio* was transformed into the rage of *The Last of England* and *War Requiem*. During the making of *The Last of England* he was writing a book of the same title with a very different sensibility from *Dancing Ledge*, completed only three years earlier. The good humour and breeziness of the earlier book are replaced by a gloomy, vitriolic tone and an introspection that finds its focus in his family, especially his father, who died in 1986.

During these years painting returned to Jarman's life. He remarks that, 'if I become ill it will be a way of working, quick, and gentle'.[35] *Caravaggio* was nominated for the Turner Prize in 1986 and Jarman showed a series of collages at the Tate in conjunction with the Turner Prize show. These were new works executed using a thick black base into which objects were pressed and then the glass cover smashed. They also sometimes included text. The contemporaneity and harsher tone of these paintings, which contain objects from present-day culture and have a strong negative quality in the broken glass and aggression of the objects collaged (bullets, a knife), reflect the mood of his films of the period. They are obviously more tactile too, Jarman using his fingers to manipulate the ground, press in the objects and fracture the glass. This coincided with his purchase of the house in Dungeness where he had space and quiet to work.

1 *Screen*, vol. 21 no. 4, 1980/1.

2 Duncan Petrie (ed.), *New Questions of British Cinema* (London: British Film Institute Working Papers, 1992), p. 22.

3 Derek Jarman, *Dancing Ledge* (London: Quartet, 1984), p. 207.

4 He had vented his spleen on the state of the industry and *Caravaggio*'s lack of funding in *Dancing Ledge*, which he began writing at Nicholas Ward Jackson's instigation in late 1982.

5 Jeremy Isaacs, *Storm Over Four: A Personal Account* (London: Weidenfeld & Nicolson, 1989), p. 120.

6 Derek Jarman, *Derek Jarman's Caravaggio* (London: Thames & Hudson, 1986), p. 133.

7 Interview with the author, 'Brittania on Trial', in *Monthly Film Bulletin*, vol. 53 no. 627, April 1986.

8 *Derek Jarman's Caravaggio*, p. 39.

9 Derek Jarman, *The Last of England*, (London: Constable, 1987), p. 54.

10 See especially Timothy Murray, *Like a Film: Ideological Fantasy on Screen, Camera and Canvas* (London: Routledge, 1993), chapter 5.

11 Ibid.

12 A phrase used by the present author in Simon Field and Michael O'Pray, 'On Imaging October, Dr Dee and Other Matters', *Afterimage*, no. 12, 1985, p. 55, and quoted in Murray, *Like a Film*, p. 126.

13 Tony Rayns, 'Submitting to Sodomy: Propositions and Rhetorical Questions about an English Film-Maker', in *Afterimage*, no. 12, 1985.

14 On the Smiths see Johnny Rogan, *Morrissey and Marr: The Severed Alliance* (London: Omnibus Press, 1992).

15 *The Last of England*, p. 169.

16 See Annette Kuhn, *Family Secrets: Acts of Memory and Imagination* (London: Verso, 1995), chapter 7.

17 Ibid., p. 112.

18 Ibid.

19 Ibid., p. 109.

20 *The Last of England*, p. 163.

21 Ibid., p. 164.

22 Gus Van Sant, *Even Cowgirls Get the Blues & My Own Private Idaho* (London: Faber & Faber, 1993), p. xxxviii.

23 Will Self, 'Birth of the Cool', *Guardian Weekend*, 6 August 1994, pp. 26–30.

24 Robert Hewison, *Future Tense: A New Art for the Nineties* (London: Methuen, 1990), p. 79.

25 Ibid.

26 *The Last of England*, p. 170.

27 *Dancing Ledge*, p. 177.

28 In Michael O'Pray, 'A Body of Political Work: Tilda Swinton in Interview', in Pam Cook and Philip Dodd (eds), *Women and Film: A Sight and Sound Reader* (London: Scarlet Press, 1994), p. 70.

29 See John Willet (ed.), *Brecht on Theatre: The Development of an Aesthetic* (London: Methuen, 1987).

30 On the background to *War Requiem* see the introductions by Don Boyd and Jarman to Derek Jarman, *War Requiem: The Film* (London: Faber & Faber, 1989).

31 Ibid., p. xi.

32 Ibid.

33 Ibid., p. 47.

34 From O'Pray, 'A Body of Political Work', p. 72.

35 *The Last of England*, p. 39.

Chapter Seven

B L A C K

The Garden, Edward II

1987–1992

In the late 80s, often ill or exhausted by his film work, Jarman turned more to his retreat in Dungeness. In 1989 and 1990 he kept a journal for publication titled *Modern Nature* in which he alludes as much to his garden as he does to his artistic pursuits. During these years he did plan three films – *The Garden*, completed near the end of 1990, *Edward II*, which he scripted, and finally a project that became *Blue*. These were also years when his health failed for the first time. In 1990, returning from a series of screenings of his work in Poland, he fell seriously ill, beginning what was to be a steady physical decline.

Modern Nature is a very different book from his previous ones. Forced to write almost daily, he displays wonderful gifts of description, especially of nature and his immediate physical environment. His preoccupations are rooted in personal problems, observations and experiences, with less polemic. The entries are studded with often comic extracts from the early English herbalists and his love of books, especially from the medieval period and beyond, shines forth on every page.

Jarman still found it difficult to raise money for his films and there were communication problems at times with the BFI over *The Garden*. But he began to achieve the status of a public figure, with young fans camping outside his flat in Charing Cross Road and newspapers and magazines running stories on his HIV positive status and film-making for the Pet Shop Boys. He became involved in the gay activist group OutRage and his short volume *At Your Own Risk* is an angry tract-cum-autobiography (some culled from previous writings) which bears the influence of militant gay politics (the book's subtitle is 'A Saint's Testament' – an allusion to Jarman's 'canonisation' by the male drag 'order' the Sisters of Perpetual Indulgence).[1] The OutRage campaign was used literally in *Edward II*.

Jarman's finances had been eased to some extent by his father's

174 'The Garden' (photo: Liam Daniel)

bequest and by videos and concert work for the Pet Shop Boys. Like the Smiths, the Pet Shop Boys were a band who wanted to express their own brand of detached irony using a film-maker of Jarman's standing. Like the Smiths', their songs articulate a critical awareness of contemporary British culture. The collaboration was not without controversy, however. Jarman's appointment was opposed by the band's management,[2] then moments of the films *Nothing Has Been Proved* and *It's a Sin* had to be censored for the Japan tour of summer 1989. Jarman's film of 'Nothing Has Been Proved', written for the soundtrack of *Scandal* (a film about the 60s Profumo affair), included the word 'Fuck' in a collage based on the story. The other film showed two young men kissing. The problems were settled by the projectionist inking out the 300 frames containing the word 'Fuck' and placing his hand over the projector lens for the offending seconds of kissing.[3]

As well as using his films as backdrops, the whole show was designed by Jarman. Lead singer Neil Tennant remarks: 'It's directed ... in the same way you direct a play or a musical.'[4] Among the props was a large mock-penis reminiscent of the one used in the opening sequence of *Sebastiane*. The long metallic artificial fingernails and brightly coloured, opulent costumes of *It's a Sin* suggest the influence of Kenneth Anger, though the mood is ironic and tongue-in-cheek.

Jarman seems to have made a distinction between his work for the Pet Shop Boys and that for the Smiths. In *Modern Nature* he recounts a row with James Mackay:

> [Mackay] We're showing the films.
> Which? *Imagining October*?
> No, the Pet Shop Boys' concert film.
> You mean the backdrops from the staging?
> (I had told James that I didn't wish them to be shown.)
> But they're like *The Queen is Dead*.
> That was a film, these weren't constructed like that, just ambient backgrounds with great big gaping holes. They looked great at Wembley with the boys singing and dancing. In any case there's only one good one, *Nothing Has Been Proved*.[5]

While the Smiths videos were heavily influenced by the harsh poeticism of the younger film–makers involved and had a strong political tone, the Pet Shop Boys films display a welter of influences:

> It's a medley that cavorts through the styles of the underground. Peter and HB have edited King's Cross like Bruce Bailies' [sic] Ode to the American Indian; at moments It's A Sin approaches Grunewald or Bosch; Domino Dancing is the most affecting, and has footage from Dungeness layered with its bullfights.[6]

In 1989, after seeing a Frank Auerbach painting while lunching at his dealer Richard Salmon's gallery, Jarman was inspired to take up his brushes again and 'stop collaging'. He immediately bought paints and returned to Dungeness determined to paint the nearby nuclear power station. At about the same time he created an installation for the Third Eye Centre, Glasgow, that was more like a film set than any of his previous art. As an invited artist to the National Review of Live Art, he took the opportunity to make an angry statement about the way the British press used the AIDS epidemic to attack gay men. Michael Coveney described the piece in a review for the *Financial Times*:

> In the gallery's centre, two naked men in a bed boarded off by barbed wire, read magazines and newspapers. Mattresses pinned to the surrounding wall were collage bases for literature, photographs, clothing. Finally, these mattresses and their defiant stuccoes had been tarred and feathered like so many victims of sectarian pillory and violence.[7]

Newspaper coverage of the AIDS epidemic from the *Sun* and other tabloids was stuck on a central pillar. Coveney judged Jarman's installation to be the only one in the show with any sense of outrage.

At the same time Jarman had a show of ten small black paintings at the Richard De Marco Gallery in Edinburgh. Jarman had been using tar as a base for his black collage paintings for some time and in December of the same year he shot the scene in *The Garden* in which the Christ-like boys are covered in treacle and feathers by the policeman, with its strong echo of the Third Eye Centre installation.

177

'The Garden'

The Garden, released in late 1990, was inspired by Jarman's love of his own garden, his ambivalence towards the almost surreal environs of Dungeness with its windswept shoreline and menacing nearby nuclear power station and a delving into his own emotions, given form by the external world and the issue of AIDS. A recounting of Christ's Passion, the film is not as unremittingly bleak as one might expect, but what violence and sadism there is surpasses anything in his prior work, including *Jubilee*. Like many of his films, *The Garden* is framed by a 'vision', this time one conjured up in the sleep of the director himself.

Christ is played by two young gay men and by a more traditional figure (the artist and actor Roger Cook who also took part in *The Last of England*). The young boy and the tattooed man (Spring) who live on the beach seem to portray the young Christ and Joseph respectively. A beachcombing young woman (Tilda Swinton) is at times a Madonna-like figure and at others an angelic presence – as with the Christ figures, there seems to be both a contemporary and a traditional rendering of her character. This tactic subverts any linear narrative and an attempt to give a straightforward synopsis of the film would be misplaced. Similarly the images move from starkly realistic shots in film to the theatrical, flattened video effects of the pop promo and television advertisement.

Tony Rayns has described the film as an '"I"-movie'[8] – a development of the psycho-drama film which began with Cocteau's *Blood of a Poet* (1930) and moved through Maya Deren's *Meshes of the Afternoon* (1943) and *At Land* (1944), Kenneth Anger's *Fireworks* (1947) and Gregory Markopolous' *Twice A Man* (1963) to the work of many other film-makers of the American underground. The psycho-drama is characterised by a hero or heroine who undergoes a rite of passage, usually in a dream-like setting. P. Adams Sitney, who helped define the genre in his classic book on the American avant-garde film tradition *Visionary Film*, understands its main concern to be with issues of personal and sexual identity encountered through personal crisis.[9] Its roots are in the Romantic tradition's emphasis on attaining self-identity through memory, imagination and knowledge.

The figure in crisis in *The Garden* is Jarman himself, depicted at the beginning of the film writing in his room in what seems a state of deep anxiety and dread. He falls asleep and water drips ominously on to a crucifix.

178

At other points in the film he is shown huddled on a bed out at sea with nymph-like figures holding burning torches dancing around him.

While *The Garden* contains sharp references to the media, education and the police, it is through its allegories that it achieves its critical force. Its mood is not too distant from the sense of loss that suffused *Caravaggio*, but its melancholy is imbued with anger which continually collapses into despair. Film, super-8, video and back-projection jostle each other, as do the clashing styles and anachronisms of the *mise en scène* and costumes. Christ in traditional clothes meets a jogger beneath high electricity pylons. Policemen disguised as Father Christmas torture the two young gays in a scene of excruciating sadism. Shrill young society women stone a man in drag while terrorist-style press photographers snap away. A recurring scene of black-shawled peasant women sitting at a long table in a parody of the Last Supper is done with a video matted-in seascape backdrop with the angel (Tilda Swinton) rising behind them. In a homage to Michael Powell's *The Life and Death of Colonel Blimp*, the two young men are harassed by leering old queens in a bathhouse. In a scene which refers to *The Angelic Conversation* two men wrestle naked in a pit of sulphurous smoke, lit by Jarman's much-loved torch flames.

In many ways, *The Garden* is a home movie devoid of the innocent certainties of that form of film-making. The film theorist Timothy Murray has remarked:

> the wistful hallucinations of *Caravaggio* seem almost to presage the traumatic realisation of Jarman's latest films, *The Garden* (1990) and *Edward II* (1991), that 'the boys emerging from the shadows reminded me of ghosts come to haunt me, all my dead friends. As always life was far more "advanced" than art'. ... AIDS has taken not only Jarman's friends from the wings of art (and, soon, Jarman himself), but also the sexual culture of Jarman's Super-8s.[10]

The Garden is framed not only by Jarman's dream but by the making of the film itself. It begins with the sounds and images of the studio, as Jarman calls on the crew to take a break. Then fairly early in the film this self-referentiality is consolidated when, immediately on the cut that ends the staged Judas scene, Jarman's voice can be heard giving a directorial instruction (it sounds like 'Go!'). There follows a montage of images shot in super-8 and video. The sequence opens with a night-shot of waves, grass, Dungeness power station and Jarman's own cottage on the shore. On the soundtrack Swinton quietly utters words that are difficult to hear ('No!' she seems to say). There is a soundtrack of children singing 'London's Burning' and shots of a young boy playing with a snail then playfully washing the hair of a tough-looking young man (the young Jesus or Joseph perhaps) outside the cottage. This is intercut with images (strong-coloured video) of the two young men playing and making love in a bath. The soundtrack begins to seem ominous and is eventually broken by a scream. There follows a shot of the young boy pointing directly at the camera which the young man approaches threateningly, his hands raised to block the lens. The men make love and then the camera cuts to a night-shot of the young man still aggressively trying to block the camera. There is then a shot of Jarman in his blue overalls sitting in a deck-chair working on some writing, obviously in the same place outside his cottage as the young boy and man. This is followed by a shot of Swinton from behind as she walks on the beach with a basket on her head. She turns and looks into the camera. Jarman is shown again mulling over the book with the pencil to his cheek and on the soundtrack a woman calls 'Derek' and he looks off-screen. There is a cut to Swinton returning with the basket on her head. We then see Jarman pursuing the young man with his super-8 camera, obviously shooting the images we have just seen.

This complex montage sequence, which ends with another staged song scene, sets up a curious interplay between elements of the story and the construction of the film. For instance, the story encapsulated in the bath scene is fractured by the scream and the camera becoming part of the action. Characters look into camera, forcing the spectator's identification with the unseen attackers and breaking the narrative space – except, of course, that the making of the film is also part of the narrative. It is the complex relationship between the narratives that gives *The Garden* its richness. Jarman's own implication of himself as Christ undermines the film's very project of a rendering of the Christian myth. The film interweaves genres – a 'home movie' which collapses into the main narrative and a constructed fictional narrative that bleeds into the 'home movie'. Perhaps the film's greatest achievement is to forge an inextricable relationship between mythology and

180

The religious iconography of 'The Garden' (photo: Liam Daniel) **181**

personal cinema that does not rely on 'dreams', simple parallelisms or juxtaposition.

Though *The Last of England* is also constructed as a vision of the film-maker, in *The Garden* Jarman has a role within his own dream-state. In *The Last of England* Jarman's appearance – besides the early one in his study – is as a young boy playing in his parents' garden with his sister and mother, shot by his father as a home movie. In *The Garden*, as the man coiled in agony and dread on the bed, he places himself in a more symbolic mode within the film text. Jarman in interview remarked that Tilda Swinton felt she was working on a collaborative venture, but when she saw *The Garden* she felt she was in his dream.[11]

The sequence of the death of Christ, following the harrowing humiliation and flogging scenes, is a *tour de force* of image montage using super-8 footage, time-lapse photography and shot-repetition. Michael Gough's voice-over accompanies a series of images of Swinton crossing the frame with a ladder representing a cross. This shot is repeated (with increasing close-up) eleven times, intercut by momentary images. Following this is another sequence in which Simon Turner's collage soundtrack of rising hysteria and horror gives the image of Christ meeting a jogger with a whistle in a desolate landscape of pylons a dark awfulness. It is followed immediately by time-lapse landscape shots of the cottage, grass, trees and skyline; of sheets being blown on a washing line; of Jarman digging; of the Jesus-Joseph figure quietly knotting a fishing rope and gazing into camera; and of Swinton. The sequence epitomises the quality of the super-8 colour (achieved through filters) and light (under the direction of lighting cameraman Christopher Hughes) that *The Garden* attains.

The end sequences of the film are unsurpassed in their beauty and invigoration of spirit. As Jarman closes his book on the beach and leaves the frame to the surrounding sea and landscape, there is an exquisite sense of being in touch with mortality ('Goodnight boys! Goodnight Johnny!') and the English landscape. There is also the feeling of tragedy, sublimely imaged in the everyday phenomena of life – the sea, a ship, fire, flowers and the sky. *The Garden* targets the Church, schools, Christian rituals, the gay world of bathhouses and old queens, advertising, press harassment, terrorist violence, police brutality, ecological disintegration, atomic threat. Yet the film at the same time suggests hope. When he was filming *The Last of England* Jarman did not know he was HIV positive; by the time of *The Garden* he had been diagnosed for some years and it was public knowledge. This perhaps explains both the thoughtful focus of the film and its note of reconciliation.

The film ends with a coda, as the two men, the young boy, an older man and Swinton eat and then light an Amaretti wrapper to watch it rise above them. Communality is asserted in a 'family' group radically different from the traditional family of contemporary Western society. Jarman's Utopianism is expressed in this final image.

Jarman was seriously ill in hospital during the editing of *The Garden* in 1990. It was acclaimed on its release and seen as one of his most personal films – his statement on AIDS and his own mortality. That Christ is a sympathetic figure but the institution of the Church is perceived as malignant did not prevent it from being awarded a Special Mention by the International Catholic Organisation for Cinema at the 1991 Berlin Festival. Nigel Andrews in the *Financial Times* described it as the 'best British film for years' and in *The Times* Geoff Brown wrote that it was 'cinema of astonishing beauty and elegiac force'. But by this time Jarman was already preparing to film Christopher Marlowe's sixteenth-century play *Edward II* for the BBC, which was to signal a return to a more orthodox style akin to the one he had adopted for *Caravaggio*.

'Edward II'

Edward II was to be made on the basis that Ken Butler, the associate director, would cover when Jarman was ill, which was necessary on quite a few occasions. Jarman was careful to pace his days to conserve his energy for filming, but there was no doubt that his health was in decline. An irritating skin rash began to disrupt his sleep and in his diary of the film he speaks of high temperatures and the regime of drugs: 'my chemical life splutters on'.[12] After this Jarman began taking AZT, a decision he made only after much thought.

That Jarman should turn to Christopher Marlowe in the early 90s was no accident. *Edward II* was made at the height of Jarman's involvement with the gay activist group OutRage, at a time when his anger was focused on the lack of government funding for research or help for victims of AIDS, on his own unravelling 'family romance' after the death of his father and, of course, on his own mortality. Frances Yates has pointed out that Marlowe's world is

183

an expression of a later and darker period of Elizabethan England than Shakespeare's, an era of increased insularity and paranoia towards foreign powers and witch-hunts at home.[13] Certainly for Jarman to have made *The Tempest* at this point would have been virtually impossible – reparation and forgiveness were not the watchwords of these years, particularly not for a gay man who was HIV positive in a society which had condoned the official negligence towards the AIDS crisis and the homophobic legislation of Clause 28, which aimed to restrict expressions of homosexuality. The script of *Edward II* is dedicated to the repeal of 'all anti-gay laws particularly clause 28'.

In conversation with myself and Colin MacCabe on the day he handed in the script to the BBC, Jarman with some glee promised an *Edward II* which would be a 'blue movie' filled with explicit fucking – an orgy of sex. In his writing too he expresses this desire, yet sex in his films is almost always either muffled by violence or verging on the platonic, as in *The Angelic Conversation*. His sexual imagery is often self-conscious and coy, as if he were not comfortable with it and realised that his interests as an artist lay elsewhere.

Edward II was produced by Working Title producers Steve Clark-Hall and Antony Root and financed by the BBC and British Screen to a budget of £850,000. Jarman in the press notes asserts:

> What is so interesting about *Edward II* ... is it touches on areas that still aggravate people, unlike *Henry V* for example. In fact it's remarkable for a play written in the 16th century, and that's why I wanted to do it.

On the appearance of OutRage in the film, he notes that 'the whole central relationship between Edward and Piers Gaveston is mirrored by what's happening right now with Section 28 and Clause 25 [later to become Clause 28] and so on'. He argues that by making the film he is 'reclaiming history because there's been a long tradition of denying the homosexual side of the relationship between Edward and Gaveston'.[14] (Interestingly, Brecht's adaptation of the play accepts the central relationship as homosexual but is more overtly political.[15]) In his notes to *Edward II* Jarman compares Shakespeare with Marlowe:

184

On 'The Media Show' A. L. Rowse said Shakespeare was a conservative, Marlowe much more radical. Shakespeare's wilful misinterpretation of the 15th century to bolster Tudor dynastic claims has blighted our past. ... For the 'Sonnets' though, all Shakespearean historical inaccuracy is forgiven. 'Shall I compare thee to a summer's day?' – I thought of using them as voice-over, then I decided against. 'The Angelic Conversation' is my film of the 'Sonnets'. I have a deep hatred of the Elizabethan past used to castrate our vibrant present.[16]

Jarman seems here to be attacking not Shakespeare himself but the present-day Establishment's use of Shakespeare to prop up a reactionary view of Britain and of English history. For Jarman, his film of *Edward II* was a political attack on a tradition that had repressed the homosexual since the Elizabethan period as well as an 'outing' of Marlowe.

Edward II is the story of the early fourteenth-century King of England who neglects his state and his wife Isabella for his love of a French courtier, Piers Gaveston. In order to wrest control away from him, his wife, aided and abetted by Mortimer and other lords, plots to overthrow him. Gaveston is killed and Edward is eventually imprisoned, tortured and brutally murdered, to be succeeded by his son Edward III. In Jarman's version the executioner Lightborn frees Edward and the horrific execution by the insertion of a red-hot poker in the King's anus is reduced to a nightmare.

Edward was a perfect subject for Jarman. Not only is his love for Gaveston a homosexual one but he is also an extremely passive character whose only activity is dedicated to the pleasures of the senses. His lack of interest in matters of state lies at the centre of the play and he suffers the consequences of choosing his own desires before his kingly responsibilities. Characteristically Jarman had found a drama which depicts not only the homosexual condition, but also its relationship to the social and the political. Like Caravaggio, Edward is compromised by the competing demands of the private and the public. The play was also particularly pertinent at a time when the British government was introducing a new wave of anti-homosexual legislation and persecution.

The play is renowned for the extreme and rather puzzling switch of sympathies that occurs half way through. Initially Edward's rejection of his wife Isabella's love and his infatuation with the Machiavellian Gaveston place

185

our sympathies clearly with her. But after Gaveston's death, Isabella becomes a brittle schemer adulterously involved with Mortimer, who is transformed from an honourable opponent of Edward to a usurper who uses his sexual desires for political ends (it is Mortimer who is given the most virulent anti-gay sentiments in Jarman's film). Our sympathies thus switch to Edward.

As in Jarman's other films, there is a disjunction between the idealisation and the eroticisation of the gay object (in this case Edward). Gaveston's homosexuality is much more dangerous, and if idealised at all, it is as a form of masculinity that is sexually voracious (his cruel 'attempt' to seduce Isabella is entirely convincing), swaggeringly arrogant and overweeningly ambitious. As with Caliban in *The Tempest*, Gaveston is portrayed not as a foreigner but as a northern working-class character. The film's violence is both sexual (the disembowelling of the soldier and Edward's dream of death at the hands of Lightborn) and sadistic (as in the scene when Gaveston runs the gauntlet of spitting clergymen). Curiously Jarman chose to make Edward's sexual refusal of his wife a painful one on his part at which he beats his head against the wall in frustration and anger.

At the outset Tilda Swinton's Isabella alternates a gruesomely shallow snobbishness with a heartfelt sense of loss at Edward's rejection of her. In the end, however, humane feelings desert her – she becomes an almost mechanical political figure, monstrous in her cruelty. In the scene when she fatally bites her brother-in-law Kent's neck, her vampiric slurpings horrify even the battle-hardened Mortimer.

Childhood plays an important role in Jarman's films from *Caravaggio* on. In *Edward II*, the young prince Edward (the future Edward III), played by Jody Graber, is forever at the scene of events, an ignored witness to his family's tragic journey. Gradually through the film he begins to adopt female attire – earrings and make-up. In a key scene the young prince, as if in a dream, witnesses a rugby scrum of naked men shot in a steamy darkness. The image of maleness is muscular, slow-moving, quietly combative. (It is of this scene that Jarman remarked that it: 'reminded me of ghosts come to haunt me, all my dead friends'.[17]) For the young boy, it is as if the scene is one of Oedipal discovery – an all-male variant of copulating parents. The young boy also represents to some extent the film-maker himself – his marginal role in the action denotes a sensibility that lies outside events, enduring and in the end defeating them. Perhaps Jarman's implication is that despite the agonies

of the present, homosexuality will endure so that there is hope for future generations.

The film's sexual complexity is furthered by the relationship between Isabella and Lightborn. It is to the Queen and not, as in the play, to Mortimer that Lightborn describes his torture techniques. Jarman loads the scene with sexual charge: as Isabella dips her head to kiss Lightborn she holds back at the last moment – an echo of Gaveston's last-minute, malicious withdrawal from kissing her.[18]

Mortimer's masochistic sexual tastes are revealed when he is shown being bound and 'abused' by three 'wild girls'. In Jarman's script there is the suggestion that this represents one face of heterosexuality, the other supplied by the decline in Isabella and Mortimer's desire for one another as they are depicted lying in bed together like a stereotypical middle-class suburban couple, she wearing a face mask and he reading a book. Homosexual love, by contrast, is portrayed as fun. Edward and Gaveston smooch in their pyjamas while Annie Lennox sings 'Every Time We Say Goodbye'. In another scene they dance camply in tuxedos; later Gaveston crouches naked on the throne. (It is true that Mortimer and Isabella also have their fun on the throne, but their actions have less to do with their feelings for each other than with the bloody fulfilment of their ambitions.) As with the dancing matelots in *The Tempest*, it is in the intertextuality of *Edward II* that Jarman proclaims gay sexuality. The fracturing of the narrative can be seen as an action against the strict, repressive, supposedly 'rational' law of heterosexuality. Homosexuality is the eruption of excess, of *jouissance*, something that cannot be held in the rigid control of narrative.

The film is probably the most post-modern of Jarman's works. He retains the theme of kingship central to the original play, juxtaposing it with costumes, actor techniques and a *mise en scène* that speak of the oppression of two gay lovers. Modern-day figures of authority – bishops, politicians, businessmen and the military – are represented fairly straightforwardly while Edward and Gaveston are the meshing of Marlowe's courtly figures caught up in past historical events with universal gay-lovers-in-crisis. In post-modern fashion, Jarman posits the original play as an interpreted text, foregrounding the very processes of adaptation and interpretation. The dungeon scenes, for instance, shot in dark shadows in which the anachronistic costumes are not apparent, occur next to scenes in contemporary mode. Other incongruous scenes are those between the Establishment characters and the two lovers, who are not given authoritative costumes, accents or postures (we cannot believe that bishops, army leaders and politicians could be ruled by these two men). In this way the play is overtly usurped by its subtext; Jarman reclaims Marlowe's play for contemporary purposes but resists the full absorption of the original into his polemical interpretation (for instance, he keeps references to Gaveston's exile to France which jar with his depiction as a working-class northerner, and so on).

Colin MacCabe has provided a fascinating interpretation of Jarman's film which connects it thematically with *The Tempest*.[19] His argument rests on the transition during the Elizabethan period from a loose organisation of power in the hands of the bishops and so on to a modern state with a repressive secret service and terror at its heart. According to MacCabe, Shakespeare's last play depicts the new repressive state apparatus: 'we can read Ariel in *The Tempest* as an allegory of [the] Secret Service'.[20] Jarman elides this historical repression so that it is at one with the repression of the homosexual in English society.

MacCabe remarks of *Edward II*: 'At its heart is the constitutive relation which founds the modern English state on a repressive security apparatus and a repressed homosexuality.'[21] According to MacCabe, torture and espionage are the twin means by which this is achieved, and both find their place in *Edward II* and in *The Tempest* (Ariel is Prospero's spy and *agent provocateur* and Caliban the tortured foreigner or misfit). MacCabe argues persuasively that Jarman's *Edward II* presents 'homosexuality as the key term in the understanding of the structure of English society'.[22] Class conflict is rendered in sexual terms (Edward's People's Army, ranked against barons and the military, is made up of OutRage demonstrators; Swinton plays Isabella as a King's Road 'aristocrat', high heels teetering, handbag swinging, while Gaveston is a working-class northerner).

Jarman has also spoken of the connections between alchemy and homosexuality – the secrecy, the signs and codes and the impulse which values passion over reason in a society in which order is established according to the rationale of the heterosexual family. To push MacCabe's argument further, the establishment of the heterosexual family as the basis for the new capitalism (because of the need to reproduce the labour force) against the

heterogeneity of the pre-capitalist period is represented in *The Tempest* by the marriage of Miranda and Ferdinand. That the gay aspect of the film is distributed between Caliban and the sailors reduces it to carnival – an exiling of homosexuality to the margins of a society centred around the heterosexual couple.

Jarman's *Edward II*, like Marlowe's original, is a piece about a homosexual relationship which takes place in a real world that wreaks its bloody revenge. There is no reconciliation or forgiveness here, no visionary idealism, even though Jarman unhappily gave his film a 'happy ending'. The years of Thatcher, the tragedy of the AIDS epidemic, the rise in anti-homosexual legislation and Jarman's own HIV positive condition surely influenced his decision to turn to Marlowe's relentless bleakness and violence as his source. Dee's rhapsodies about the sweet sounds of the angelic conversation have no place in *Edward II*.

Edward II was made at a period when Jarman's involvement in queer politics was at its most intense. His public profile was high and he used interviews to preach the radical gay cause. His involvement lasted from the anti-Clause-28 movement of the mid-80s to the campaign for the lowering of the age of consent for gay men (he died the night before Parliament lowered it to eighteen). In September 1991 Jarman was canonised as a 'saint' by the Sisters of Perpetual Indulgence, for which ceremony he wore Edward's golden cape from the film. From being a famous gay, he became a living icon for the queer movement.

1 See also Simon Garfield, *The End of Innocence: Britain in the Time of AIDS* (London: Faber & Faber, 1994).

2 Chris Heath, *Pet Shop Boys, Literally* (London: Penguin, 1991), p. 161.

3 Ibid., p. 74.

4 Ibid., p. 5.

5 Derek Jarman, *Modern Nature: The Journals of Derek Jarman* (London: Century, 1991), p. 189.

6 Ibid., p. 93.

7 *Financial Times*, 21 October 1989.

8 Tony Rayns, 'The "I" Movie', in *The Garden* press notes (London: Artificial Eye Film Co., 1990), unnumbered.

9 P. Adams Sitney, *Visionary Film: The American Avant-Garde 1943–1978* (Oxford: Oxford University Press, 1979), chapter 2.

10 Timothy Murray, *Like a Film: Ideological Fantasy on Screen, Camera and Canvas* (London: Routledge, 1993), p. 166.

11 Derek Jarman interview, *Artscribe*, September – October 1990.

12 Derek Jarman, *Queer Edward II* (London: British Film Institute, 1991), p. 2.

13 Frances Yates, *The Occult Philosophy in the Elizabethan Age* (London: Ark, 1983), chapter 11.

14 There are exceptions, of course. For instance, Harry Levin fully accepts the homosexual relationship. See Harry Levin, *Christopher Marlowe: The Overreacher* (London: Faber & Faber, 1967), especially chapter 4.

15 See Bertholt Brecht, 'The Life of Edward II of England', in John Willett and Ralph Manheim (eds), *Berholt Brecht: Collected Plays 1* (London: Methuen, 1994).

16 *Queer Edward II*, p. 112.

17 Ibid., p. 52.

18 In Jarman's script she actually kisses Lightborn, but the half-given kiss is much more powerful.

19 Colin MacCabe, 'Edward II: Throne of Blood', *Sight and Sound*, vol. 1 no. 6, October 1991, pp. 12–14.

20 Ibid., p. 14.

21 Ibid., p. 12.

22 Ibid.

Chapter Eight

COLOUR
Wittgenstein, Blue

1992–1994

After he made *Wittgenstein* in 1992 there was a rapid deterioration in Jarman's health. He lost weight and his sturdy frame became frail. His involvement in gay activism did not slacken and with assistance he managed still to paint. Ironically, he ended his career simply painting, as if his life had described a full circle. His final film, *Blue*, is a pure colour field.

Jarman's public profile in these last years was enormous. Interviews proliferated, usually about AIDS or his famous garden. Jarman had never been indifferent to publicity – he drew enormous energy from it and was a charming, witty and provocative interviewee. His relationship with Keith Collins, or 'HB' as he described him in his writings, was a steadying force and a source of love and comfort as his illness progressed. Rock star Holly Johnson, himself diagnosed HIV positive in 1991, speaks of how Jarman had been a 'workhorse' for the AIDS movement and had 'burned very brightly since his AIDS diagnosis'. Johnson relates how:

> I'd read a couple of Jarman's books by then [February 1992] and Derek had become my kind of spiritual hero, he was like this god to me, because he was so fabulous in this way that he dealt with the media.[1]

Johnson also voiced a view held by others that Jarman 'had constructed a fabulous legend of Derek Jarman … that perhaps wasn't there before'.[2] According to his art dealer Richard Salmon, Jarman was receiving 'a stream of letters from all over the world' and felt he had 'inspired a whole generation'.[3]

'Wittgenstein'

Like *War Requiem*, *Wittgenstein* was a commission, this time from a company not known for its involvement in artistic ventures. Tariq Ali, Marxist, writer

and *bête noire* of the student movement in the 60s, was the head of Bandung, a film company set up largely to make documentaries about Third World issues. *Wittgenstein* was a programme in a series Ali had planned on philosophers – Socrates, Locke, Spinoza and Wittgenstein – which he set out to make after being approached by Gwynn Pritchard, commissioning editor for education at Channel Four. Pritchard wanted a series of 52-minute plays on great philosophers with the emphasis on their lives and ideas rather than the usual talking-heads approach. Ali commissioned scripts from well-known left-wing writers – dramatists Howard Brenton and David Edgar for *Socrates* and *Locke* respectively, academic and Marxist theorist Terry Eagleton for *Wittgenstein* and Ali himself for *Spinoza*. The budget was 'considerably under £200,000 per programme'.[4] Pritchard shortly left the channel and subsequent budget cuts meant dropping *Socrates*. Peter Wollen was asked to direct *Locke* and *Spinoza* was to be directed by Bandung regular Christopher Spencer.

Curiously, Ali asked Jarman to direct *Wittgenstein*. He was an admirer of the film-maker's work and felt that *Wittgenstein* needed a director 'with a fantastic amount of vision and imagination ... and Jarman came to mind'.[5] Jarman thought the script 'quite cheerful and good fun'. The low budget was not a problem except that he wanted to shoot the programme on film rather than video. Ben Gibson, head of production at the British Film Institute, was 'tickled' by the idea of Jarman and Eagleton working together. He offered extra finance if the programme was made on super-16 as a feature film with the hope of a theatrical release and a place in the Berlin Film Festival. The theatrical and television rights were sold to Uplink, the distributors of Jarman's films in Japan, who wanted a blown-up 35mm version. All this meant that the film increased to roughly seventy-five minutes in length. Jarman shot the entire film in ten days in late 1992 in a studio near London's Waterloo Station, using mainly black drapes as background.

The Eagleton script, set in Cambridge and using outside locations, was heavily rewritten for the change in circumstances and to incorporate Jarman's own view of Wittgenstein. When Eagleton saw the final film he was affronted by the changes to his script and interpretation of the philosopher and wrote a piece for the press expressing his objections and anger. A peace was achieved when Colin MacCabe agreed to both scripts being published by the British Film Institute with introductions and statements by both collaborators.[6] Such a dispute would hardly be newsworthy in the world of mainstream cinema with its countless rewrites of scripts, but in the small field of independent film-making it is a rare occurrence. The idea that an academic, however highly acclaimed, is qualified to turn his or her hand to the skilled practice of script-writing is seriously misguided. Equally, the likely effects of Jarman's idiosyncratic style of film-making and way of working with scripts should have been recognised at the outset.

Jarman gathered his friends around him once more for this final orthodox film. Tilda Swinton, Michael Gough, Karl Johnson and Keith Collins were the main actors and an array of friends played minor parts. Ken Butler, who had assisted on *Edward II*, was associate director. Sandy Powell designed the costumes, oddly reminiscent of the designs Jarman had done for the ballet *Silver Apples of the Moon* in 1973.[7]

Jarman thought *Wittgenstein* was one of his few humorous films, and this is indeed the case. The overall effect is of Jarman at his most irreverent, treating the cornerstone of modern British philosophy with wit and high spirits. Swinton's rendition of Isabella as a stilted debutante-type in *Edward II* is reworked more for laughs for her portrayal of Lady Ottoline Morrell. The repressive effects of education are made much of in an excellent scene in which the tutors reciting (ironically from Wittgenstein's own writings) encircle the boy at his desk, their voices rising in a screaming crescendo as he desperately places his hands over his ears. The high society of the philosopher's family is visualised as part of a Roman dynasty gathered formally around a grand piano (interestingly, the father is not included in this family portrait), an example of Jarman's ongoing fascination with ideas of Empire.

The film traces Wittgenstein's life from his childhood in a powerful Austrian industrialist's family with strong leanings towards the arts, through his meeting with Bertrand Russell at Cambridge University in the years leading up to the First World War and the discovery of his 'genius' as a philosopher, to the writing of his revolutionary philosophical work the *Tractatus* in the trenches. On his return to Cambridge, after an abortive attempt to forsake philosophy and teach in an Austrian junior school, he imparts his difficult ideas to perplexed seminar groups and embarks on a painful relationship with a young working-class student whom he manages to convince that a career as a philosopher is a bad thing and he should

197

become a mechanic. The film ends with Wittgenstein's death from cancer in the early 50s in Cambridge. The death scene is finely judged, no doubt assisted by Eagleton's excellent dialogue.

The pared-down visuals of vividly coloured costumes set against a black backdrop with a minimum of props go against the rich detailing usually employed to give bio-documentaries authenticity and conviction. Yet Jarman's austere *mise en scène* is enormously successful. The use of primary colours is rare in Jarman's later films and it is interesting that at about the same time as he made *Wittgenstein* he was also painting canvases in strong oranges, yellows and reds, as if the combination of his failing eyesight and a renewed confidence had led him to discard the blacks and golds of his earlier work. In his notes to the film, Jarman remarks that Wittgenstein's book *Remarks on Colour* led him back to the *Tractatus*. It seems that for Jarman *Remarks on Colour* supplied not only a means of coding the design of the film, but more importantly a way of approaching the philosopher through the visual arts. Nowhere are Jarman's imaginative powers so well represented as in this use of colour in a film whose sober subject matter does not readily suggest such a solution. The bold, schematic celebration of colour in *Wittgenstein* signalled the beginning of a process that culminated in the single colour field of *Blue*.

The use of bright costumes and black background, with only Wittgenstein dressed normally in tweeds and grey flannels, also vividly evokes the dream-like state in which the philosopher existed, forever alienated and at odds with the world. Wittgenstein's isolation and awkwardness are further highlighted by the contrast between Karl Johnson's naturalist performance as Wittgenstein and the high camp and caricature of the other actors. In addition, the use throughout of the young Wittgenstein as the narrator contrasts the boy's seemingly normal behaviour and attitudes with the intense puzzlement of the adult man. The boy figure who had lurked in the sidelines in previous films is now confidently established, as if Jarman had put behind him the horrors of childhood.

Throughout, the film uses unsettling, often anachronistic, juxtapositions. For instance, the three taunting cyclists are in fashionable 80s cycle wear; Hermine Wittgenstein's model in one scene is from the present; and so on. Wittgenstein is thus portrayed as a figure condemned to roam twentieth-century England, lost and excluded by all, a strategy which

198

facilitates his identification with the marginalised gay. Wittgenstein's sense of alienation is economically achieved through this disjunctive device which also allows for humour.

Biographical accounts of Wittgenstein give the keen sense of a tortured sensibility. His remark that in philosophy he wanted to get rid of 'the age-old picture of the soul brooding in isolation'[8] is ironically very much the image he presented of himself and his practice. Wittgenstein would have conceded that the whole business of philosophising is an insane one and not a proper way to conduct a life.[9] As Jarman became more aware of his own mortality he insisted similarly that gardening and most other activities are more important than film-making. We can believe that he identified strongly with a character who experienced continually the state of self-questioning others only arrive at when faced with death.

Jarman had considered a film on Wittgenstein some years earlier at the instigation of the gay novelist Edmund White. In conversation he told me that it was the torture of the philosopher's repressed sexuality that made him an appealing subject (along the same lines as Sebastian, Caravaggio, Wilfrid Owen and Edward II). As in his other 'biographical' films, Jarman places his protagonist in a corrupt social context, here the upper classes of turn-of-the-century Vienna and London's Bloomsbury group, represented by Bertrand Russell, Maynard Keynes and Lady Ottoline Morrell. This rendering of Wittgenstein's situation is simplistic and one-sided but typically Jarmanesque, echoing the schematic scenarios of *Caravaggio* and *War Requiem*. Russell, Keynes and Lady Ottoline are loosely connected by sexual openness, intellectual arrogance and a sense of their country as having lost its status at the head of a great empire facing virtual collapse in the slump of the 20s and 30s. In a film about an Austrian philosopher, Jarman returns once more to his favourite theme of the state of his country.

As Colin MacCabe states in his preface to the published script, 'Eagleton sees [in Jarman's film] the substitution of a figure of English eccentricity for his European philosophical modernist.'[10] But Jarman does not make Wittgenstein an English eccentric so much as use him to highlight English eccentricity in the form of the Bloomsbury group, whose decadence and superficiality are contrasted with the philosopher's austerity of life and purpose and pained intensity. While finding Russell, Keynes and Ottoline Morrell to some extent figures of fun, Jarman is also aware of their

199

progressive role in matters of sexual freedom and highlights the tensions between their sexual proclivities and the demands of public life. The compromises between these two areas are not embraced by Wittgenstein, whose intense egotism does not allow him either the comfort of sex or the rewards of a professional career. His anguish and sublimation are reminiscent of Sebastian's denial of his sexuality and religious martyrdom.

Yet Jarman's Wittgenstein can also be interpreted as a modernist. Jarman's conception of modernism was not simply about reflexivity in art (painting being about painting and a return to materials) but about the role of the self. Jarman states, 'Ludwig said, "How can I be myself?" That is modern.'[11] This is not in conflict with Eagleton's view but is rather a different angle on modernism that takes the ethical and psychological as central. Jarman had always been a modernist in his paintings and design work, but not one who subscribed to abstraction, formed as he was by a generation, of which Pop Art was one strand, in which the object, the collage and form were paramount. To put it in a rather old-fashioned way, subject matter always counted.

'Blue'

In May 1989 Jarman noted in his journal discussions he had had about a television programme on artist Yves Klein which he complains threatened to be a 'travesty' of Klein's ideas and work. The germ of the idea for his own film *Blue* is contained in his remarks:

> I agreed to cooperate only if the work explained Yves and didn't turn him into a circus – perhaps an interview followed by as many minutes or seconds of blank blue soundless TV?[12]

The idea of Jarman as someone who likes to shock for its own sake is belied by his objections to the programme's cultural associations, whereby 'Body art, tattoos and piercings [are] thrown in with Yves Klein'.[13] Jarman seizes upon the secret nature of the performances of Klein's *Symphonie Monotone* and *Anthropometry* before invited audiences in formal dress which he recognises as not so far removed from the way much of his own cinema was screened before an invited audience of initiates. Later in the same entry he speculates:

200

Maybe the best way would be to black out TV sets. Furious phone calls: 'I've paid my license.' Yes, but it doesn't give the right to pry – this is a private programme of the void; if you wish to see it you'll pay the dues as well and if you fail you'll be fined.[14]

Jarman had first spoken about the Yves Klein project in 1987 at the time of the release of *The Last of England*. He had then had discussions with Sony, Tokyo, about a documentary on Klein along the lines of *Caravaggio* but less detailed. The project became more tangible shortly after he completed *The Garden* and as he was launching into *Edward II*. By then Jarman had replaced the documentary idea with the notion of doing a minimalist blue-field film. It amused him enormously to imagine his detractors faced with a film comprising a blank blue screen. There was little doubt that he was playing with the double meaning of the word 'blue' as he was also enthusiastic at the time to make *Edward II* a 'blue' film with explicit sex in an almost pantomime rendering of the tragedy. Working Title, who produced *Edward II*, made some reels of lab-generated blue film but they failed to raise money for the new project.

At a special AIDS benefit screening of *The Garden* at the London Lumière cinema on 6 January 1991, Jarman and Tilda Swinton put on a pre-screening event titled 'Symphonie Monotone'. They sat at a table on stage creating sounds by running their moistened fingers around the rim of wine glasses, as in the Last Supper sequence of *The Garden*, and recited passages from various writers on the theme of 'blue'. On the cinema screen was projected a 35mm film of a detail from an Yves Klein blue painting shot at the Tate Gallery. At various points slide images were projected on to the blue field. Sitting on the floor before the stage was a group of musicians led by Simon Turner playing gentle, almost hippie-style music. Now and then the young boy actor Jody Graber from *The Garden* would run out into the audience with small blue and gold painted stones which he gave to individuals. The whole performance lasted about a hour and was mesmeric, a reminder of the range of Jarman's reference points.

The event was transformed in 1993 into a 70-minute film and radio piece called *Blue* for Channel Four and BBC Radio 3. The sound was broadcast in stereo and the television screen was filled with a blue colour field produced by film processing techniques. The music performance piece

201

was toured in various forms, without Jarman, by James Mackay and Simon Turner. In Japan a blue film loop was shown with slide images from Jarman's super-8 films and a recording of Jarman's poems recited by the actor Michael Gough. For Italy John Quentin read from the film script of *Blue*, which by then existed, and the British Council produced a catalogue. By now, Mackay had produced blue gels instead of the film loop as this was proving difficult to project. In the film *Blue* the quotations used in Jarman and Swinton's performance are supplemented by the monologue of an AIDS victim – Jarman himself – based on his observations and experiences as a patient at Queen Mary's Hospital in London. The experience of *Blue* in the cinema with the scale of the screen and the concentration cinema demands is much more intense and evocative than its televisual rendering. Just listening to the sound with one's eyes closed achieves a similar intensity.

Blue is the most autobiographical of Jarman's films, its script made up largely of excerpts from his journals recounting hospital visits and the progress of his illness. It shares with much of his work the conjunction of realism and reverie. Curiously, its account of boredom and enforced inactivity – the hours spent in hospital waiting rooms, lying around in his flat, sitting in cafés, incapacitated by his illness and always waiting – is reminiscent of the soldiers' lives in *Sebastiane*. And as in *Sebastiane*, this narrative is interrupted constantly by tender memories and reveries of love. The film's central figure – Jarman himself – is a man 'blinded' by 'love' and doomed to die. It is as if Jarman's own life had come to resemble that of the protagonists of his earlier films – passive doomed figures trapped by their circumstances and memories. In *Blue* Jarman was able to give artistic form to his experiences, eschewing self-indulgence and the purely confessional mode.

A theme of 'seeing' pervades the film. The 'invisibility' of gay men, which has contributed to the number of gay casualties of AIDS, is touched on by Jarman, as is his own refusal of what he calls 'the pandemonium of images' in favour of the 'universal Blue'.[15] The image has always been the site of Jarman's most aggressive feelings: the manic, almost frenzied editing of *The Last of England*, for instance, implies a reading of the film as a struggle between Jarman's violent feelings towards the reality captured by his camera and his attempts to regain control of it. His aesthetic saturation of the image through graphic composition, colour and movement is reminiscent of

Eisenstein's obsessive aesthetisation of the image in films such as *October* and *Ivan the Terrible*.

The blue colour field in *Blue* is offered as a denial, perhaps a transcending of his enthralment with the real. It is such an extreme negation of his imagistic sensibility that it is perhaps an instance of Freud's notion that a feeling can be so intense that its only outlet is through its opposite. Just as the young Wolf Man in Freud's case history fantasised the secretly observed frantic coupling of his parents through the image of the perfectly still wolves in the tree, so Jarman's last filmic sighting of the world is imaged in blue, just blue. What he wants so dearly and is soon to lose, the ever pulsating real, must be relished in an exquisite passivity. It can be hypothesised that perhaps that was what he always wanted – the passivity of the subject. To be loved, to be fucked, to be held.

The film's release coincided with the publication of his last book *Chroma*, which contained the *Blue* script. As Jarman became more assailed by his illness, one of whose symptoms is partial blindness, visual images became almost inimical. The enforced cessation of meaningful activity was strongly felt and *Chroma* is full of descriptions of enforced idleness. In a passage of despair he speaks of facts, the reality of the world which is primarily visual, as being a lost cause:

> These facts, detached from cause, trapped the Blue Eyed Boy in a system of unreality. Would all these blurred facts that deceive dissolve in his last breath? For accustomed to believing in image, an absolute idea of value, his world had forgotten the command of essence: Thou Shalt Not Create Unto Thyself Any Graven Image, although you know the task is to fill the empty page. From the bottom of your heart, pray to be released from image.[16]

Jarman's consistent anti–realism is a mark of his continued refusal of the ready image, the facile realism he believed deceived us. In *Blue* and *Chroma*, this refusal becomes even more urgent.

Chroma is a distillation of Jarman's previous books and the nearest any of his writing comes to a statement of his philosophy. Its intermingling of discourse, diary, poetry and personal and social history, of thoughts, feelings, desire, hopes and passions, is typical of the man and his work. In *Chroma* no

single voice dominates, but instead each voice struggles against others, occasionally connecting only to be dashed apart so that complacency cannot set in. *Blue* has many of these qualities: the militancy of *At Your Own Risk* and *The Garden* meshes with the poeticism of *The Angelic Conversation*, the angry passion of *The Last of England* and the cool irony and sad humour of *Caravaggio* and *Jubilee*. But above all it tells of Jarman's humanism. For all his anti-realism, we see in *Blue* and *Chroma* the humane observation of people he meets in waiting rooms, cafés and taxis together with his painter's eye for the world – the peeling walls of a hospital room, the clothes of a fellow-patient, and always his memories of nature: the sky, flowers, landscapes and the sea. Very few of Jarman's films have not encompassed at some point a view of the natural world; many of them are richly embellished with such images, as in *The Garden*, *The Last of England* and *The Angelic Conversation*.

Blue is a peculiarly difficult film to discuss. This is not entirely because its image is blue throughout, for there is a well-established discourse for the discussion of minimal art and avant-garde cinema from the 60s and 70s has included directors who have subscribed to a minimalist or abstract aesthetic. But Jarman is not using the colour field in a modernist way, or at least there are other ways in which it has meaning. For Jarman, the blue is primarily a metaphor. It is also a self-reflexive statement about the medium of cinema. Interestingly for this project Jarman rejected a use of film that stressed its inevitable patina – the scratches, the slight flicker – in favour of a blue akin to the electronic video field, unadulterated by the human hand and sheer in the way only a pixel can attain (in this it is like Yves Klein's own use of vertiginous blue). Within the most electronic of the popular media, and one which he had resisted, Jarman found a ground for his most discursive and profound piece.

By early 1993 Jarman could barely concentrate enough to read, sleeping was difficult and he had lost weight and looked frail. I met him on Good Friday of that year; he was eating alone in Presto in Soho where he usually lunched. He had often claimed that the current film would be his last, or at least feared that it might be. When he told me on this occasion that *Blue* was to be the last, I believed him.

After completing *Blue*, Jarman's health failed rapidly. He had major operations on his eyes and being denied the pleasure of reading and all the other activities that had given him his *raison d'être* made him unhappy. His

206

last interview for the British Council was shocking for any who knew him.[17] His fragility and exhaustion were piteous to watch as he raised his head with some effort to focus on the questions. But the spirit was very alive when he answered: the same sense of humour, love of life and passion. Behind him was one of his last canvases – the large-scale, free and energetic gestures and confidence with colour of his final paintings had brought him enormous pleasure and a recognition by the art world that had previously been denied him. The Tate Gallery's purchase of *Ataxia: Aids Is Fun* (a reference to the loss of control of limbs incurred in AIDS) in 1993 and the dinner they gave in his honour was a high point of his life and career. As many of his friends knew,[18] he had always been a painter who made films rather than the other way around. The success of his painting perhaps meant more to him in the long run than that of his films, though it was the films that filled the life he lived. He died having achieved all he had wanted. A remarkable life.

1 Holly Johnson interviewed in Simon Garfield, *The End of Innocence: Britain in the Time of AIDS* (London: Faber & Faber, 1994), pp. 252–3.

2 Ibid., p. 252.

3 Ibid., p. 269.

4 For production details see Michael O'Pray, 'Philosophical Extras', *Sight and Sound* vol. 3 no. 4, April 1993, p. 24

5 Ibid.

6 See Terry Eagleton and Derek Jarman, *Wittgenstein: The Terry Eagleton Script – The Derek Jarman Film* (London: British Film Institute, 1993).

7 Super-8 footage exists of a rehearsal of this ballet showing the costumes and sets designed by Jarman. See Derek Jarman, *Dancing Ledge* (London: Quartet, 1984), p. 132.

8 Ibid., p. 65.

9 See Ray Monk, *Ludwig Wittgenstein: The Duty of Genius* (London: Cape, 1990), p. 425.

10 Eagleton and Jarman, *Wittgenstein*, p. 2.

11 Ibid., p. 64.

12 Derek Jarman, *Modern Nature: The Journals of Derek Jarman* (London: Century, 1991), p. 82.

13 Ibid.

14 Ibid.

15 See Paul Julian Smith, 'Blue and the Outer Limits', *Sight and Sound* vol. 3 no. 10, October 1993.

16 Derek Jarman, *Chroma: A Book of Colour – June '93* (London: Century, 1994), pp. 114–15.

17 See Ken McMullen's film *There We Are, John …* (1994).

18 Christopher Hobbs thought so in interview with the author, August 1994.

Bibliography

For a fairly comprehensive bibliography, including Italian and German writings, see Vincenzo Patane (ed.), *Derek Jarman* (Venice: Circuito Cinema no. 53, 1995).

Abel, Richard, *French Film Theory and Criticism, 1907–1939, Vol. 1: 1907–1929* (Princeton: Princeton University Press, 1988).

Afterimage no. 12, 1985, 'Special Issue: Derek Jarman ... of Angels and Apocalypse'.

Artscribe, September – October 1990, 'Eastward in Eden: Interview with Derek Jarman'.

Auty, Martyn, 'The Tempest' (review), *Monthly Film Bulletin*, vol. 47 no. 555, April 1980.

Auty, Martyn, and Nick Roddick, *British Cinema Now* (London: British Film Institute, 1985).

Bailey, David, and Peter Evans, *Goodbye Baby & Amen: A Saraband for the Sixties* (London: Corgi, 1971).

Barnes, Rachel, 'A Different War' (review of Jarman's paintings at Newlyn Art Gallery, Penzance), *Guardian*, 12 October 1993.

Barr, Charles, *All Our Yesterdays: 90 Years of British Cinema* (London: British Film Institute, 1986).

Baxter, John, *An Appalling Talent / Ken Russell* (London: Michael Joseph, 1973).

Berke, Joseph, *Counter Culture* (London: Peter Owen, 1969).

Birnbaum, Alfred, 'Derek Jarman: Fade to Blue', *Together* magazine, February 1993.

Blackwell, Trevor, and Jeremy Seabrooke, *The Politics of Hope: Britain at the End of the Twentieth Century* (London: Faber & Faber, 1988).

Booker, Christopher, *The Seventies: Portrait of a Decade* (Allen Lane, 1980).

—— *The Neophiliacs: A Study of the Revolution in English Life in the Fifties and Sixties* (London: Collins, 1969).

Boy George (with Spencer Bright), *Take It Like a Man: The Autobiography of Boy George* (London: Sidgwick & Jackson, 1995).

Brecht, Bertolt, *The Life of Edward II of England* in *Collected Plays 1*, eds John Willett and Ralph Manheim (London: Methuen, 1994).

Clare, Anthony, *In the Psychiatrist's Chair* (London: Heinemann, 1992).

Collick, John, *Shakespeare, Cinema and Society* (Manchester: Manchester University Press, 1989).

Collins, Bruce, and Keith Robbins (eds), *British Culture and Economic Decline* (London: Weidenfeld & Nicolson, 1990).

Comino, Jo, 'Recent British Super 8', *Film and Video Umbrella Broadsheet*, 1985.

Cooper, Emmanuel, *The Sexual Perspective: Homosexuality and Art in the Last 100 Years in the West*, 2nd edition (London: Routledge, 1994).

Coudert, Allison, *Alchemy: The Philosopher's Stone* (London: Wildwood House, 1980).

Culpepper, Nicholas, *Complete Herbal* (London: Bloomsbury Books, 1992; first published in 1653).

Curran, James, and Vincent Porter, *British Cinema History* (London: Weidenfeld & Nicolson, 1983).

Curtis, David (ed.), *The Elusive Sign: British Avant-Garde Film 1977–1987*, catalogue (London: Arts Council of Great Britain / British Council, 1987).

Davies, Christie, *Permissive Britain: Social Change in the Sixties and Seventies* (London: Pitman Publishing, 1975).

Davies, Terence, *A Modest Pageant: Six Screenplays* (London: Faber & Faber, 1992).

Dixon, Wheeler Winston (ed.), *Re-Viewing British Cinema, 1900–1992* (Albany: State University of New York Press, 1994).

Docherty, David, Dave Morrison and Michael
Tracey, *The Last Picture Show? Britain's
Changing Film Audience* (London: British
Film Institute, 1987).

Dodd, Philip, *The Battle over Britain* (London:
DEMOS, 1995).

Dwyer, Simon, 'Through a Screen, Darkly:
The Derek Jarman Interview', *Rapid Eye*
no. 1 (London: Annihilation Press, 1993).

Dyer, Richard, *Now You See It: Studies on
Lesbian and Gay Film* (London: Routledge,
1990).

Eagleton, Terry, and Derek Jarman,
*Wittgenstein: The Terry Eagleton Script –
The Derek Jarman Film* (London: British
Film Institute, 1993).

Eberts, Jake, and Terry Iliott, *My Indecision
Is Final: The Rise and Fall of Goldcrest Films*
(London: Faber & Faber, 1990).

Erdman, David V., *Blake: Prophet Against
Empire*, revised edition (Doubleday Anchor,
1969).

Evans, Caroline, and Minna Thornton,
Women and Fashion: A New Look
(London: Quartet Books, 1989).

Faithfull, Marianne (with David Dalton),
Faithfull (Harmondsworth: Penguin, 1995).

Field, Simon, and Michael O'Pray,
'On Imaging October, Dr Dee and Other
Matters: An Interview with Derek Jarman',
Afterimage, no. 12, 1985.

Finch, Mark, 'Caravaggio' (review), *Monthly
Film Bulletin*, vol. 53 no. 627, April 1986.

French, Peter, *John Dee: The World of an
Elizabethan Magus* (London: Ark, 1987).

Frith, Simon, and Howard Horne, *Art into Pop*
(London: Methuen, 1987).

Garfield, Simon, *The End of Innocence: Britain
in the Time of AIDS* (London: Faber & Faber,
1994).

Garr, Gillian G., *She's A Rebel: The History of
Women in Rock & Roll* (London: Blandford,
1993).

Gomez, Joseph A., *Ken Russell: The Adaptor as
Creator* (London: Frederick Muller, 1976).

Grundman, Roy, 'History and the
Gay Viewfinder: An Interview with
Derek Jarman', *Cineaste*, vol. 18 no. 4,
December 1991.

Hacker, Jonathan, and David Price,
Take 10 Contemporary British Film Directors
(Oxford: Oxford University Press, 1991).

Hamlyn, Nicky, 'The Garden' (review),
Performance, no. 63, March 1991

Haynes, Jim, *Thanks for Coming*
(London: Faber & Faber, 1984).

Heath, Chris, *Pet Shop Boys, Literally*
(London: Penguin, 1991).

Hebdige, Dick, *Subculture: The Meaning of Style*
(London: Methuen, 1979).

Hewison, Robert, *Culture and Consensus:
England, Art and Politics since 1940* (London:
Methuen, 1995).

—— *Future Tense: A New Art for the Nineties*
(London: Methuen, 1990).

—— *The Heritage Industry: Britain in a Climate
of Decline* (London: Methuen, 1987).

—— *Too Much: Art and Society in the Sixties,
1960-75* (London: Methuen, 1986).

Higson, Andrew, 'A Diversity of Film
Practices: Renewing British Cinema in the
70s', in Bart Moore-Gilbert (ed.), *The Arts in
the 1970s: Cultural Closure?* (London:
Routledge, 1994).

Hobbs, Christopher, 'In Memory of Derek
Jarman', *Sight and Sound*, vol. 4 no. 6,
April 1994.

Hoberman, J., and Jonathan Rosenbaum,
Midnight Movies (London: Harper & Row,
1983).

209

Hodkinson, Mark, *As Tears Go By: Marianne Faithfull* (London: Omnibus Press, 1991).

Holden, Anthony (ed.), *Greek Pastoral Poetry* (Harmondsworth: Penguin, 1974).

Holmes, Richard, *Firing Line* (London: Pimlico, 1985).

Isaacs, Jeremy, *Storm Over Four: A Personal Account* (London: Weidenfeld & Nicolson, 1989).

Jackson, Russell, 'Shakespeare's Comedies on Film', in Anthony Davies and Stanley Wells (eds), *Shakespeare and the Moving Image: The Plays on Film and Television* (Cambridge: Cambridge University Press, 1994).

Jarman, Derek, *derek jarman's garden* (London: Thames & Hudson, 1995).

—— *Freeze Frame* (Tokyo: Uplink, 1994).

—— *Chroma: A Book of Colour – June '93* (London: Century, 1994).

—— *Queer* (Manchester: Manchester City Art Galleries, 1992).

—— *At Your Own Risk: A Saint's Testament* (London: Hutchinson, 1992).

—— *Queer Edward II* (London: British Film Institute, 1991).

—— *Modern Nature: The Journals of Derek Jarman* (London: Century, 1991).

—— *The Exhibition of Derek Jarman: Luminous Dark* (Tokyo: Uplink, 1990).

—— *War Requiem: The Film* (London: Faber & Faber, 1989).

—— *The Last of England* (London: Constable, 1987).

—— *Derek Jarman's Caravaggio* (London: Thames & Hudson, 1986).

—— *Dancing Ledge* (London: Quartet, 1984).

Jenkins, Steve, 'The Last of England' (review), *Monthly Film Bulletin*, vol. 54 no. 645, October 1987.

—— 'In the Shadow of the Sun' (review), *Monthly Film Bulletin*, vol. 48 no. 569, June 1981.

Jongh, Nicholas de, 'History Is Punk', *Guardian*, 2 February 1978.

Julien, Isaac, and Colin MacCabe, *Diary of a Young Soul Rebel* (London: British Film Institute, 1991).

Jung, C. G., A*ion: Researches into the Phenomenology of the Self* (London: Routledge, 1991).

—— *Alchemical Studies* (London: Routledge & Kegan Paul, 1983).

Klein, Yves, *Yves Klein, 1928-1962; Selected Writings* (London: Tate Gallery, 1974).

Kuhn, Annette, *Family Secrets: Acts of Memory and Imagination* (London: Verso, 1995).

Le Grice, Malcolm, *Abstract Film and Beyond* (London: Studio Vista, 1977).

Levin, Bernard, *The Pendulum Years: Britain and the Sixties* (London: Pan, 1977).

Levin, Harry, *Christopher Marlowe: The Overreacher* (London: Faber & Faber, 1967).

Lewis, Peter, *The Fifties: Portrait of a Period* (London: Heinemann, 1978).

Lippard, Chris, and Guy Johnson, 'Private Practice, Public Health: The Politics of Sickness and the Films of Derek Jarman', in Lester Friedman (ed.), *British Cinema and Thatcherism* (London: UCL Press, 1993).

Lydon, John, *Rotten: No Irish, No Blacks, No Dogs* (London: Coronet Books, 1994).

Lynton, Norbert, 'Bare Landscape, an Invitation To Play', *Guardian*, 12 March 1969.

MacCabe, Colin, 'Edward II: Throne of
Blood', *Sight and Sound*, vol. 1 no. 6,
October 1991. Extended version
'A Post-National European Cinema:
A Consideration of Derek Jarman's
The Tempest and *Edward II*', in Duncan Petrie
(ed.), *Screening Europe: Image and Identity in
Contemporary European Cinema* (London:
British Film Institute Working Papers, 1992).

Mackay, James, 'Low-budget British
Production: A Producer's Account', in
Duncan Petrie (ed.), *New Questions of British
Cinema* (London: British Film Institute
Working Papers, 1992).

Maitland, Sara (ed.), *Very Heaven: Looking Back
at the 1960s* (London: Virago, 1988).

Marcus, Greil, *In the Fascist Bathroom: Writings
on Punk 1977–1992* (London: Viking, 1993).

Marwick, Arthur, *Culture in Britain Since 1945*
(Oxford: Blackwell, 1994).

—— *British Society since 1945*, 2nd edition
(Harmondsworth: Penguin, 1990).

Masters, Brian, *The Swinging Sixties*
(London: Constable, 1985).

Meek, Scott, 'Jubilee' (review), *Monthly Film
Bulletin*, vol. 45 no. 531, April 1978.

Mellor, David, *The Sixties Art Scene in London*
(London: Phaidon, 1993).

—— (ed.), *A Paradise Lost: The Neo-Romantic
Imagination in Britain 1935-55* (London: Lund
Humphries and Barbican Art Gallery, 1987).

Melly, George, *Revolt into Style: The Pop Arts in
Britain* (London: Allen Lane, 1970).

Mercer, Kobena, *Welcome to the Jungle:
New Positions in Black Cultural Studies*
(London: Routledge, 1994).

Meyer, Moe (ed.), *The Politics and Poetics of
Camp* (London: Routledge, 1994).

Monk, Ray, *Ludwig Wittgenstein: The Duty of
Genius* (London: Cape, 1990).

Moore-Gilbert, Bart (ed.), *The Arts in the
1970s: Cultural Closure?* (London: Routledge,
1994).

Murphy, Robert, *Sixties British Cinema*
(London: British Film Institute, London,
1992).

Murray, Timothy, *Like a Film: Ideological
Fantasy on Screen, Camera and Canvas*
(London: Routledge, 1993).

Nash, Mark, 'Innocence and Experience',
Afterimage, no. 12, 1985.

Nicholl, Charles, *The Reckoning: The Murder of
Christopher Marlowe* (London: Picador, 1993).

—— *The Alchemical Theatre* (London:
Routledge & Kegan Paul, 1980).

Nuttall, Jeff, *Bomb Culture* (London: Paladin,
1971).

O'Pray, Michael, 'If You Want to Make Films',
Sight and Sound, 'Art into Film' supplement,
July 1994.

—— 'Between Slapstick and Horror',
Sight and Sound, vol. 4 no. 9, September
1994.

—— 'A Body of Political Work: Tilda
Swinton in Interview', in Pam Cook and
Philip Dodd (eds), *Women and Film: A Sight
and Sound Reader* (London: Scarlet Press,
1994).

—— 'Philosophical Extras', *Sight and Sound*,
vol. 3 no. 4, April 1993.

—— 'The Garden' (review), *Monthly Film
Bulletin*, vol. 58 no. 684, January 1991.

—— 'The B Movie Phenomenon:
British Cinema Today', *Aperture*, no. 113,
Autumn 1988.

—— 'Fierce Visions: Derek Jarman',
Art Monthly, June 1988.

—— 'Brittania on Trial: Interview with
Derek Jarman', *Monthly Film Bulletin*, vol. 53
no. 627, April 1986.

211

—— 'Derek Jarman's Cinema: Eros and Thanatos', *Afterimage*, no. 12, 1985.

—— 'Gerald's Film'; 'Pirate Tape (W.S.B. Film)'; 'Waiting for Waiting for Godot' (reviews), *Monthly Film Bulletin*, vol. 51 no. 605, June 1984.

—— 'News from Home', interview with Derek Jarman, *Monthly Film Bulletin*, vol. 51 no. 605, June 1984.

Orton, Joe, *The Orton Diaries*, ed. John Lahr (London: Methuen, 1986).

Orwell, George, 'The Lion and the Unicorn: Socialism and the English Genius', reprinted in I. Angus and S. Orwell (eds), *The Collected Essays, Journalism and Letters of George Orwell* (Harmondsworth: Penguin, 1970).

Palazzo delle Esposizioni, *Blueprint suoni e immagini dal cinema di Derek Jarman* (Rome: British Council, 1993).

Park, James, *Learning to Dream: The New British Cinema* (London: Faber & Faber, 1984).

Paulin, Tom, *Minotaur: Poetry and the Nation State* (London: Faber & Faber, 1992).

Petrie, Duncan (ed.), *New Questions of British Cinema* (London: British Film Institute Working Papers, 1992).

—— *Screening Europe: Image and Identity in Contemporary European Cinema* (London: British Film Institute Working Papers, 1992).

Pevsner, Nikolaus, *The Englishness of English Art* (Harmondsworth: Penguin, 1976).

Procktor, Patrick, *Self-Portrait* (London: Weidenfeld & Nicolson, 1991).

Raine, Kathleen, *William Blake: Poems and Prophecies* (London: Everyman, 1975).

—— *William Blake* (London: Thames & Hudson, 1970).

Rayns, Tony, 'Queendom Come', *Time Out*, 24 February–2 March 1978.

—— 'The "I"-Movie', *The Garden* press notes (London: Artificial Eye Film Co., 1990).

—— 'Submitting to Sodomy: Propositions and Rhetorical Questions about an English Film-maker', *Afterimage*, no. 12, 1985.

Rees, A. L., 'Warhol Waves: Andy Warhol and the British Avant-Garde', in Michael O'Pray (ed.), *Andy Warhol: Film Factory* (London: British Film Institute, 1989).

Roberts, John, 'Painting the Apocalypse', *Afterimage*, no. 12, 1985.

Rogan, Johnny, *Morrissey and Marr: The Severed Alliance* (London: Omnibus Press, 1992).

Russell, Ken, *A British Picture: An Autobiography* (London: Mandarin, 1989).

Savage, Jon, 'Tuning Into Wonders', *Sight and Sound*, vol. 5 no. 9, September 1995.

—— *England's Dreaming: Sex Pistols and Punk Rock* (London: Faber & Faber, 1991).

Self, Will, 'Birth of the Cool', *Guardian Weekend*, 6 August 1994.

Shakespeare, William, *The Tempest*, ed. Frank Kermode (London: Arden, 1983).

Sitney, P. Adams, *Visionary Film: The American Avant-Garde, 1943–1978* (Oxford: Oxford University Press, 1979).

Smith, Paul Julian, 'Blue and the Outer Limits', *Sight and Sound*, vol. 3 no. 10, October 1993.

Sontag, Susan, 'Notes on "Camp"', in *Against Interpretation* (London: Vintage, 1994).

Stansill, Peter, and David Zane Mairowitz, *Bamn: Outlaw Manifestos and Ephemera, 1965–70* (Harmondsworth: Penguin, 1971).

Stringer, Julian, 'Serendipity into Style: The Queen is Dead', *Millenium Film Journal*, no. 27, Winter 1993–4.

Suster, Gerald (ed.), *John Dee: Essential Writings* (London: Crucible, 1986).

Talvacchia, Bette, 'Historical Phallicy: Derek
Jarman's *Edward II*', *The Oxford Art Journal*,
vol. 16 no. 1, 1993.
Tillman, Lynne, 'Love Story' (review of
Caravaggio), *Art in America*, January 1987.
Van Sant, Gus, *Even Cowgirls Get the Blues &
My Own Private Idaho* (London: Faber &
Faber, 1993).
Vaughan, Keith, *Journals 1939–1977*
(London: John Murray, 1989).
Walker, Alexander, *National Heroes: British
Cinema in the Seventies and Eighties*
(London: Harrap, 1985).
Walker, John A., *Cross-Overs: Art into Pop/
Pop into Art* (London: Comedia, 1987).
Watney, Simon, 'Derek Jarman 1942–94:
A Political Death', *Artforum*, May 1994.
—— 'Derek Jarman: Home Movie Man',
Marxism Today, October 1987.
Webb, Peter, *Portrait of David Hockney*
(London: Chatto & Windus, 1988).
Whitworth Art Gallery, *Derek Jarman Evil
Queen: The Last Paintings* (Manchester:
Whitworth Art Gallery, 1994).
Willet, John (ed.), *Brecht on Theatre:
The Development of an Aesthetic*
(London: Methuen, 1987).
Williams, Raymond, *Orwell*, revised edition
(London: Fontana, 1984).
Wollen, Peter, 'Possession', *Sight and Sound*,
vol. 5 no. 9, September 1995.
—— 'The Last New Wave: Modernism in the
British Films of the Thatcher Era', in Lester
Friedman (ed.), *British Cinema and
Thatcherism* (London: UCL Press, 1993).
Woodward, Marcus (ed.), *Gerard's Herbal*
(London: Senate, 1994; first published in
1597).
Yacower, Maurice, *The Films of Paul Morrissey*
(Cambridge: Cambridge University Press,
1993).

Yates, Frances, *The Rosicrucian Enlightenment*
(London: Ark, 1986).
—— *The Occult Philosophy in the Elizabethan
Age* (London: Ark, 1983).
—— *Shakespeare's Last Plays: A New Approach*
(London: Routledge & Kegan Paul, 1975).
York, Peter, *Style Wars* (London: Sidgwick &
Jackson, 1980).
—— *Theatre of the World* (London:
Routledge & Kegan Paul, 1978).
Yorke, Malcolm, *Keith Vaughan: His Life and
Work* (London: Constable, 1990).
Yule, Andrew, *David Puttnam: The Story So Far*
(London: Sphere, 1989).

Filmography

The best Derek Jarman filmographies compiled to date have appeared in *The Complete Derek Jarman*, ed. Lindsay Merrison (Arbeitgemeinschaft Kummunales Kino e.V., Stuttgart, 1988), and in *Derek Jarman*, ed. Vincenzo Patane (*Circuito Cinema* no. 55, Comune di Venezia Assessorato alla Cultura, 1995). Both these publications were supported by the British Council. In compiling the filmography which appears here I have had the benefit of consulting the super-8 archives held by James Mackay at Basilisk Communications and of discussions with Jarman's biographer, Tony Peake, who I believe will produce the definitive filmography in the near future.

The super-8 material presents certain difficulties for the historian. Many of the films were screened initially to private gatherings of friends and other film-makers though by the mid-70s Jarman was showing some of these films at public screenings and festivals. Titles used during this early period were often changed in the early 80s. So there are different titles for what we believe to be the same film and, at times, the same title used for slightly different films.

In 1976 Jarman became part of the new Arts Council of Great Britain's 'Film-makers on Tour' scheme. The following titles and times were included in the accompanying booklet printed in December 1976: *Bankside* 4 mins, *New York Walk Don't Walk* 10 mins, *Duggie Fields* 5 mins, *Andrew Logan Smith's* [*sic*] *World* 10 mins, *Ula's Fete* 10 mins, *Burning the Pyramids* 15 mins, *Laetitia's Pot Plant* 4 mins, *In the Shadow of the Sun* 40 mins and *The Art of Mirrors* 16 mins. In the equipment requirements for this programme Jarman states the need for *three* super-8 projectors (plus 'turntable, cassette player and amplifier'). It is believed that the three-screen film was called *The Art of Mirrors* and involved *Burning Pyramids*, *In the Sun's Shadow* and *Fire Film*. In an undated letter written at the time the German Cinemathek/Forum was making a 16mm print of *In the Shadow of the Sun*, Jarman states that '*In the Shadow of the Sun* is part of a series of films called *The Art of Mirrors* which were made in London from 1970–1974.' Thus *The Art of Mirrors* was a generic title for a series of films.

In April 1975, in a letter to the Arts Council, Jarman states that he is involved with *A Film That Will End in Death* which is 'mostly devoted to landscape [and] consists of three minute sections which preserve the entity of the [film] cassette with short link passages'. The cassettes in this section (the fifth) are 1. *Nostalgia*; 2. *Miss Gaby Prepares a Meal*; 3. *The Eye of the Storm*; 4. *1000 Molehills*; 5. *The Puddle*; 6. *Breakfast at the Pines*; 7. *Going North*; 8. *A Violent Moment*.

Some super-8s were only projectible on

214

super-8 projectors which could show at a variety of speeds (*Gerald's Film, Pontormo and Punks at Santa Croce, B2 Taper Film* and *Jordan's Dance*). When I toured the super-8 films in 1985–6 as part of the Film and Video Umbrella, I used Jarman's own excellent super-8 Bolex projector which I projected at three frames per second. I synchronised manually the music tapes accompanying the films.

It was James Mackay who first organised the distribution of some of the super-8s in the early 80s. For a brief period this was done in association with the Film and Video Umbrella, of which I was the director. These were by and large the films shown at the ICA retrospective in 1984. They were available on U-matic and on super-8 (prints were made). Since then new titles such as *Jordan's Wedding* (1981) and *The Pantheon* (1978) have entered into proper existence. At the ICA screening Jarman provided a commentary to the films which included important factual information as well as soundtracks which have tended to become fixed, though a year later when many of the same films were toured by the Film and Video Umbrella other soundtracks were chosen.

Jarman handed all but one (a film of the Sex Pistols which Jarman sold, something which he subsequently regretted) of the super-8s in his possession to James Mackay before his death. They were in boxes dated, numbered and sometimes named by Jarman either at the point when the film was completed, or later. Some of these titles are purely descriptive but others are the title of an intended film (not always realised). Some of the boxes are dated, but whether this is the date of filming or editing is not clear. Similarly, dates given for completed films have

been misleading, as it is uncertain whether these refer to filming date (many home-movie films were reworked after filming), completion of editing or first screening. About thirty-two hours of material shot from 1971 to the late 80s have been transferred by Mackay on to videotapes and it is very likely that films from the collection will be distributed in the near future. With this fact in mind I have included below films not in distribution at present but which constitute a film, as opposed to a fragment, off-cut or technical experiment. In some cases (as with some of the earlier music videos) it has not been possible to track down full filmographical details.

1970–3
Studio Bankside, super-8, colour and black and white, 6 mins (blown up to 16mm and included in *Home Movies Reel 1*)

1971
A Journey to Avebury, super-8, colour, 10 mins (formed part of *In the Shadow of the Sun*)

1972
Miss Gaby (aka *Miss Gaby I'm Ready for My Close-up* and *Miss Gaby Gets It Together*), super-8, colour, 5 mins
Garden of Luxor (aka *Burning the Pyramids*), super-8, colour, 6 mins
Andrew Logan Kisses the Glitterati, super-8, colour, 8 mins (features Gerlinda von Regensburg and Peter Schlesinger)

1973

215

1973

A Walk on Møn, super-8, black and white,
12 mins

Tarot (aka *The Magician*), super-8, colour,
7 mins (features Christopher Hobbs; formed
part of *In the Shadow of the Sun*)

Miss World 1973, super-8, black and white
(also a pink version), 6 mins

The Art of Mirrors, super-8, colour, 6 mins
(features Gerald Incandela, Kevin Whitney,
Luciana Martinez)

Sulphur, super-8, colour, 16 mins

Stolen Apples for Karen Blixen, super-8, colour,
3 mins

1974

The Devils at the Elgin (aka *Reworking The
Devils*), super-8, black and white, 15 mins
(shot by Jarman with black and white super-
8 in a cinema in Manhattan)

Ula's Fete (aka *Ula's Chandelier*), super-8,
colour, 10 mins

Fire Island (aka *My Very Beautiful Movie*),
super-8, colour, 5 mins (formed part of *In
the Shadow of the Sun*)

Duggie Fields (aka *Duggie Fields Earls Court
Elegance*), super-8, colour, 5 mins

1975

Sebastiane Wrap, super-8, colour and black and
white, 10 mins (shot on location in Sardinia;
blown up to 16mm and included in *Home
Movies Reel 1*)

Picnic at Rae's, super-8, colour, 10 mins

1976

Art and the Pose, super-8, black and white,
8 mins, (features Gerald Incadela and Jean
Marc Prouveur)

Sea of Storms (aka *Kingdom of Outremer*),
super-8, black and white, 3 mins

Gerald's Film, super-8, colour, 12 mins (features
Gerald Incandela; originally screened at
three frames per second with music by
Mahler)

Sloane Square (aka *Removal Party*), super-8,
colour and black and white, 10 mins (blown
up to 16mm and included in *Home Movies
Reel 2*, retitled *Sloane Square: A Room of
One's Own*)

Sebastiane, 16mm (blown up to 35mm), colour,
85 mins *p* Howard Malin, James Whaley;
ph Peter Middleton; *m* Brian Eno;
ch Lindsay Kemp; *cast* Leonardo Treviglio
(*Sebastian*), Barney James (*Severus*), Neil
Kennedy (*Max*), Richard Warwick
(*Justin*), Ken Hicks (*Adrian*), Donald
Dunham (*Claudius*), Janusz Romanov
(*Antony*), Staffano Massari (*Marius*), Gerald
Incandela (*Leopard Boy*), Robert Medley
(*Diocletian*). Also featuring Lindsay Kemp
and Troupe, Peter Hinwood, Christopher
Hobbs, Oula, Philip Fayer, Luciana
Martinez, Nicholas de Jongh, Norman
Rosenthal, James Malin, Peter Logan,
Michael Davis, Eric Roberts and
Graham Cracker

1977

Jordan's Dance, super-8, colour, 12 mins
(formed sequence in *Jubilee*)
Every Woman for Herself and All for Art, super-8,
black and white, 1 min (blown up to 16mm
and included in *Home Movies Reel 2*)

1978

Jubilee, 16mm and super-8 (blown up to
35mm), colour, 103 mins *p. c.* Whaley-Malin
Productions; *p* Howard Malin, James
Whaley; *asst. d* Guy Ford; *ph* Peter
Middleton; *ed* Nick Barnard; *cost.*
Christopher Hobbs; *m* Brian Eno; *songs*
'Right to Work' by Chelsea, 'Paranoia
Paradise' by Wayne County and the Electric
Chairs, 'Love in a Void' by Siouxsie and the
Banshees, 'Jerusalem', 'Rule Britannia' by
Suzi Pims (arranged by Danny Beckermann,
Will Malone),. *cast* Jenny Runacre
(*Bod/Queen Elizabeth I*), Little Nell (*Crabs*),
Toyah Wilcox (*Mad*), Jordan (*Amyl Nitrate*),
Hermine Demoriane (*Chaos*), Ian Charleson
(*Angel*), Karl Johnson (*Sphinx*), Linda
Spurrier (*Viv*), Neil Kennedy (*Max*),
Orlando (aka Jack Birkett) (*Borgia Ginz*),
Wayne County (*Lounge Lizard*), Richard
O'Brien (*John Dee*), David Haughton (*Ariel*),
Helen Wellington-Lloyd (*Lady-in-Waiting*),
Adam Ant (*Kid*), Claire Davenport
The Pantheon, super-8, colour, 3 mins

1979

Broken English, super-8 and 16mm colour and
black and white, 12 mins (Marianne
Faithfull's three songs 'Broken English',
'Witches Song', 'Ballad of Lucy Jordan')
The Tempest, 16mm (blown up to 35mm),
colour, 95 mins
p. c. Boyd's Company; *p* Guy Ford, Mordecai
Schreiber; *sc* Derek Jarman; *ed* Lesley Walker,
Annette D'Alton; *p. des.* Yolanda Sonnabend;
cast Heathcote Williams (*Prospero*), Karl
Johnson (*Ariel*), Toyah Wilcox (*Miranda*), Peter
Bull (*Alonso*), Richard Warwick (*Antonio*),
Elisabeth Welch (*Goddess*), Jack Birkett
(*Caliban*), Ken Campbell (*Gonzalo*), David
Meyer (*Ferdinand*), Neil Cunningham
(*Sebastian*), Christopher Biggens (*Stephano*),
Peter Turner (*Trinculo*), Claire Davenport
(*Sycorax*), Kate Temple (*Young Miranda*),
Helen Wellington-Lloyd and Angela
Whittington (*Spirits*)

1974–1981

In the Shadow of the Sun, super-8 (blown up to
16mm), colour, 54 mins *p. c.* Dark Pictures
with assistance from Freunde der Deutschen
Kinemathek (Berlin); *ph* Derek Jarman;
rostrum camera Marek Budyzinsky; *16mm
blow-up* John Hall; *m* Throbbing Gristle; *cast*
Christopher Hobbs, Gerald Incandela,
Andrew Logan, Kevin Whitney, Luciana
Martinez, Lucy Su, Karl Bowen, Frances
Wishart

217

1981

TG Pychic Rally in Heaven, super-8 (blown up to 16mm), colour, 8 mins (film of the band Throbbing Gristle performing at the nightclub Heaven, London; perhaps also known as *Throbbing Gristle*; made in December 1980 and shown at the ICA in March/April 1981).

Jordan's Wedding, super-8, colour, 5 mins

1982

Pirate Tape/Film (WSB), super-8 (transferred to 16mm and video), colour, 17 mins (film of Burroughs at time of Final Academy Event, 1982, with a soundtrack by Psychic TV)

Pontormo and Punks at Santa Croce, super-8, colour, 10 mins

Ken's First Film, super-8, colour, 5 mins (made by Ken Butler but usually included in Jarman's filmographies)

Diese Machine ist meine antihumanistisches Kunstwerk, super-8, 6 mins (for Psychic TV)

1983

Waiting for Waiting for Godot, super-8 and video, colour, 18 mins (film of a video of John Maybury's set design for Beckett's play produced at the Royal Academy of Dramatic Arts, London in October 1982)

Dance with Me, colour, 4 mins *p. c.* Aldabra (music video for The Lords of the New Church)

My Heart Beats (music video for Jimmy the Hoover)

Willow Weep for Me, colour and black and white, 3 mins *p. c.* Aldabra (music video for Carmel)

Dance Hall Daze, colour, 4 mins *p. c.* Aldabra (music video for Wang Chung, includes interesting home movie footage of the Jarman family)

Stop the Radio, *p. c.* Aldabra (music video for Steve Hale)

B2 Tape/Film, super-8 (transferred to video), colour, 30 mins (features Dave Baby, John Scarlett-Davies, Volker Stokes, Judy Blame, Hussain McGaw, James Mackay, Padeluum, Jordan)

1984

The Dream Machine, super-8 (blown up to 16mm), colour, 35 mins (four films made individually by Jarman, Michael Kostiff, Cerith Wyn Evans and John Maybury)

Catalan, 16mm, colour, 7 mins (made for Psychic TV and Spanish television)

Tenderness Is a Weakness, 16mm and video, colour, 6 mins (music video for Marc Almond)

Imagining October, super-8 and video (blown up to 16mm), colour, 27 mins *p* James Mackay; *sc* Derek Jarman, Shaun Allen; *c* Derek Jarman, Richard Heslop, Cerith Wyn Evans, Sally Potter, Carl Johnson; *ed* Derek Jarman, Cerith Wyn Evans, Richard Heslop, Richard Cartwright; *m* Genesis P. Orridge and David Ball; Paintings by John Watkiss (featuring John Watkiss, Peter Doig, Keir Wahid, Toby Mott, Angus Cook)

What Presence, 16mm, colour, 4 mins *p. c.* Aldabra (music video for Orange Juice)

1985

The Angelic Conversation, super-8 and video (blown up to 35mm), colour, 78 mins *p* James Mackay; *ph* Derek Jarman, James Mackay; *ed* Cerith Wyn Evans, Peter Cartwright; *m* Coil (John Balance, Peter Christopherson), Benjamin Britten; Shakespeare's Sonnets recited by Judi Dench; *cast* Paul Reynolds, Philip Williamson

Windswept, *p. c.* Aldabra; *ph* Gabriel Beristain (music video for Bryan Ferry)

1986

Caravaggio, 35mm, colour, 93 mins *p. c.* BFI
in association with Channel Four, Nicholas
Ward-Jackson; *ph* Gabriel Beristain; *ed*
George Akers; *p. des.* Christopher Hobbs; *m*
Simon Fisher Turner; *cost.* Sandy Powell; *cast*
Nigel Terry (*Michelangelo Caravaggio*), Sean
Bean (*Ranuccio Thomasoni*), Garry Cooper
(*Davide*), Dexter Fletcher (*Young Caravaggio*),
Spencer Leigh (*Jerusaleme*), Tilda Swinton
(*Lena*), Nigel Davenport (*Giustiniani*),
Robbie Coltrane (*Cardinal Scipione Borghese*),
Michael Gough (*Cardinal del Monte*), Noam
Almaz
(*Boy Caravaggio*), Dawn Archibald (*Pipo*),
Jack Birkett (*Pope*).

The Queen Is Dead, super-8 (transferred to
35mm), colour and black and white, 15 mins
p James Mackay; *ph & ed* Derek Jarman,
Christopher Hughes, Richard Heslop, John
Maybury (music video for The Smiths)

Ask Me, super-8 for video, colour, 3 mins
p. c. Rough Trade; *p* James Mackay; *ph & ed*
Derek Jarman, Christopher Hughes, Cerith
Wyn Evans (music video for The Smiths)

1969, super-8 for video, colour and black and
white, 3 mins *p. c.* Anglo International Films;
p James Mackay; *ph & ed* Derek Jarman,
Christopher Hughes, Richard Heslop,
Cerith Wyn Evans (music video for
Easterhouse)

Whistling in the Dark, super-8 for video,
4 mins. *p. c.* Anglo International Films; *p*
James Mackay; *ph & ed* Derek Jarman,
Christopher Hughes, Richard Heslop,
Cerith Wyn Evans (music video for
Easterhouse)

1987

Aria ('Depuis le jour' segment), super-8 and
35mm (transferred to video then blown up
to 35mm), colour, 5 mins *p* Don Boyd; *seq.
p.* James Mackay; *composer* Gustave
Charpentier aria 'Depuis le jour' from *Louise*
(features Amy Johnson, Tilda Swinton,
Spencer Leigh).

The Last of England, super-8 and 16mm
(blown up to 35mm), colour, 87 mins
p. c. Anglo International Films for British
Screen, Channel Four, ZDF; *p* James
Mackay, Don Boyd; *ph* Derek Jarman,
Christopher Hughes, Cerith Wyn Evans,
Richard Heslop; *ltg* Christopher Hughes; *ed*
Peter Cartwright, Angus Cook, John
Maybury, Sally Yeadon; *p. des.* Christopher
Hobbs; *cost* Sandy Powell; *cast* Spring,
Gerrard McCarthur, John Phillips, Gay
Gaynor, Matthew Hawkins, Tilda Swinton,
Spencer Leigh; *voice-over* Nigel Terry

It's a Sin, 35mm for video, colour, 5 mins
p.c. Anglo International Films; *p* James
Mackay (music video for The Pet Shop
Boys)

Rent, 35mm for video, colour, 4 mins
p.c. Basilisk; *p* James Mackay (music video
for the Pet Shop Boys).

Out of Hand, super-8 and 16mm, colour
p. c. Basilisk; *p* James Mackay/Anglo
International Films (music video for the
Mighty Lemon Drops)

I Cry Too, super-8 and video 8 for video,
colour and black and white, 4 mins *p. c.*
Anglo International Films; *p* James Mackay
(music video for Bob Geldof)

In the Pouring Rain, super-8 and video 8 for
video, colour and black and white, 4 mins
p. c. Anglo International Films; *p* James
Mackay (music video for Bob Geldof)

1988

L'Ispirazione, super-8 (blown up to 35mm), colour, 2 mins *p* James Mackay; *ed* John Maybury, Peter Cartwright; *m* Silvano Bussotti; *cast* Tilda Swinton, Spencer Leigh

1989

War Requiem, super-8 and 16mm, colour, 82 mins *p* Don Boyd; *ph* Richard Greatrex and Christopher Hughes; *p. des.* Lucy Morahan; *cost.* Linda Alderson; *ed* Rick Elgood; *video editor* John Maybury; *m War Requiem* by Benjamin Britten; *cast* Laurence Olivier (*Old Soldier*); Nathaniel Parker (*Wilfrid Owen*); Tilda Swinton (*Nurse*); Owen Teale (*Unknown Soldier*); Patricia Hayes (*Mother*); Sean Bean (*Enemy Soldier*); Nigel Terry (*Abraham*)

Pet Shop Boys Concert, super-8 and 16mm (transferred to 70mm), colour, 40 mins *p. c.* Basilisk; *p* James Mackay; *asst. d* Keith Collins, Julian Cole; *ph* Christopher Hughes; *ed* Peter Cartwright, Keith Collins, Adam Watkins; *a. d.* Christopher Hobbs

1990

The Garden, super-8, 16mm and video (blown up to 35mm), colour, 92 mins *p. c.* Basilisk in association with Channel Four, British Screen, ZDF, Uplink; *p* James Mackay; *asst d* Matthew Evans; *ph* Christopher Hughes; *additional photography* David Lewis, James Mackay, Nick Searle; *camera operators* Steve Farrer, Richard Heslop, Christopher Hughes, Derek Jarman; *ed* Peter Cartwright; *p. des* Derek Brown, Christopher Hobbs; *m* Simon Fisher Turner; *cast* Tilda Swinton (*Madonna*), Johnny Mills and Kevin Collins (*Lovers*), Pete Lee-Wilson (*Devil*), Spencer Leigh (*Mary Magdalene/Adam*), Jody Graber (*Young Boy*), Roger Cook (*Christ*), Jessica Martin (*Singer*), Philip MacDonald (*Joseph/Jesus*), Dawn Archilbald (*Nature Spirit*), Michael Gough (*Voice-overs*), Maribelle La Manchega (*Spanish Dancer*), Orlando (*Pontius Pilate*)

Red Hot and Blue Compilation video of Cole Porter songs sung by various artistes. Annie Lennox's 'Ev'ry Time We Say Goodbye' directed by Ed Lachman uses extracts from Jarman's father's home movies

1991

Edward II 16mm (blown up to 35mm), colour, 90 mins *p* Steve Clarke-Hall, Antony Root; *exec. p* Sarah Radclyffe, Simon Curtis, Takashi Asai (Japan); *assoc. d* Ken Butler; *ed* George Akers; *ph* Ian Wilson; *p. des.* Christopher Hobbs; *sc* Derek Jarman, Stephen McBride; *m* Simon Fisher Turner; *cast* Steven Waddington (*Edward II*), Keith Collins (*Lightborn*), Andrew Tiernan (*Gaveston*), John Lynch (*Spencer*), Dudley Sutton (*Bishop of Winchester*), Tilda Swinton (*Isabella*), Jerome Flynn (*Kent*), Jody Graber (*Prince Edward*), Nigel Terry (*Mortimer*); (based on Chrstopher Marlowe's play *Edward II*)

1992

Wittgenstein 16mm (blown up to 35mm), colour, 75 mins *p. c.* Bandung Production for Uplink (Japan), BFI and Channel Four; *assoc. d* Ken Butler; *ltg & ph* James Welland; *cost.* Sandy Powell; *m. d.* Jan Latham-Koenig; *ed* Budge Tremlett; *a. d.* Annie Lapaz Cast Karl Johnson (*Ludwig Wittgenstein*), Clancy Chassay (*Young Wittgenstein*); Jill Balcon (*Leopoldine Wittgenstein*), Sally Dexter (*Hermine Wittgenstein*), Gina Marsh (*Gretyl Wittgenstein*) Nabil Shaban (*Martian*) Michael Gough (*Betrand Russell*); Tilda Swinton (*Ottoline Morrell*), John Quentin (*John Maynard Keynes*) Keith Collins (*Johnny*), Lynn Seymour (*Lydia Lopokova*)

1993

Blue, 35mm, colour, 75 mins *p. c.* Basilisk Communications/Uplink (Japan) in association with Channel Four/Arts Council of Great Britian/Opal/BBC Radio 3; *p* James Mackay, Takashi Asai; *assoc. p & assoc. d* David Lewis; *sc* Derek Jarman; *m* Simon Fisher Turner; *sd* Marvin Black; *voices* John Quentin, Nigel Terry, Derek Jarman, Tilda Swinton

So Young, super-8 and 16mm for video, colour and black and white, 3 mins *p. c.* Basilisk Communications; *p* James Mackay, David Lewis, Andy Crabb (music video for Suede)

Projections, super-8 and 16mm (transferred to 70mm), 40 mins, UK video release version includes two re-edited super-8 films, *Garden of Luxor* and *Studio Bankside*, *p. c.* Basilisk Communications; *p* James Mackay; *asst. d* Keith Collins, Julian Cole; *ph* Christopher Hughes; *ed* Peter Cartwright, Keith Collins, Adam Watkins; *a. d.* Christopher Hobbs (music videos for Pet Shop Boys)

Little Emerald Bird, super-8, colour, 2 mins *p. c.* Basilisk Communications; *p* James Mackay; *ed* Keith Collins, Andy Crabb (music video for Patti Smith; super-8 material from *The Garden*)

The Next Life, super-8, colour, 3 mins *p. c.* Basilisk Communications; *p* James Mackay; *ed* Andy Crabb, David Lewis (live video of Suede concert at Clapham Grande with back projection of *Jordan's Dance*)

1994

Glitterbug, super-8 to 35mm, colour and black and white, 60 mins *p. c.* Basilisk Communications/BBC; *p* James Mackay; *asst. d* David Lewis; *ed* Andy Crabb; *m* Brian Eno

Selected Exhibitions

Most of this material has been culled from *Derek Jarman Evil Queen: The Last Paintings*, Whitworth Art Gallery, University of Manchester, in collaboration with Richard Salmon, 1994, and *Derek Jarman Queer*, Manchester City Art Galleries in collaboration with Richard Salmon, 1992.

1960 *Michael Jarman – True Lover's Knot*, Northwood, London (exhibition of 25 paintings)

1961 *University of London Union Art Exhibition* sponsored by *Daily Express* (awarded 1st prize in Amateur Artists category; David Hockney awarded 1st prize in Professional Artists category)

1961 *Michael Jarman*, Watford Public Library (exhibition of 40 paintings)

1966 *Derek Jarman*, Rimmell Gallery, London (exhibition of 45 drawings, 2 silkscreen prints, 8 paintings)

1967 *Young Contemporaries*, Tate Gallery, London (winner of Peter Stuyvesant Foundation Prize)

1967 Lisson Gallery, London, opening exhibition (10 works shown)

1967 *Edinburgh Open Hundred*, David Hume Tower, Edinburgh University (group show organised by Richard Demarco and Edinburgh University)

1967 *September Exhibition*, Lisson Gallery, London

1967 *Cinquième Biennale de Jeunes Artistes*, Musée d'Art Moderne, Paris (showed designs for Prokofiev's *The Prodigal Son)*

1969 *The English Landscape Tradition in the Twentieth Century*, Camden Arts Centre, London

1969 *Derek Jarman*, Lisson Gallery, London (exhibition of 14 paintings, theatre designs, environmental sculpture)

1971 *Drawings, Paintings and Designs for The Devils*, 13 Bankside, London (one of three studio shows with Michael Ginsborg, *Recent Work* and Peter Logan, *Models and Kinetic Pieces)*

1971 *Drawing*, Museum of Modern Art, Oxford

1976 *American Biennial Exhibition*, Houston, Texas, US (curated by Bryan Alexander)

1978 *Still Lives, Paintings, Film Scripts, Photographs and Drawings by Derek Jarman*, Sarah Bradley's Gallery, London

1981 *Group Show*, B2 Gallery, London (8 paintings in exhibition curated by David Dawson)

1982 *Derek Jarman*, Edward Totah Gallery, London (exhibition of 22 paintings)

1984 *Derek Jarman*, ICA, London (retrospective exhibition of paintings, installations and films)

1986 *Turner Prize Show,* nominated with Art & Language, Victor Burgin, Gilbert & George, Stephen McKenna and Bill Woodrow (nine paintings – the Caravaggio group – exhibited)

1987 *Nightlife and Other Paintings by Derek Jarman,* Herbert F. Johnson Museum of Art, Cornell University, Ithaca, New York, US

1987 *Derek Jarman – Paintings from a Year,* Richard Salmon, London (132 new paintings)

1988 *Derek Jarman,* Dom Kulture Studenski Grad, Belgrade (retrospective of films and exhibition of 18 paintings)

1989 *Derek Jarman – New Paintings,* Richard Salmon, London (30 new paintings and assemblages).

1989 *Derek Jarman – Peintures,* Accatone, Paris (retrospective of films and exhibition of 40 paintings with catalogue)

1989 *Derek Jarman – Paintings,* Galeria Ambit, Barcelona (exhibition of 39 paintings coinciding with Barcelona Film Festival)

1989 *National Review of Live Art,* Third Eye Centre, Glasgow; installation and large paintings.

1989 *Derek Jarman – New Works,* Lyth Arts Centre, Lyth, Scotland, and Richard Demarco Gallery, Edinburgh, Scotland

1990 *Luminous Darkness,* Terrada Warehouse, Tokyo, Japan (exhibition of paintings, assemblages and sculptures with catalogue)

1991 *At Your Own Risk,* Museum and Art Gallery, Kelvingrove, Glasgow (part of Glasgow Museums New Art Season; exhibition of paintings and assemblages)

1992 *Derek Jarman Queer,* Manchester City Art Galleries (exhibition of 44 new oil paintings)

1992 *Derek Jarman – New Paintings,* Karsten Schubert Ltd, London, in conjunction with Richard Salmon, London

1993 *Derek Jarman Queer Exhibition,* Palazzo delle Esposizione, Rome (from Manchester City Art Gallery with amendments; organised by British Council and Richard Salmon, London)

1993 *Derek Jarman – Queer Exhibition,* Filmmuseum, Potsdam, Germany (organised by Richard Salmon, London)

1993 *Dead Sexy,* Newlyn Art Gallery, Cornwall (first showing of 8 new paintings 1992–3 with selected earlier works; organised by Richard Salmon, London)

1993 *Paintings by Derek Jarman,* Marsh Gallery, New Romney, Kent, (selection of small works organised by Richard Salmon, London)

1994 *Derek Jarman – Painter, Filmmaker and Poet,* Chesil Gallery and Portland Lighthouse, Portland, Dorset (organised by Richard Salmon, London)

1994 *Derek Jarman: Evil Queen – The Last Paintings,* Whitworth Art Gallery, University of Manchester (in collaboration with Richard Salmon, London)

223

Index

All film titles by Derek
Jarman unless stated
otherwise.

Sources for illustrations

The publishers would like to express their gratitude to Mike Laye, James Mackay and Richard Salmon for their assistance with the visual material.

Colour section

BFI stills, posters and designs; 24/25, 31.
Mike Laye; 16, 17, 21, 22, 23, 26 top, 27, 28, 29.
James Mackay; 18/19, 20, 26 bottom.
Richard Salmon Ltd; 30.

Black and white

Arts Council of England; 53, 75.
Basilisk Communications; 33, 175, 181.
BFI stills, posters and designs; 81, 87, 90/1, 101, 103, 106/7, 111, 115, 117, 123, 133, 164/5, 169, 171, 187, 190/1, 195, 204/5.
Mike Laye; 14, 37, 139, 145, 157.
James Mackay; 63, 69, 155.
Private collection; 47.
Richard Salmon Ltd; 41.

DATE DUE

HIGHSMITH #45115